THE BIG BOOK OF

CH'I

THE BIG BOOK OF
CH'I

99 01182252/613.714

PAUL WILDISH

Thorsons
Directions for Life

Thorsons
An Imprint of HarperCollins*Publishers*
77–85 Fulham Palace Road,
Hammersmith, London W6 8JB

The Thorsons website address is:
www.thorsons.com

Published by Thorsons 2000
10 9 8 7 6 5 4 3 2 1

Text copyright © Paul Wildish 2000
© Thorsons 2000

Paul Wildish asserts the moral right to
be identified as the author of this work

Editor Nicky Vimpany
Designer Jacqui Caulton
Production David Hearn and Monica Green

Photographs by Guy Hearn
Text illustrations by Jane Spencer
Calligraphy by Manny Ling

A catalogue record for this book
is available from the British Library

ISBN 0 7225 3852 9

Printed and bound in Singapore

To my sensei, sempai and students
who guide my steps along the Way.

Acknowledgements

My thanks must go first to my partner and dearest friend, Joanna Leigh, who proof read my drafts, corrected my grammar, gave good critical advice and supported my efforts throughout the making of this book. I must also thank my friends and fellow students of the 'Ways', Louise Parkin, Alex Hannant, Melinda Courtney, Sathees Kana and Aaron Fuest who took repeated falls, posed patiently in difficult stances and allowed themselves to be stretched, pressed and punctured to illustrate this book. Acknowledgements are also due to Tony Dove and Gemma Twigg who gave such good advice for illustrating the t'ai chi ch'uan and acupuncture sections of this book.

Thanks also to the team at Thorsons, in particular Louise McNamara, who put my idea for this book on Belinda Budge's desk, who liked it and took it to Nicky Vimpany, who watched and worried over its emerging text before taking it to Jacqui Caulton who made my words and Guy Hearn's photographs into such a beautiful book.

Carrying vitality and consciousness,

embracing them as one,

can you keep them from parting?

Concentrating energy,

making it supple,

can you be like an infant?

Purifying hidden perception,

can you make it flawless?

'Tao-te Ching', translated by Thomas Cleary,
Vitality Energy Spirit, Boston, 1991

Since first coming to rational self-consciousness, humankind has carried the burden of the question 'why?' Unlike other animals we are compelled to solve problems and seek answers to questions that at first seem unexplainable. No larger question arises than the question of life itself. What force animates us? Who or 'what' created this universe? Can we ever understand the power that formed planets, moves constellations and created a force such as gravity? Despite our undoubted success in providing rational answers and making profound scientific discoveries, we still seem able to explain only *how* things work and not *why*. For those of a scientific rationalist view, this is more than enough. They are prepared to wait upon new discoveries and insights and see little need to speculate whether this universe has a purpose, or a powerful consciousness at work within it. For others the question – 'why is there life at all?' – is much more significant.

In trying to understand and explain our world we have developed sophisticated philosophies, arts and religions, which have tutored and civilized our technological ingenuity. Indeed science, often the critic of religion, has itself grown from the sages' observations of the heavens and the experiments of shamans with herbal remedies and alchemical potions. Ancient civilizations looked out on a vast, unknowable world where, even with their emergent technology, they were weak in the face of the elemental forces loose within it. Humankind has, historically, sought either to control and harness these forces with technology, to placate them with faith and ritual, or to harmonize itself with this elemental energy and allow it to structure the rhythm of daily life.

These are never exclusive impulses. The history of our civilizations demonstrates that all three strategies are at work at the same time. However, there is a sense of unease alive in the world that questions whether we have taken the technological strand too far and expected too much from it. When we see the mounting environmental problems that our attempts to control the planet have produced, or witness wars, famine and disease, we know that despite our technology we are no more spiritually or morally advanced than our ancestors.

Real peace, the spiritual peace that we imagine might bring some sense of a compassionate order to our world, works to a different agenda. Compassion does not have the ability to conquer poverty or eliminate suffering on its own. Without the assistance of technology and the provision of material resources we are unlikely to meet the needs of the millions of people that inhabit this planet. However, we must ensure that moral integrity, humanitarian concern and a broad appreciation of spiritual values inform the application of our technology and the deployment of our resources. Only then may we hope to prevent people from acting without regard to the effects their actions may have on others, or the environmental impact on the planet.

The ancient faiths of Hinduism, Buddhism and Taoism regard the universe as one inter-connected reality, which we all form a part of. There is no real 'self' apart from this universal oneness and there is no place we can stand outside of it. Everything we do and touch and feel is only a manifestation of one universal life force given shape by our consciousness. In India this universal life force is described as prana, in China it is called ch'i (qi) and in Japan it is known as ki. It is the vital energy that animates all existence and is present in all things.

Eastern tradition holds that this vital energy has a tendency towards equilibrium that establishes a harmonious balance throughout the universe. As this energy flows within us, we too have a natural tendency towards equilibrium. When the balance of energy within our bodies is altered or disturbed, our mental and physical health is affected. So too the balance of vital energy in nature. Denude the hillsides of trees and you create a cycle of destructive erosion that leaves only barren slopes. Divert a great river for industrial agriculture and you dry out an internal sea. To establish a harmonious balance, cut only some trees and replant what you have taken. Take only a reasonable share of the water and fishermen can still provide food from the inland sea. These are obvious, commonsense principles that we all see value in, yet still seem so often to ignore.

Although the belief in a life force and a common animating energy is shared throughout the East, there are differences both in how it is understood and how it is interpreted. In India the venerable traditions of

Ayurvedic medicine and yoga have channelled the subtle power of prana to sustain a healthy balance of the mind, body and spirit. In China and Japan this harmonious balance has been pursued via a wide variety of complex and sophisticated disciplines encompassing all aspects of human endeavour. It is beyond both the scope and intention of this book to make a comprehensive exploration of how the concept of vital energy has shaped all the cultures of the East. Instead it sets itself the more limited aim of surveying a selection of the many diverse Chinese and Japanese arts and ways whose purpose is to integrate and harness the energies of ch'i for physical, mental and spiritual well-being. Some of these arts and ways have become very familiar and are practised enthusiastically in the West, while others are less well known. Each of these arts in its own unique and characteristic way illuminates a different path to the same end; an exploration of energy, form and spirit. It is an exploration of ch'i, an energy that is within us and without us and of which all matter is only a manifestation. It is an exploration of the forms through which this energy is internalized and expressed, and finally it is an exploration of the spirit that guides our actions, governs our will and gives us the potential to heal ourselves and our planet.

道

THE WAY

It is to the ancient philosophies and religions of the East that we must look for the origins of the concept of ch'i, the spirit energy that breathes life into our bodies and moves the stars around the cosmos. The most sophisticated of these theories have cross-fertilized and developed in parallel within India and China and have gone on to influence all the great civilizations of the East. In India this force is known as *prana* and it has given birth to yoga and Ayurvedic medicine. Within China it is known as ch'i, and as *ch'i kung*, the 'work of energy,' it has grown many branches. Virtually all Chinese or Japanese systems of exercise, traditional medicine and martial arts are constructed around this single concept and have designed a methodology to summon and use it. What then is ch'i and from where did this concept develop?

The Chinese concept of ch'i as a theory to explain the world emerged from its roots in shamanistic traditions to be given coherence and clarity by the early philosophers of China's Classical period from the eighth to the third centuries BCE. This was the time that produced many of China's greatest and most creative thinkers whose work and influence have etched their character on the civilizations of the East. Foremost among these intellectuals were the Taoist philosophers Lao Tse and Chuang Tse and the great moralist and social philosopher, Confucius. All three made major contributions to the development of the idea of the *Tao*, which acts in our world through the energy called ch'i.

Tao translates simply as 'road' or 'path' but is more commonly described as the 'way', which, if followed correctly, will realize the individual's potential to interact harmoniously with creation. For thinkers such as Lao Tse and Chuang Tse, the Tao is a way whose dynamic we are all compelled to comply with but have no ability to alter or affect. Unlike the Christian concept of God as the creative source and energy of the universe, the Tao cannot be influenced by good deeds or loving action. To be in harmony with the Tao requires no prescription of faith or code of moral conduct, but an acceptance and surrender to the way of nature. Taoist thought sees no supreme being but only what John Blofield, the eminent popularizer of Taoism, described as a 'supreme state of being'.

For Confucius, the Tao is a path that we follow by conforming to correct action and the observance of a refined moral and ethical code of divine inspiration. This correct behaviour, *li*, if observed, demonstrates virtue, *te*, and by following the Tao we will find virtue. The Taoist philosophers saw this principle differently. In their view the Tao is the ultimate reality that gives form to all things and thereby gives reality to virtue. The Tao is thus an abstract concept, not an ethical principle. The Tao is therefore unknowable, beyond description, eternal and unmeasurable. It is the void that exists as pure spirit, it is the non-void that surrounds and contains the universe. The Tao is all-pervading and

flows in all directions and, like water, overcomes by softness. Lao Tse taught a way of non-interference, trusting in the Tao's innate capacity to arrange and form all things and therefore be the source from which all positive things flow. Lao Tse said the Tao, 'is the weakest thing in heaven and earth, it overcomes the strongest; proceeding from no place, it enters where there is no crack. Thus do I know the value of non-activity. Few are they who recognize the worth of the teaching without words and of non-activity.'

This is the doctrine of *wu wei*: to take no action which is not in harmony with the laws of nature. Non-action is not to be interpreted as opting out of responsibility to sit idly watching the world go by. Wu wei is spontaneous action performed with skill and commitment, but only to meet the present need. It is energetic when required but never calculated or pursued for profit or greed. This action is always relaxed and never pursued to the point of stress or strain and is part of the Taoist recipe for well-being and longevity. The Taoist sage only acts when circumstances dictate and makes no more effort than that which is appropriate and natural. Without the burden of ambition, avarice or conceit, the sage does not stop to receive plaudits for achievement, but moves on to meet whatever the Tao brings.

The Tao is considered to act in the world through the processes of 'yin' and 'yang' and the 'Five Elements'. These theories were in existence before Lao-tsu and his successors began to formulate a comprehensive cosmology. The *I Ching*, or *Book of Changes*, held in great esteem by both Taoists and Confucians, predates Lao Tse's *Tao-te Ching*, and is the source of these ideas. Both Taoist cosmology and the practices of Traditional Chinese Medicine are sophisticated developments of these theories and form the conceptual basis for many health, callisthenic and martial arts systems.

Yin and yang is the process that makes the Tao discernible in the world. The basic dynamic of this universe is ch'i, the primordial 'energy' from which all existence is derived. Chuang Tse considered form or substance as only a condensation of ch'i to a greater or lesser extent. Life or material form is condensed ch'i. In its diluted state ch'i becomes indefinite potential. Ch'i spreads itself across space and time filling every dimension, animating the world and turning it through the great cycles of change. Ch'i cannot be detected except by being present as condensed form or substance. In this state it can be transformed, for example from water to mist, but when these forms disappear, it becomes ch'i once again. Ch'i does not exist separately alongside the forms it takes, it becomes them. Life is ch'i, matter is ch'i and is both the void and the non-void.

The transformations of the primordial breath began with a division into yang breath, which flowed upward and formed heaven, and yin breath, which moved downwards and formed the earth. Yin breath is opaque and heavy, where yang is a pure, light breath, thus the nature of heaven is to be pure and always in motion while that of the earth is to be opaque and static. In human terms the yang represents the positive self of

identity, continuity and change, while yin represents the 'other', in contradistinction limiting and contracting.

Yin and yang are two opposing forces that constantly cross and intermingle, each one always containing the seed of the other within it. Mankind exists in the realm between the yang of heaven and the yin of earth. In this plane, where their passages cross and coalesce there can be no pure yin or pure yang. Once each polarity reaches its extreme limit it reverses to become its opposite. Yin and yang give birth to each other, the 'one', the primordial energy producing the 'two'. Thus the presence of yin and yang is only realized in the exchange made between the one and the other.

The Taoist sage strives therefore to be at once yin, expressing receptive 'feminine' qualities and at the same time yang, manifesting active 'male' characteristics, and cannot exist without both. To harmonize the inter-play of yin and yang is to follow the Tao and to construct the platform from which spiritual enlightenment can be reached. The Taoist takes care to balance the forces of yin and yang within all aspects of existence. Maintaining his health and developing wisdom through exercise, meditation, diet and study, the sage sits in the monastery on the mountain top, breathing in the pure ch'i from the surrounding mists. The legends speak of these Taoist mystics living lifespans over centuries. However, longevity is not to be pursued for its own sake, but in the expectation of achieving a mystical or spiritual revelation.

Although the interchange of yin and yang is responsible for much of the dynamic of phenomena, another set of principles is at work. This is the so called *wu hsing*, or 'Five Elements', doctrine, which divides all natural processes into five characteristic activities resembling the interplay between wood, fire, metal, earth and water. Observing nature in lonely contemplation the sages noticed that all the forces at work depend on a system of fine checks and balances. These forces work together or against each other and their relative strengths or weakness are the dynamic of each situation.

The 'Five Elements' theory is combined with that of yin and yang, so that Wood is called 'young yang', Fire 'great yang', Metal 'young yin', Water 'great yin' and the Earth is the element of 'central harmony'. As the seasons succeed themselves and the day makes its passage from light to dark, so each element has its ascendance. These elements are also 'breaths' as are yin and yang, each influencing a season or a part of the body in an alternating cyclic rhythm. Earth is the centre of this cycle. The world is divided into four sectors with Wood governing the east and the spring, Fire governing the south and summer, Metal governing the west and the autumn, and finally Water is ascendant in the north and during the winter. The conditions for equilibrium are established through a cycle of change, with no element ever able to dominate for longer than their allotted space. The Taoist sees that this cycle resolves all disharmonies in due time and is the basis for their confidence in following the laws of the natural order.

Within each of us is a mirror image of this universe as each of us is made up of these polarities of ch'i, yin and yang. In men yang is on the outside and yin within while in women these poles are reversed. Yang rules the left side and upper part of the body while yin dominates the lower half and the left. Our external organs such as eyes, nose, mouth and ears and our internal organs all correspond to the Five Elements. So that Water, for example, is associated with the kidneys and the bladder and externally with the ears. As the seasons and the heavens rotate through the cycles so does the body, marked both by outside elemental influences and by those within.

As this change is cyclical, it may also be predictable, and the experienced Taoist practitioner will be able to forecast events through reading the *I Ching*, the *Book of Changes*, and observing the passage of the seasons. Or within the body the sage may diagnose an imbalance of ch'i by feeling the regions of yin and yang and the constantly changing influences of the Five Elements. Thus the sage is a microcosm of the universe itself, reflecting within himself all the laws and structures that govern creation. Ch'i is the energy that drives this whole process and thus it is with ch'i that the adept must work, conserving and replenishing it, to fuel a long life with limitless potential for spiritual development.

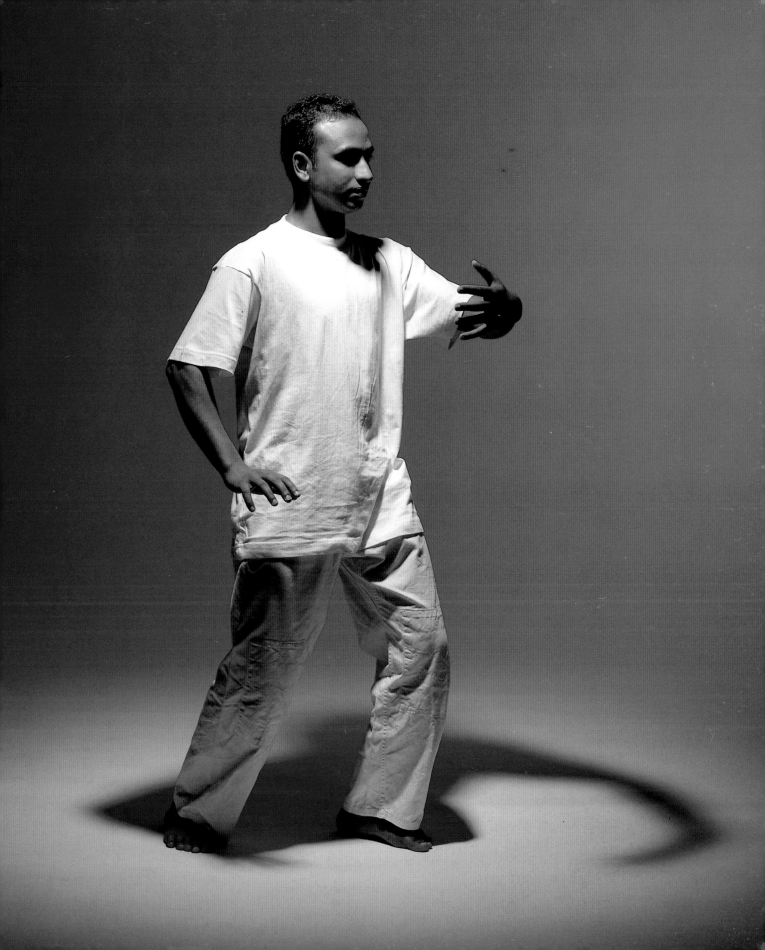

THE QUEST FOR ETERNAL LIFE

Taoism is the force that inspired Chinese society's close and sustained relationship with the concept of ch'i. The idea that all matter, be it inert or active, is part of the vast sea of universal energy, led many Taoist sages to speculate on how best to tap into this limitless supply of life-giving ch'i. All human societies wish to heal and prolong life and have evolved complex mythologies and religious doctrines that speak of life beyond death. The Chinese Taoist philosophers believed that the Tao was an eternal force. If that force is eternal then it must be possible to use that energy, not just to sustain life but to prolong it to the point of immortality.

The quest for eternal life became one of the greatest motivations for the development of Traditional Chinese Medicine and the disciplines of the body that have their root in ch'i kung, or 'energy work'. Taoist mystics began to experiment with a variety of practices in an attempt to distil the elixir that would endow the individual with eternal life. The quest of these mystics soon gave birth to legend and abundant stories are told of Taoist adepts who managed to live for centuries. Peng-tsu, the most famous of these 'immortals' is said to have lived for 800 years sustained by the daily practice of meditation, rising at 3am and sitting until dawn, and by the assiduous practice of energy work. The exercise system Peng-tsu developed to sustain ch'i through his long life is called *tao yin*. It involves the combination of deep abdominal breathing with the slow projection and extension of the limbs; breath and movement in harmony. Through this measured balance between the poles of stillness and movement, Peng-tsu emulated the perfect symmetry of yin and yang.

Peng-tsu found his elixir of longevity in the disciplines of body and mind, but not all Taoist adepts believed this to be the answer to the secret of eternal life. The Taoists of the religious school that formalized Lao Tse's 'Way of the Tao' into a faith with ritual and observance, sought the answer in an external source. This became a quest similar to that of the medieval European alchemists, an attempt to find a chemical or herbal means to unlock the door of eternity. If all substance is ch'i, then it must be possible to break down its composition and distil its energy into an elixir, or the 'Great Pill', the goal of the Taoist alchemists.

Gradually Taoist alchemical thought divided itself into two traditions of practice, the *wai-dan* or outer elixir and the *nei-dan* or inner elixir schools. The outer, or external, school believed that the pursuit of yoga or meditation could not of itself deliver immortality. Although their benefits for sustaining health, vitality and longevity were apparent, they could not gift eternity. The answer could only be found in an external source, towards which end these sages dedicated their research into the properties of metals, minerals and herbs and their effects on the human body.

The legendary Yellow Emperor, Huang Ti, who lived during China's Golden Age between 2852 and 2255 BCE,

laid the foundation of Chinese medical practice with his famous text *The Yellow Emperor's Classic of Internal Medicine* (*Huang Ti Nei Ching*). Legend credits Huang Ti with teaching the Chinese people the arts of agriculture, the use of fire, the cultivation of the silk worm, metal working and of course medicine. Although he frequently practised sexual yoga with the 1,200 women of his harem, forgoing ejaculation to preserve the life essence in his sperm, he was also interested in creating the Great Pill. After living for 111 years Huang Ti is said to have taken the elixir, mounted the back of a dragon and flown off to the world of the immortals.

The pursuit of the inner elixir was not only different in method, but also in concept; the very question of what constituted immortality itself. For the Taoist philosophers pursuing the inner elixir, immortality was a spiritual concept whereby the yang soul was liberated from the yin physical body to become part of the universal Tao at the point of death. Beyond death there was no necessity to concern oneself with an ego identity. Personal consciousness would be absorbed into the universal spirit. The only objective for the sage was to understand the principles of the universe and to harmonize with them.

Some sages believed that through the pursuit of spiritual yoga this transfer of the soul from the physical body could be achieved before death. By this practice the production of chemical change is transferred to the inside of the body. Spiritual yoga transforms the organs which correspond to Fire, Water, Metal and other elements, and mixes their energies to forge the inner elixir.

The inner school came to rely on practices that would sustain and replenish the body's store of ch'i. If one practised ch'i kung, maintained a modest diet, drank infusions of herbs, and meditated, then it was thought possible to achieve unity with the Tao within one's lifetime. It is this strand of Taoism that came to be accepted as the most likely to deliver the benefit of good health, vitality and great age, rather than the wai-dan's fruitless quest for an immortality 'pill'.

Although the wai-dan school believed in the development of the Great Pill through the mixture of herbal medicines and chemical distillations of metals and minerals, this did not preclude them from practising tao yin and other exercises to sustain health. Nor would a follower of the internal nei-dan school reject an efficacious external remedy to sustain his blood and the flow of ch'i. The Chinese attitude to spiritual practice and philosophy has always been eclectic. Chinese society has long managed to combine belief in Taoism, Confucianism and Buddhism with a rich mixture of reverence for ancestors and the gods of hearth and fortune without any apparent philosophical or spiritual dilemma.

In this way it was possible for Ge Hong, a famous teacher of the external elixir school, to believe that the Great Pill would grant immortality only to those who lived an upright life in accordance with Confucian virtues. If an evil man without a pure heart drank from the cup of immortality, he was doomed to an unexpectedly early death. This was an outcome similar to those found in our own Grail legends where only the most worthy can drink from the chalice.

By the time of the Three Kingdoms and the Northern and Southern dynasties (200–580 CE), the inner elixir school had become the predominant influence on the development of ch'i kung and Chinese medicine. The philosophical basis of their practice was the theory of the Three Treasures: *jing* (essence), ch'i (vital energy) and *shen* (spirit). Each of these treasures had a physical and a spiritual dimension. Jing, associated with male sperm and female sexual fluids, has a physical location in the genitals, while its non-corporeal aspect represented creativity and the seed of life. Ch'i, located in the *tan t'ien* within the stomach, is sustained by breath and is the source of internal energy and vitality. While shen, the spirit, is associated with the head, heart and lungs and governs not only our everyday thoughts and emotions but also our spiritual consciousness. By cultivating a balance between these Three Treasures not only could longevity be encouraged but it would provide the time to deepen one's insight and gain spiritual immortality.

The Taoist philosophers of the nei-dan believed it was possible to reverse the process of life and restore the pre-natal energy, or ch'i, with which one is born. The baby inside its mother's womb takes in ch'i through the umbilical cord directly into the tan t'ien. This is the store of pre-natal ch'i with which he or she will be born and the quality of that energy will vary according to the condition of the mother and the baby's genetic inheritance. When the baby is born, a process of change begins as soon as the child starts breathing through the nose and throat. Gradually, if it is not replenished, our pre-natal ch'i will be used up. It moves from the abdomen to the lungs, rising higher and higher in the body as we age. Eventually our remaining ch'i passes out of our throat and mouth with the expulsion of our last breath. By controlling our breath and learning to take it deep into the abdomen, the store of pre-natal ch'i can be replenished and the ageing process delayed. The practice of ch'i kung and *t'ai chi ch'uan* were the practical means for deepening breath control and restoring the energy levels within the tan t'ien. Sitting meditation could reinforce this process by using internal focus and visualization techniques to govern the movement and consumption of ch'i. This combination of sitting meditation and moving meditation through the practice of ch'i kung, was established as the sages' pathway to spiritual immortality.

A seminal influence on the subsequent development of ch'i kung and meditative practice was made by the unlikely figure of the Indian monk, Bodhidharma. Known to the Chinese as Ta Mo, he had arrived in China during the Southern Ling dynasty (502–557 CE) and taken residence in the famous Shaolin Temple. Here, with a determination to pierce the truth and receive final enlightenment, he is said to have sat facing a wall in the seclusion of his chamber meditating in absolute silence for nine years. His long and lonely spiritual struggle convinced him that if a monk was to have the mental strength to sit through long periods of meditation, he would also need physical stamina. The Chinese monks of the Shaolin Temple were not able to imitate Bodhidharma's resolve and were physically weak from lack of exercise. To overcome this problem he introduced Indian pranayama breathing methods and yoga, combined with Chinese tao yin and the 'Play of the Five Beasts', an exercise based on the movements of animals. The Shaolin Temple became a centre for the development of ch'i kung and the practice of martial arts, not for crude fighting ability, but to govern the mind and discipline the spirit.

Bodhidharma taught that we cannot make distinctions between 'this' or 'that' for all things have a commonality that transcends arbitrary divisions. The enlightened mind senses the stillness within movement and movement within stillness. Sitting meditation or moving meditation are but different reflections of the same state. By moving between these two states we can understand the energetic processes which unite them and enter Bodhidharma's 'sublime state'. Ch'i, the vital energetic force, makes this connection between the body and mind. When we move through the forms of ch'i kung we are practising for both spiritual and physical gain in the same moment.

The legacy of Bodhidharma's teachings extends well beyond the devising of new forms of physical and spiritual exercise. He is also recognized as the founder of Ch'an Buddhism. Ch'an Buddhism spread from China through Korea to Japan, where in its Zen incarnation it profoundly influenced all aspects of Japanese culture.

The influence of the Taoist schools and particularly the nei-dan confirmed energy work as the primary means of ensuring physical health and mental equilibrium. Traditional Chinese Medicine, acupuncture and internal martial arts, such as t'ai chi ch'uan and *pa kua*, all work directly with flowing ch'i energy lines within the body. Ch'i is summoned and directed either to help restore balance to depleted energy centres or to deliver the focused kick, deflection or punch. Whether it is calligraphy or astrological divination, ch'i drives it. It is the ability to summon the power of ch'i and put it to good purpose that the devotee of any of these disciplines strives for.

Taoism framed the principles upon which Confucianism, Budhhism and secular traditions were to build their own ch'i kung practices. The purpose of Taoist energy work is to 'achieve immortality', *cheng-shien*. This is brought about by the cultivation of the spiritual embryo, *ling-tai*. At the moment of death the spiritual embryo serves as the platform for conveying consciouness to the highest realm of the spirit within the heart of the Tao. To be able to achieve this, the Taoist sage must devote himself to conserving, cultivating and replenishing his ch'i. Within his body the practitioner converts his store of ch'i into spiritual energy, *ling ch'i*, from which the spiritual embryo of immortality is grown. When this process of internal alchemy is successfully concluded the spirit is returned to 'emptiness'.

To achieve this immortality, the devotee must start with the most basic of considerations which will set the disciplined pattern of his or her life. His or her primary responsibility is to take care of the body and ensure that he is constantly charging his life energy. Without a healthy, energized body there can be no vital mind. Mind, body and spirit are indissoluble, which demands that the devotee must pursue all the elements of Taoist practice. The adept must practice physical exercises to stimulate the body and the energies of the mind. He should study the principles of movement and change in the universe and adapt his life to move in tune with their cyclic rhythm. Finally, the practitioner must meditate to bring about that state of inner tranquillity and calm that help both body and mind to relax and function naturally without stress or imbalance. This is the minimum one must do to follow *yang sheng Tao*, 'the Tao of cultivating life'.

Despite the importance set on developing the spiritual embryo through individual action upon your own body, outside forces can assist the process. In Taoist sexual yoga practices, the male partner inhibits ejaculation in order to stimulate and prolong the secretions and sexual energies of his lover. This brings their sexual ch'i energy into a heightened state of balance enabling this sexual energy to be reabsorbed and drawn up the spine to nourish the brain.

The Taoist path of energy work, like the philosophy of Lao Tse himself, is open and inclusive. As the Tao itself flows freely through the universe, so can the human spirit, which should not be constrained by cultural or religious dogma. Each individual comes to practice with their own personality and needs, and is free to map their own pathway to their goals, be they physical, spiritual, or both.

The idea that a healthy body produces a healthy mind was endorsed by the Confucianists who concluded that healthy minds must also lead to a healthy body politic and a harmonious society. Confucianism looked for a stable, ordered state administered by well-educated, incorruptible officials who conducted the business of the empire with a profound sense of dignity and duty. From the emperor, the 'Son of Heaven', down to the lowliest peasant, each had their place and their responsibilities to fulfill. It was the Confucian view that just as disease can be brought about by imbalance in an individual's mental and emotional state so too can it bring social and political disharmony. Energy work was to be encouraged to balance the mind and govern the will, so that the individual can fulfill his destiny according to the rules of nature and heaven. Through ch'i kung Confucianism sought to discipline the individual spirit to fit in with the rigid social and political hiearchies of their ideal harmonious state. In contrast, Taoism emphasized the liberation of the spirit and the individual's right to determine their own pathway to enlightenment.

Although Confucianism is a philosophy of life rather than a faith, there were historical attempts to give it the characteristics of an established state religion. During the Sung Dynasty the Confucian scholars were bitterly opposed to the evangelizing presence of Buddhism, which they regarded as a subversive alien import. The Mahayana Buddhism that had crossed the Himalayas from India and Tibet had entrenched itself and grown strong in its Chinese character. Whereas Confucianism regarded the individual as the servant of the state, Buddhism offered individual salvation and the compassionate intervention of the Buddhist saints. This was a religion of personal hope, and philosophically owed no allegiance to a particular view of the state, save that each should live in accordance with the moral and ethical principles of Buddhist theology. To the reformist Confucian scholars of the Sung, this individual right to conscience needed to be opposed in order to prevent any possibility of a breakdown of public order and social harmony.

Inspired by figures such as Chu Hsi (1130–1200), a famous scholar and moral philosopher, these Neo-Confucianists proposed to meet the people's need for spiritual fulfilment. Whereas Taoism and Buddhism spoke authentically to the human heart, Confucianism spoke to the mind. Until now it could only offer a secular philosophy, concerned with the daily pragmatic concerns of social morality and public ethics. Abstract philosophy may satisfy the enlightened scholar, but for the people, the toiling mass of the people, this held out no hope of personal salvation or spiritual comfort. Borrowing extensively from their Taoist and Buddhist rivals, Chu Hsi and his fellow Neo-Confucianists embarked on reform. Man's spiritual needs would be addressed by encouraging the practice of ch'i kung and meditation to cultivate the spirit and the mind, thus forming a new element of Confucian practice.

The concept of the alchemy of the inner elixir, borrowed from the Taoists, was transformed by the Neo-Confucianists into a project for the good society. Through the disciplines of reflective physical and mental practice, man's emotional and immoderate behaviour may be subdued and equanimity of the spirit restored. The healthy man, balanced by a 'spiritual' acceptance of purpose and place and guided by the laws of 'heaven', would provide the backbone of civilized order. Charged with duty, as well as the cultivation of a calm, modest spirit, this was a creed for the ordinary member of society engaged in the pragmatic business of daily affairs. This was to be a religion of public conduct and collective concern, not a withdrawal to the lone struggle of the Buddhist monk in a monastery cell, or the Taoist sage in a mountain hermitage. This was a religion of social restraint for a political purpose; the longevity and good rule of the Chinese Empire and its civilization.

These Neo-Confucianist ideas, like all Chinese thought, permeated and influenced neighbours in the East, particularly Korea and Japan. Perched on the edge of a giant empire, ruled by the 'Son of Heaven' and with the backing and authority of thousands of years of civilization, no neighbouring country could resist China's power. As Greek and Roman culture have permeated and moulded the West, China cast much of the East in its image. The Neo-Confucianism of Chu Hsi was taken up by the Tokugawa *Bakufu*, or military government, of Japan to serve as the ethical justification of its political policies. During the 'Edo' period (1603–1868 CE) Japan enjoyed a period of unparalleled peace, undisturbed by major civil conflict or foreign wars. City society flourished as did the pursuits of the cultivated life through devotion to poetry and the expressive arts, which were considered to be the proper business of the samurai military class. With large numbers of armed and trained men forming a privileged but under-employed ruling caste, there was a need for a social cement to bind their loyalty to the Bakufu. Selecting those principles from Chu Hsi that emphasized public decorum, piety to one's family and ancestors and inflexible loyalty to one's superiors, the Tokugawa Bakufu framed a Neo-Confucianist ideology for their state.

During the Edo period, the Japanese martial arts were reinvented. The samurai turned from the practice of *bujutsu*, or martial 'arts', designed for the very practical purpose of killing, to training in *budo*, a martial 'Way' of self transformation. The Tao, or 'Way' in its Japanese incarnation *do* was synthesized through the filter of native Shinto religion and Japanese feudal obligations, and interpreted as a 'Way' or 'road' to travel through life.

Japanese budo began to concern itself more with application of martial skills as a process whereby ch'i, or ki in Japanese, is generated to stimulate the health of the body-mind in the quest for perfect physical form. The struggle for physical and aesthetic form represents an active, disciplined struggle for control of one's thoughts and emotions and ultimately the realization of one's 'original mind'. The ideal of the self-perfected man is one who is so calmed and tuned by this practice of the do, or the 'Way', that he may act spontaneously, appropriately and morally in all situations.

Japanese society of the Edo Period developed a highly sophisticated concept of do that harnessed many secular pursuits to the purpose of spiritual improvement of the body-mind. Tea-making, flower arranging, calligraphy, the martial arts and healing systems have all been influenced and transformed by this view of practice. Each is influenced by the concept of ch'i, the external and internal energy of life and the importance of regulating the breath, keeping the body centred and maintaining a good posture. In the smallest act there can be the biggest meaning. If each action is pursued with the original mind, unclouded by pre-judgment, then the action will follow a natural path in harmony with ch'i, the force that moves the universe. As the individual practitioner transforms and improves him or herself; their health and vitality; their spiritual and moral mind, so will society be transformed by their actions and example.

As ever with the Tao, the borrowing of practice and ideas always flowed both ways. The sage Liu Hua-yang (1736–1846? CE) had been a Buddhist who came to Taoist practice in his middle life. He believed that internal alchemy, immortality and the enlightened Buddha-mind, were different names for the same spiritual condition; the original mind. Liu Hua-yang believed that on their own, Buddhism and Taoist internal alchemy were incomplete systems. He believed that while Taoist inner alchemy cultivated robust health and vitality and prolonged life, it had no real insight in finding original mind. Contrastingly, the meditative practices of Buddhism could deliver the enlightened experience but, with the exception of Bodhidharma, had no developed practice for health and longevity. By synthesizing the practice of Taoist internal alchemy and the techniques of Hua-yen and Zen meditation,

Liu Hua-yang believed that the highest spiritual level could be attained.

Everyone holds ch'i, the energy of the Tao, within their body. Liu Hua-yang believed that the negative forces of greed, desire and emotional attachment not only inhibited enlightenment but caused ch'i to leak from the body. This leakage could be stemmed by stilling the mind and restraining the emotions. Once stilled, the non-attached mind allows free and unimpeded passage for ch'i to circulate around the body. Liu Hua-yang thought that this process would in turn incubate the spiritual embryo within to create a spirit-body that can travel through many spheres of consciousness and reality. When the body is left behind at the moment of death, the fully matured spirit will emerge as pure ch'i to achieve a union with the energy of the cosmos.

Taoist internal alchemy practice eventually developed a recognizable body of techniques that were used to develop the spiritual consciousness. Spiritual training, as Bodhidharma noted, requires stamina, suppleness and strength of both mind and body. The weak body, full of physical imbalance, is a poor vehicle for the maintenance of an alert mind through hours of contemplation. Sitting requires flexibility of muscles, joints and tendons and the ability to reduce tension and stress in the body. Proper breathing, when still or moving, increases the store of energy and moves ch'i to the head and the mind. Muscle and bone strength provide the supporting structure within which the energy flows. Taoist techniques were developed as a web of complementary exercises that would work on each aspect of the body's needs to support the health and vitality of the practitioner. These techniques include exercises for external and internal strengthening of the body and those which combine both the internal and external.

The Taoist experience, supported by the contribution of Confucian and Buddhist models of ethics and spiritual awareness, has, since the time of the Sung, provided the philosophical impetus and the practical means for the exploration of internal energy work, or ch'i kung. The developed modern systems that utilize the internal power of ch'i to heal, to provide longevity, to defend, or to awaken the spiritual mind are the inheritors of this tradition. In the course of the 20th century, these ch'i-based systems have tended to focus and specialize in a particular area of interest, be it healing, the exercise of the body, the practice of martial arts or spiritual development. Few of us can hope successfully to develop a full and comprehensive ability in all these practices to match the abilities of the Taoist internal alchemist. However, although defined by their specialisms, each makes a unique contribution to our understanding and ability to work with the vital energy of ch'i. It is the purpose of the succeeding chapters to examine how both Chinese and Japanese culture have given shape to these practices and to demonstrate the part they can play in developing vitality of the body and mind and prescience of the spirit.

Internal Strengthening Techniques

- The regulation of breath through the nine methods of breathing to enhance the flow of ch'i through the blood and the body's energy channels or meridians.
- Directing the breath through mindful intention but without conscious control, so that the breath circulates naturally through the open channels of the body.
- Ch'i kung postures and exercises, designed to promote the flow of internal energy.
- Absorbing energy from nature.

External Strengthening Techniques

- I-chin, or tendon-changing. The ability to soften and relax all the muscle groups, tendons, ligaments and nerve fibres in the body to enhance speed of reaction and performance.
- Hsi-sui, or marrow-washing, designed to clean and regulate marrow content in the bone, increase bone size and density and make them soft, elastic and resistant to fracture.

External and Internal Strengthening Techniques

- Massage and kneading of the body, used for both the external toning of the body and also deep internal strengthening of the organs.
- The use of herbs and foods for curative and preventative medicine and for assisting the process of generating and moving ch'i around the body.
- The practice of the internal martial arts as means of combining external and internal strengthening with the cultivation of the alert consciousness within the stilled mind. The four internal Chinese martial arts of t'ai chi ch'uan chuan, pa kua chang, *hsing-i chuan* and *liu-he pa-fa* are all practised for the generation and channelling of ch'i and as forms of moving meditation.

乾

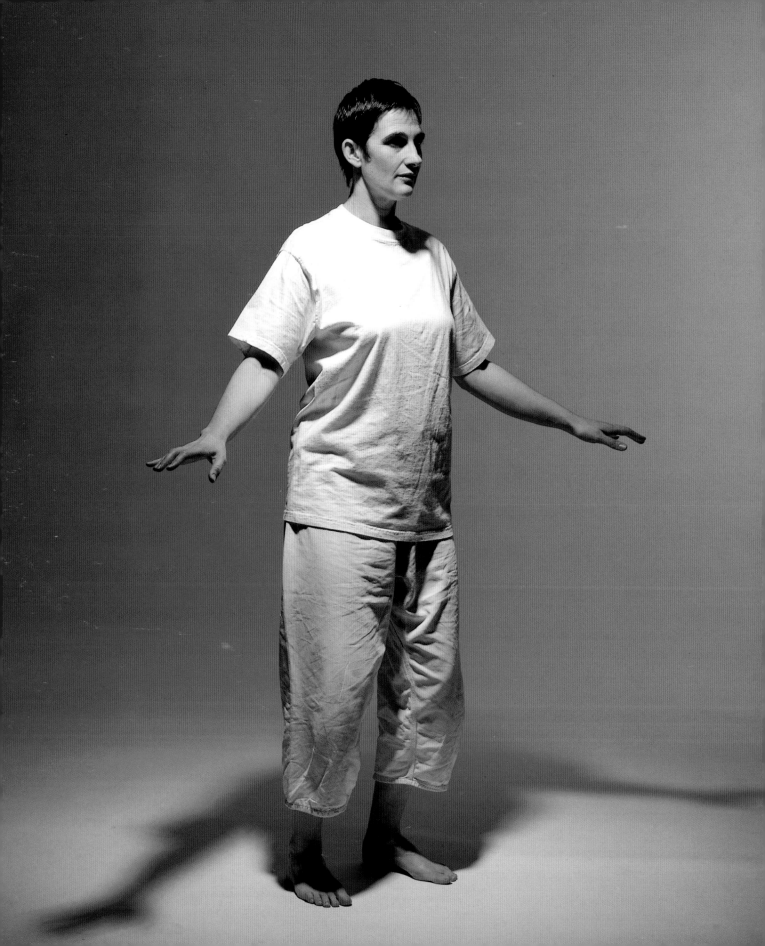

Ch'i is 'breath', it is the air that we breathe and at the same moment the energy and vitality that sustain us. Everything we see, or touch, or experience is composed of ch'i and is merely an arrangement of this energy into recognizable form. It is a concept comparable to the explanation of quantum physics for the structure of atoms and molecules as accumulations of energy organized into distinct patterns. Our whole existence is determined by this energy. All facets of human life, our physical health, mental alertness and emotional stability are conditioned by the levels and the relative flow of ch'i in and around our bodies. Summoning, conserving and using ch'i is therefore vital to maintaining a happy and healthy life. This is the premise upon which the work of energy, the ch'i kung of inner alchemy rests.

Ancient Chinese philosophers of all major traditions accepted the centrality of working with ch'i as an element of their practice, and constructed an elaborate schema to explain how it actually functions within the body. Ch'i operates through the bipolar dynamic of yin and yang, in a constant process of transmutation. When we breathe in it is yin and when we breathe out it is yang. This bipolarity is the constant of the inner alchemy schema and is present in each aspect of the functions and movement of ch'i.

Yin–Yang Trigrams

the trigrams of yin and yang

Central to all Oriental health practices is the theory of yin and yang, first set down in the *Book of Changes,* or *I Ching* during the second millennium BCE. Yang, represented by a strong, continuous line —, is balanced by the yielding, broken line – – yin. These forces, grouped in eight combinations of three, the eight trigrams of the pa kua, represent all the possible permutations of elements and natural forces at work in creation. Our health and vitality, our moods, needs and desires are all expressions of the exchange of these forces, one into the other.

Heaven, the strongest combination of three yang lines, is understood to be the active, creative male force and is associated with warmth, light, the sun and the

passage of time. While the most yin trigram, the three broken yin lines, symbolizes earth. This feminine force nurtures and provides food, shelter and rest and is seen as still, dark and cold. These forces are constantly in flux, for yin can only be yin relative to yang and as one force expands the other will contract. Within each force is the character of the other, as yin contains an element of yang, so yang surrounds a complementary element of yin.

This interaction of yin and yang is the dynamic of the phenomenon of ch'i, the primary energetic force from which the basic substance of all life and matter is formed. As we have seen through the previous chapter, ch'i can be substance or it can exist without form, it can be thought or action, the spiritual or the material. The non-material states, which are closer to being pure energy, tend to the yang, while the coalescence of material form is more yin. Good health is founded on establishing a natural cyclic equilibrium of these two forces.

The Three Treasures

Lao Tse said:

Tao produces one.
One produces two.
Two produces three.
Three produces ten thousand things.

In Taoist cosmology it is the Three Powers of Heaven (yang), Earth (yin) and Man (yin and yang) that govern the flow of ch'i. Yang ch'i flows downwards from Heaven. Yin ch'i flows upwards from Earth and in the zone of Man that lies between them, the flows meet and combine. Within the human body this trinity is mirrored in the Three Treasures of jing, or essence, ch'i, or vital energy and shen, the spirit. In distinction to the laws of yin and yang, which affect *all* the processes at work within the universe, the Three Treasures relate directly to the phenomenon of life. They conceptualize three planes of existence for all living beings; the mental, physical and energetic. Once again it is their relative strengths, and the balance that can be achieved between them, that will determine our health and longevity. In the culture of China, to be a 'superior person', is to be strong in all Three Treasures; body, breath and mind in natural harmony. The Three Treasures are the gift of the Tao bestowed on us at birth.

Within the body the Three Treasures are located in the *san tan t'ien*, the three elixir fields. Jing, the primordial essence, is positioned in the lower elixir field below the navel and is associated with our sexual glands. Ch'i, is located in the middle elixir field around the solar plexus and is linked to the adrenal glands. Shen, or spirit, is centred in the head and is related to the pituitary and pineal glands. The internal alchemy of Taoism transforms essence into energy, energy into spirit and spirit into the vital qualities of the universe, the mysterious resonance of power, compassion and wisdom.

The Five Elements

Taoists believe that all creation is subject to the rule of the Five Elements of Wood, Fire, Earth, Metal and Water. These elements have a season and a time of day when their influence is strongest and give way to each other's influences and powers as the cycle of creation turns. Within all things these Five Elements are present in ever-shifting proportions. Sometimes these elements block each other's influence, at other times they combine and assist each other. It is the

continuous cycle of blockage, interaction and fusion that contributes to the ultimate stability of the universe. Within ourselves the balance of these forces is sought in order to establish harmony of the mind, body and spirit; the dragon's back upon which we may fly to the stars.

As a tool of medical practice the Five Element theory may be employed to counteract imbalances, by using the forces of one element to support or oppose another and restore equilibrium to the body. There are two transformational cycles at work in this process, the creative cycle and the control cycle. In the creative cycle the energies of one element are passed on to stimulate and reinvigorate the next. Each element is described colloquially in Chinese as being both mother and son. Thus Water is the mother of Wood, which is the mother of Fire, which is the mother of Earth, which creates Metal and completes the cycle by creating Water. Similarly, these elements inhibit each other through a cyclic progression. In the control cycle, Water impedes the effects of Fire, which reduces the quality of Metal, which restrains Wood, which reduces Earth, which goes on to complete the cycle by blocking Water.

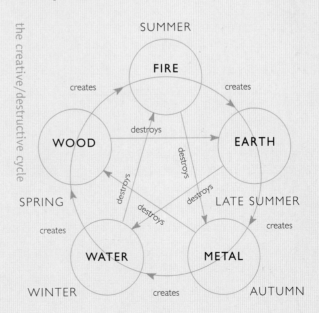

These energies have associations which assist both the medical practitioner and the energy worker to restore or enhance the balance of certain organs and unblock the flow of ch'i. Fire is associated with the heart, so a weak heart might be strengthened and conditioned by exercise or treatment to the meridians that channel ch'i to it. Further amplification of the Fire quality might be obtained by wearing the colour red or eating food with 'hot', bitter tastes, but always in balanced moderation. The external manifestation of Fire can be recognized in the complexion, while our emotional capacity for sadness and grief are also influenced by this element. To counteract any excessive effects of the Fire element we amplify the qualities of Water by working with meridians associated with the kidneys and bladder.

An intricate web of correspondences to colour, taste, smell, climate, season, emotions, time, sounds, organs and meridians are associated with each of the Five Elements. All the organs of the body are matched in sets of yin and yang with a particular element. So that, for example, the liver, which is yin, is matched to the gallbladder, which is yang, and both are associated with the Wood element.

The Meridians

Within the body, ch'i circulates along the meridian lines; the non-material pathways of energy that form an intimate relationship with the flow of blood. Ch'i is the energetic yang force that moves blood around the body, while blood is a material form of ch'i, nourishing and sustaining the organs where ch'i is generated. As ch'i moves the blood, the blood moves ch'i, each according to the principles of yin and yang containing an element of the other. When ch'i is blocked it will be reflected in the slowing down of the blood flow, which

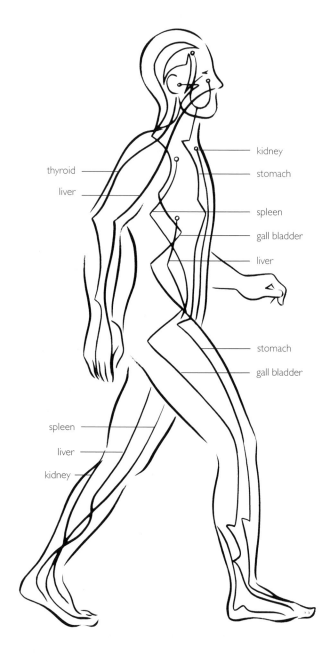

thyroid
liver
kidney
stomach
spleen
gall bladder
liver
stomach
gall bladder
spleen
liver
kidney

the energy channels of the body

in turn will affect the organs and the ability of ch'i to regenerate. So the cycle of dysfunction will go on unless there is an intervention to unblock the flow.

There are 12 main meridians. These are the yang meridians located on the back and the outside surfaces of the limbs, and the yin meridians found on the inner surface of the limbs and the front of the body. Ch'i flows down the yang channels from Heaven, while the yin meridians flow up the body from the Earth.

The early, acute phases of illness are often manifested in the yang organs as they are responsible for the digestion and processing of food and the elimination of the body's waste. These organs are the stomach, bladder, gall bladder and the large and small intestine. They are characterized as 'hollow'.

The yin organs; heart, liver, kidneys, spleen and the lungs are the 'solid' organs deep within the body. They have the essential role of storing, processing and stimulating the flow of ch'i and blood.

In addition to these 12 primary meridians, eight other channels flow a little deeper beneath the surface of the body. They are the reservoirs of ch'i and cross the 12 primary meridians. The most important of these deeper circulating channels are the Governing Vessel and the Directing Vessel meridians located centrally on the front and rear of the body. The Governing Vessel regulates all the yang channels and runs up the spine and over the top of the head, while the Directing Vessel runs up the front of the body, over the stomach and chest to the throat and mouth. All the yin channels are controlled by the Directing Vessel meridian. Together with a number of subsidiary channels that have been identified through experience and therapeutic observation, this intricate web of meridians distributes ch'i around the body, complementing and stimulating the healthy circulation of blood and the body's fluids.

Ch'i, the vital energy, is the basic energy of the universe but as it is 'one', so it is also 'two' and 'three', so that it may be divided into different qualities or types of ch'i that we are born with, or absorb, or generate inside ourselves.

Yuan-ch'i: The Primordial Energy

We come into this world already full of yuan-ch'i, the primordial energy, which has been passed on to us at conception through the semen and ovaries of our parents. Yuan-ch'i is held in the ovaries of women, in the testes of men and in the adrenal cortex of both sexes. This is our pre-natal energy, which provides a reservoir from which we will draw throughout our lives. This reservoir is not limitless. Like any reserve it requires careful management and replenishment to last the course of a satisfactory, healthy lifetime. If we fail to maintain an adequate diet, subject ourselves to overwork, too much indulgence or succumb to frequent bouts of illness we will use up this store of yuan-ch'i more rapidly. Yuan-ch'i is posed in bipolar relationship to our postnatal energy, *jen-ch'i*, or 'true energy'.

Jen-ch'i: The True Energy of the Day

Jen-ch'i is the energy of our daily existence, distilled and converted by our metabolism from the food that we eat and the air that we breathe. It is generated by our digestive and respiratory systems and begins to operate within our bodies the moment the umbilical cord is cut and our lungs take over breathing independently of our mothers. If we therefore seek to improve the quality of our diet and use exercise and breathing techniques to increase the capacity and function of our lungs, we increase our intake of jen-ch'i and consume less of our prenatal energy. Jen-ch'i operates within the body as *ying-ch'i*, the nourishing energy and wei-ch'i the protecting energy.

Ying-ch'i: The Energy of Nourishment

Ying-ch'i is the vital energy that flows through our blood and, in the Chinese medical schema, through the meridians, the energy channels of the human body. Through the circulatory system and the meridian pathways, ying-ch'i is distributed to every part of our body, from the vital organs within us to the smallest cell.

The vigour of our ying-ch'i is necessarily dependent on the quality of our intake of food, drink and air. If we live on a diet of junk food and stimulants, the vitality of our ying-ch'i will not be able to keep pace with our consumption of prenatal energy. The purer our intake of air and the more natural and nutritious our food, the further this nourishing ch'i will take us. Naturally, having a strong heart, efficient lungs and a good, well-nourished blood supply is the ideal profile and can be conditioned by exercise, diet and mental balance.

Wei-ch'i: The Protecting Energy

Wei-ch'i stands as a barrier against the influence of harmful external energies. Running evenly throughout the subcutaneous layer of the skin and covering the surface of the body, it protects us from the elemental energies of nature such as extremes of climate, the radiation of the sun and the transmission of disease from other human beings and animals. It is the function of wei-ch'i to balance the force of internal energy against external, as it reacts to the influence of the environment. All the functions of the skin that we are familiar with from Western biology, such as the regulation of temperature through perspiration, are

affected by the strength of this protecting energy. The lungs are important to the condition of the skin and by improving our breathing we strengthen our protecting energy and our capacity to fend off malign influences.

Dzang and *Fu Ch'i*: The Solid and Hollow Energy of the Organs

As we have described briefly above, all the organs of the body are considered to have a yin and yang aspect and to be subject to the natural cycle associated with the Five Elements. Each organ is either yin and 'solid' (dzang), or yang and 'hollow' (fu), and is in turn governed by one of the Five Elements. For example, the element of Fire governs the heart and small intestines, while the element of Wood governs the liver and gall bladder. Dzang and fu ch'i respond both to the influences of the Five Elements, as they progress through seasonal change and as they affect the quality of our nutrition, and also to internal factors. Our emotional health and hormonal and metabolic processes are equally important factors in the generation of this energy.

The two remaining human energies have a more metaphysical character and function. They are jing-ch'i, or essential energy and ling-ch'i, the energy of the spirit.

Jing-ch'i: The Essential Energy

Jing-ch'i results from the conversion of the most vital essences of the body, such as hormones secreted by the glands of the endocrine system, and hormones generated by our semen-essence, both male and female, resident in testes and ovaries. It is the Taoist view that the latent potency of these essences should be conserved and refined into this energy, which will increase vigour and longevity and amplify the clarity of the mind.

Ling-ch'i: The Energy of the Spirit

Ling-ch'i, the energy of the spirit, gives shape to the ling-tai, the spiritual embryo from which we emerge to expand our consciousness into the universe. It is therefore the most highly prized of the energies and the most difficult to obtain. Only when we gain wisdom and insight and perfect our control of our energies can we hope to transform them into the pure spiritual energy of ling-ch'i. Then we stand in reach of the immortal.

This is the theoretical framework upon which the Eastern understanding of the function and powers of ch'i is erected. Ch'i is conditioned by the dynamic relationship of yin and yang and the cycle of influence generated by the Five Elements. It is stored in the elixir fields within the body and flows through both the blood and the meridian channels to animate and sustain our lives. Ch'i is the energy of both the mind and the body and when we work on and replenish these, they activate our spirit. All traditional Eastern practices of medicine, health maintenance, meditation and the cultural and martial arts are to some greater or lesser degree based around these principles. In the following chapters we will explore the many directions that Eastern culture has taken in its long exploration of the life-generating power of ch'i.

CH'I KUNG: MOVEMENT, STILLNESS AND BREATH

The arrival in the West of ch'i kung (*qi gong*) as a distinct system of working with energy to promote health and vitality has been a phenomenon of the latter quarter of the 20th century. Indeed, the term ch'i kung has come into public usage comparatively recently in China itself. Ch'i kung, though there are references to the term in the Han period, only gained acceptance in the 1950s after the publication of Liu Gui Zhen's ground-breaking book *Practical Ch'i Kung Therapy*. Since then it has been used to describe a broad category of exercises, techniques and styles of body and energy work whose origins stretch back to the practices of the shamans and the ancient Taoist sages.

The arrival of ch'i kung in the West has been piecemeal and attended by the usual misconceptions and fantastic accounts of its capabilities. This, together with our not unreasonable ignorance of Chinese culture and history, has clouded our perception of ch'i kung and what it does. After all, we have not been brought up in a society whose social mores and world view have been framed by Taoism, Confucianism and

Buddhism. Our essentially Western Christian tradition sets the relationship of God and man at the centre of its dynamic and has viewed the Earth as the dimension where this relationship is played out. In this cosmology, mankind has stewardship on earth and we may use it as we will until such time as we must give account of our 'dominion' to God.

In Chinese culture, as we have discussed above, there is no 'supreme being', only a 'supreme state of being', of which we are all a part, linked indissolubly with each other through the ch'i that powers the universe. Health and the promotion of the vitality of the body, together with the exercise of the mind, form an integrated spirituality that realises and reveals the 'supreme state of being' to us and within us. Nature is not distinct from us, given only to order and govern, it is the pattern of natural order which we must follow and integrate into our own character so that our biorhythms and spirit are in harmony with the vibration of life itself.

Although we have come to embrace such seemingly diverse practices as acupuncture, t'ai chi ch'uan, I Ching divination and feng shui, we have not clearly understood their inter-connectedness. Ch'i kung, the work of energy, is the key to reintegrating these practices so that each may complement and extend the other and deepen our understanding of the Way. Thus ch'i kung is t'ai chi ch'uan and it is feng shui. Ch'i kung is whatever therapy or 'Way' you might follow that proposes ch'i as its theory of being. Yet ch'i kung is also something very distinct, forming a core of personal practice concerned with the inner alchemy of the body and development of the power of breath.

It is ironic that the advent of ch'i kung practice in the West has been given some of its impetus through the support and encouragement of China's communist government. That an atheist, materialist philosophy should have encouraged and supported the development of ch'i kung, an essentially spiritual practice, might seem surprising until we recognize how deep ch'i as a concept is lodged in Chinese language and culture. Ch'i is as air is as breath is, with no distinction between their material and non-material states. The Chinese marxist leaders were subject to these same cultural influences and were brought up with the same traditions. Mao Tse Tung is said to have predicted that the two greatest gifts that China would give to the world would be its cuisine and its traditional medicine. As the West is witnessing, this has turned out to be one of Chairman Mao's better predictions.

Communist ideology has also shaped another aspect of this ch'i kung renaissance by insisting that its support is conditional on it being open to all. This is not the traditional way of access to ch'i kung, or any other cultural practice. Eastern culture traditionally values the group and allegiance to the group, but it is a closed group where others are admitted only if they satisfy criteria set by the group. In this cultural setting any skill, and particularly one of high order and spiritual purpose, would only be taught to a small number of selected pupils. These pupils would either be selected through family connection or by some demonstration of worthiness. Once learnt, the techniques would be secret and preserved within the group, largely for the benefit of the group.

The Chinese revolutions of the 20th century, both Nationalist and Communist, have gradually broken open these closed preserves and encouraged the open practice of all traditional arts. Traditional Chinese Medicine is practised within state-supported hospitals and the martial arts promoted as healthy exercise in public gymnasiums. This has brought the practice of inner alchemy into the open and encouraged the exchange of ideas and techniques between masters. This exchange has seen ch'i kung flourish within China. However, as much as this support has promoted the health aspects of ch'i kung to the people, its spiritual message has not received the same encouragement. Therefore, it is to the teachers of the Chinese diaspora that we owe much of our understanding of ch'i kung's inner qualities. What then are these inner qualities, if all other ch'i energetic systems have it as their root?

The Practice of Ch'i Kung

Ch'i kung is a system of self-cultivation aimed at reconciling and harmonizing the twin aspects of man, those of nature and those of life. The nature referred to here is our human nature, our self. While life refers to all the inherited elements bequeathed to us from Heaven, our primordial and immortal spirit-self. The way of ch'i kung is to cultivate both aspects through the unity of the breath. This takes two forms, still practice and moving practice: the yin and yang to which all styles of ch'i kung conform.

Moving Forms

Moving forms are those that involve the external exercise and movement of the body while the mind is stilled. This includes all forms of physical practice that encourage and develop the quality of moving meditation. The process of movement becomes a focus through which all extraneous distractions are filtered from the mind, until it is free to live in each moment. This is called *mushin* in the Japanese martial arts, where the mind has cast away self-conciousness and ego-led preoccupation. The 'no-mind' reacts spontaneously and appropriately according to the laws of nature. Thus all the internal martial arts and styles of physical and mental self-cultivation belong to the category of ch'i kung moving forms.

Within the internal martial arts such as t'ai chi ch'uan, hsing i and pa kua, moving forms include sequences of kicks, punches and blocks, with the emphasis on a flowing, seamless transfer between one action and the next. While non-martial forms, such as 'Travelling Dragon', involve the practitioner generating internal ch'i by the graceful swaying of the body. Balancing the body is also an important requirement and exercises that stretch tendons and loosen muscles to achieve complete physical relaxation are employed. In all these forms, the ch'i kung practitioner seeks to co-ordinate breathing and movement in rhythmic accord.

Still Forms

Still forms cultivate the internal movement of ch'i while keeping the body still. These forms include meditation positions such as sitting on a chair, cross-legged in lotus-position, standing and, for the sick, reclining. It is the quieting of the conscious and subconscious mind, the 'entering of silence' that is the purpose of still forms. Therefore, the form of the practice is not as important as the focus and attention of the practitioner. Whichever posture is best suited to the person is best suited to the purpose. However, it is essential that the spine is always held in central alignment with the head to stimulate the flow of ch'i through the central channels running up the back, over the head and down the front of the body to the tan t'ien, or lower abdomen area.

Standing forms, such as the 'horse stance', are adopted to increase the flow of ch'i from the head to the feet. Ch'i kung theory holds that the greater the distance between the bipolar elements of yang and yin in the upper and lower body, the greater the flow of ch'i between them. By standing still, we increase the gradient between the head and feet, requiring more effort from lungs and heart to generate the flow of blood and ch'i. Though the body remains still in these standing positions, they require intense physical effort to hold for any length of time until the practitioner trains his body to relax all tension. In these standing postures, the practitioner reflects the cosmology of the Three Treasures standing in the realm of Man where the downflow of yang ch'i from Heaven meets the up-flow of yin ch'i from the Earth. The body cannot be expected to remain in a standing posture for any length of time without hours of patient training. Martial arts practitioners sometimes hold the 'horse stance' standing position for an hour or more, as the relaxed strength required to maintain this stance is the key to dynamic action in movement. Good posture is fundamental to all forms of physical practice, whether it be walking, standing, sitting or lying down.

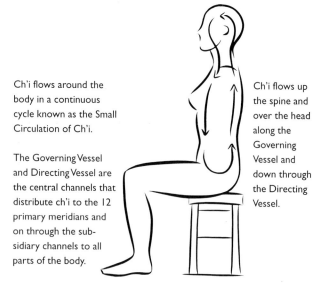

Ch'i flows around the body in a continuous cycle known as the Small Circulation of Ch'i.

The Governing Vessel and Directing Vessel are the central channels that distribute ch'i to the 12 primary meridians and on through the subsidiary channels to all parts of the body.

Ch'i flows up the spine and over the head along the Governing Vessel and down through the Directing Vessel.

Breath

The unifying element between both sitting and moving forms of ch'i kung practice is breath. Co-ordination of movement and breath, or stillness and breath unblocks the power of ch'i within the body, opening the channels to the replenishing flow of external energy. To learn to breathe is to learn to live. We all breathe, yet how many of us use our lungs to their full capacity? How many of us understand how to control and modulate breath to maximize our potential performance or to conserve energy? Ch'i kung, like its Indian counterpart yoga, places much emphasis on the learning of specific breathing techniques appropriate to both sitting and standing forms of practice. Naturally, the depth and frequency of inhalation and exhalation varies according to the energy required to activate the body or to still it. Despite the variation of rhythm and method, all ch'i kung breathing exercises aim to increase the capacity of breath and ch'i inhalation and the ability to direct meridian flow and conserve vital energy.

'Bellows breath', for example, is used to prepare the body for ch'i kung practice by ridding the body of toxins and increasing the amount of oxygen flowing through the bloodstream. This is done by inhaling three short successive breaths followed by three equally quick exhalations. The whole exercise should last no longer than one to two minutes. Inhalation is made through

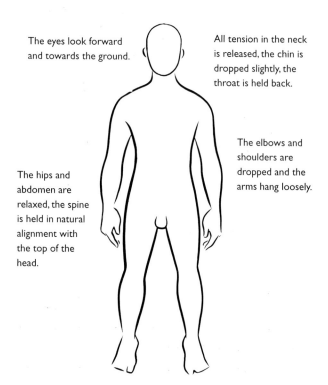

The eyes look forward and towards the ground.

All tension in the neck is released, the chin is dropped slightly, the throat is held back.

The elbows and shoulders are dropped and the arms hang loosely.

The hips and abdomen are relaxed, the spine is held in natural alignment with the top of the head.

Wu Ch'i: the first position

the nose while air can be expelled through the nose or through the mouth.

The two most familiar breathing methods used in ch'i kung are natural and reverse abdominal breathing. Natural abdominal breathing involves drawing air slowly and evenly in through the nostrils to the bottom of the lungs. Simultaneously, the diaphragm is pressed downward to expand the abdomen. As the practitioner

energy into the lower elixir field and stimulates the conversion of hormone essence into vital ch'i.

Reverse abdominal breathing is, as its names implies, the opposite of the natural abdominal method. In this cycle, instead of expanding the stomach on inhalation it is contracted and relaxed on exhalation. The relative pressure difference between the lungs and the abdominal cavity that this cycle creates, produces a stronger

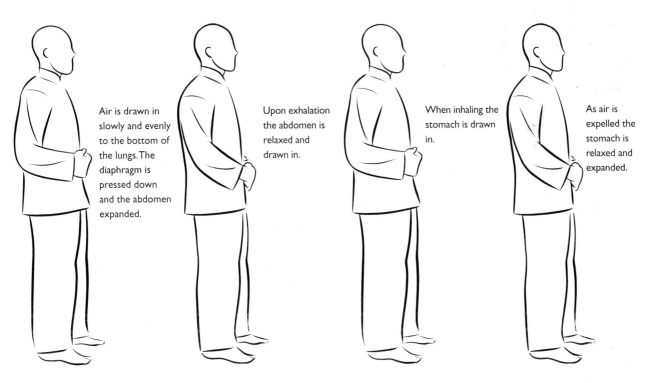

Air is drawn in slowly and evenly to the bottom of the lungs. The diaphragm is pressed down and the abdomen expanded.

Upon exhalation the abdomen is relaxed and drawn in.

When inhaling the stomach is drawn in.

As air is expelled the stomach is relaxed and expanded.

natural abdominal breathing

reverse abdominal breathing

breathes out slowly, the abdomen is relaxed and drawn in. Between each cycle the body is relaxed and allowed to recover its natural posture. Abdominal breathing stimulates and massages organs and glands and converts the diaphragm into a second heart, assisting circulation and the efficiency of the lungs. It is also important to the processes of internal alchemy, as it concentrates

pumping action than natural abdominal breathing.

Other breathing techniques include vibratory sounds, using the syllable 'ah' or mantras familiar to yoga and Buddhist practice. The intention in this case is not specifically religious, but is to give a vibratory massage to the lungs, stimulating oxygenation and the flow of blood and ch'i to the brain.

In ch'i kung practice it is the breath that leads the body, harmonizing the body's movements with its rhythmic cycle at the signal of the mind. As a general rule, the extension of head and arms upwards or inward is made when inhaling, and downward and outward movements are made upon exhalation. This cycle of inhalation and exhalation is carried by concentrating the mind firmly on the process until body and breath harmonization is effective and consistent.

Movement and Stillness

The ideal outcome of ch'i kung practice is to seek the point of balance between stillness and movement and achieve a seamless integration of function and form. To acquire an intimate knowledge of how to regulate energy flow and the relaxation of muscle groups and tendons when the body is still, speeds the pathways to successful dynamic action. The trained body begins to understand the optimum flow of energy required to meet all situations and circumstances. It is the calmed mind in the relaxed body that is unclouded by stress or exhausted by physical tension. This is the reflection of yin and yang, mirrored in the physical world; 'stillness in movement and movement in stillness'. The integration ch'i kung practice sets out to achieve.

The Centre

No lesser concept than that of stillness, is that of the tan t'ien as the central focus of all the body's spirit-mind and energy. This centre is located approximately two inches below the navel in the lower elixir field. In the martial arts of Japan this is called the *tanden* and described as the 'one point'. Not only does this one point represent the centre of the body's spiritual energy, but it is also its centre of gravity. It is the focal point where psycho-physical forces are integrated and stored. To be able to summon and release this energy we must learn to centre both mind and body. The body must be taught how to keep balanced, relaxed and low, with the spine always in central alignment to the hips, while the mind must learn to visualize and concentrate on this centre. When body and mind can move as one, the body leading the mind and the mind leading the body, they are united in stability. The focusing of the mind into the one point cuts out distractions and calms the mind. If the mind is calm the body will immediately start to relax. Conversely, we can return calm to the distracted mind by relaxing the body. Only when all the processes we have learnt are combined through the balance of breath, body and mind, are we are able to command our energy and utilize our full potential.

Ch'i Kung as a Healing Force

Ch'i kung as a force for healing has been traditionally expressed in the practices of Chinese medicine, acupuncture and forms of massage that work on the ch'i energy channels of the body. Traditionally ch'i kung has been practised as the pathway to longevity and for spiritual purposes. Practitioners have generally worked on their own bodies and have concerned themselves with prevention rather than cure. However, within traditional Chinese medical institutions today, ch'i kung is increasingly being used as a therapy to combat disease by a new generation of qualified medical ch'i kung practitioners. Healing is achieved by the transmission of positive energy directly to the patient from the practitioner's hands.

The ch'i kung healer transmits a beam of emitted energy, *fa ch'i*, to the patient through what is termed the *lao-gung*, or energy gates, in the centre of the palms. These energy gates on the palms, together with those on the crown, brow, heart, navel, perineum and the soles of the feet, form the major entry points for receiving ch'i from the Earth and Heaven. By a process of concentration and focus, the practitioner is able to summon and draw upon the flow of his own energy and pass it to the patient. The ch'i kung healer usually has no direct contact with the patient, relying instead on holding his palms over the area of the body that needs rebalancing. It is the force of the healer's own balanced ch'i and higher energy level that overrides the weak meridian flow of the patient to flush through and dissipate the patient's imbalances. The emitted flow of energy carries with it the memory of its source, and imprints its pattern into the patient's energy system. This charges the patient's energy flow to follow the direction and intention set by that of the healer. The patient's energy system reproduces the rhythm, pace and eventually the strength of the healer's, to become an identical copy of its source.

It is also possible for the healer to draw upon the focused power of the mind to visualize and transmit specific concentrations of beam to kill cancer cells or, by the emission of an 'intelligent' hunter-killer ch'i, locate and destroy specific infection within the body. Extravagant claims you may think, but much scientific research is being conducted in China today which offers evidence for surprising clinical results in the treatment and elimination of disease. The Chinese government is sufficiently confident of its efficacy to sponsor three-year training programmes in ch'i kung therapeutic practice within its colleges of Traditional Chinese Medicine.

The medical ch'i kung practitioner adopts five major therapeutic approaches to the treatment of disease, which involve the use of techniques for the emitting of ch'i, the teaching of self-regulatory ch'i kung exercises to the patient, massage and visualization. These are:

■ Distance therapy

The medical ch'i kung practitioner focuses on the external channels and meridian points of the body, manipulating and directing the flow to restore function. Holes can be punched through this field where it is weak and low in energy, letting disease through to invade the internal energy field. The healer directs the energy flow to recover equilibrium and restore the defences of the body. The ch'i kung therapist may do this at a close distance, with the palms held over the body, or from some miles away by using the power of focused visualization.

■ Invisible needle therapy

Here the practitioner visualizes the insertion of invisible needles into the acupuncture points of the meridians. This is used in the same way as the acupuncturist uses real needles to stimulate the flow of ch'i to particular organs or specific areas of the body that require treatment.

■ Energetic point therapy

In this therapy the patient and healer join together to concentrate their focus on a specific channel point and direct ch'i to the place where it is most needed.

■ Massage therapy

This form of massage is totally unlike acupressure or older practices of hands-on massage such as tuina. The medical ch'i kung practitioner lightly brushes the surface of the patient's body with his or her hands, skimming off some of the patient's external energy field. In response, the internal energy field is stimulated and charged as it flows to replace what is lost.

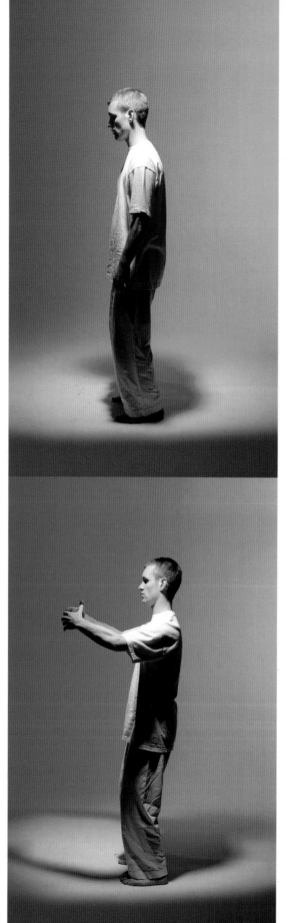

Zhan Zhuang form: Wu Chi, the first position

Zhan Zhuang form: the second position

Through these therapies the medical ch'i kung practitioner 'teaches' his patient to get better, by the direction of emitted ch'i and by developing the patient's powers of visualization and energy-control to fight disease. It is an uncompromisingly holistic approach and depends as much on the patient's will to participate actively in their own recovery as it does on the therapist's energy. For the ch'i kung doctor it also involves total commitment to a healing therapy which can involve a risk to their own health. Each treatment that involves the transmission of energy to a patient depletes the energy levels of the practitioner. This is particularly true for patients being treated for life-threatening illnesses such as cancer. Often the patient's energy levels have been reduced even further by chemotherapy and other Western medical interventions undertaken before coming to the ch'i kung therapist. Much energy must be transmitted into the cancer patient before the levels of ch'i are sufficient for the patient to join the fight. This transfer of ch'i by the practitioner gives a vital kick-start to the process.

As the ch'i kung healer treats patients with his or her own energy, it is essential that he or she maintains his or her own health and generates high levels of energy. Commentators have observed the effects of treatments on practitioners, noting how they take on some of the physical symptoms of their patients. If a ch'i kung practitioner fails to take care of their own health, it will fail and ultimately they will fail the patient. To be a healer you must first look to your own practice and ensure that spirit, mind and body are in harmony and that you are open to receive the flow of ch'i from all around you. Practically, this means the daily practice of ch'i kung physical forms, meditation and visualization techniques to both develop the ability to restore personal energy levels and to understand how to concentrate and command its flow. As the healer heals himself so he heals the patient.

The Schools of Ch'i Kung

In China, and wherever it has found a welcome in the world, ch'i kung offers three major traditions or categories of practice, the medical, the martial and the meditative. Although their primary goals and intentions may differ, these traditions are never mutually exclusive. That the head-teacher of a martial arts school should also be a healer or that the doctor should practise t'ai chi ch'uan is part of the fabric of Eastern life. In China's past, when medical care might be hard to find, who would know more about the need to keep the body fit or how to treat injury and soothe pain than the martial arts teacher. Similarly, the Chinese doctor understands, through his intimate knowledge of body energies, that the practice of t'ai chi ch'uan provides him with the strength and mental peace necessary to be an effective healer.

The following chapters explore these three great themes, the medical, the martial and the meditative, and examine how they have been formed and moulded for their separate purposes. We will not be able to look at all the disciplines that we could include within our broad definition of ch'i kung practice, for the task would be immense. Instead we shall examine those disciplines that have grown roots in our own Western culture. Some of these are freshly grown, while others are well-established. But all share a common purpose, the integration of mind, body and spirit through the power of breath.

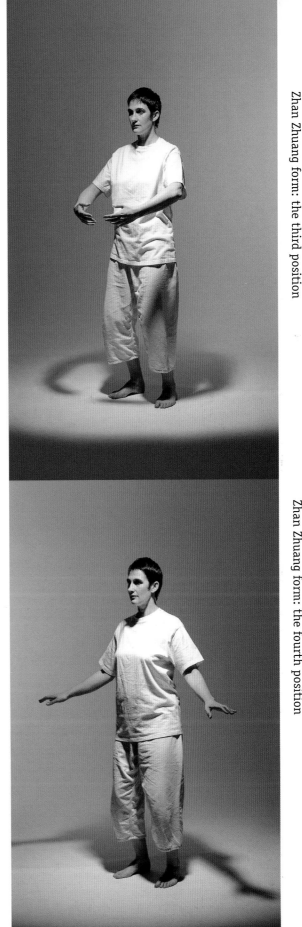

Zhan Zhuang form: the third position

Zhan Zhuang form: the fourth position

文

THE HEALING TOUCH

Many Western scientists still regard the traditional Chinese medical practice of acupuncture as a therapy without any scientific basis, whose efficacy can be dismissed as either psychosomatically induced or provided by chance. Indeed, they suggest you might as well stick needles into the patient at random to have the same likelihood of cure.

Western doctors who are prepared to give acupuncturists a hearing listen to their concerns for the total care of the patient, both physiological and psychological. In their view, Western medicine has strayed too far from providing a patient with total care to become obsessively concerned with total cure. Here the individual's psychological and spiritual states are far less important in diagnosis and prognosis, and are often seen as irrelevant to the question of cure.

This does not mean that one should accept acupuncture uncritically. It may be a therapy founded on ancient texts and venerated over centuries, but that does not confer infallibility. It may use a diagnostic language that is both exotic and poetic, but it is not sanctified or made more 'true' by these characteristics. The uncritical acceptance of any philosophy without examining its consequences is both logically preposterous and spiritually unmindful. Those who seek treatment from acupuncturists just because it is Oriental and ancient do it a great disservice.

Although the scientific case for acupuncture is being pressed in the West today, this is essentially irrelevant to the perspective Chinese medicine takes on the human body and how it functions. For an acupuncturist, it is not so important to locate and describe the human anatomy or isolate the purpose of specific cells. Traditional Chinese Medicine has no concept of a nervous system or an endocrine system, but it does treat conditions arising from their malfunction. Disease may be described as stemming from an excess of Fire in the lungs or 'dampness' in the spleen, yet they still remain conditions that have a parallel Western medical identity. The essential difference between Eastern and Western medicine lies in their opposing views of how disease is caused and the diagnostic judgments they make.

Western medicine is centred upon detecting and analysing the patient's symptoms and then focusing on a specific disease or malfunction. This perspective is fixed on the condition and isolates its cause for treatment. The Chinese medical practitioner by contrast looks at what is termed 'patterns of disharmony'.

A healthy person is one who shows no signs of illness or distress and demonstrates a balance of mind and spirit. Disease stems from imbalance, which is detected in both the physiological and psychological state of the patient. Treatment is founded on a diagnosis tailored to the patient's individual needs. Western medicine generally identifies two patients with similar symptoms as having a common illness and will prescribe the same course of treatment. In Chinese medicine this is very unlikely to happen, for although the centre of the disharmony might be the same in both patients, each will display differences in how they are affected that require individual adjustment. The purpose of Chinese medicine is to bring about the necessary changes that restore harmony to the whole person.

Yin Yang

The premise upon which acupuncture's medical logic is built assumes that a part cannot be understood except in relation to the whole. In Chinese philosophical thought this is described by the theory of yin yang. The Chinese medical tradition has translated this theory into five general principles of yin yang, which provide a structure for diagnosis.

■ All things have a yin and yang aspect.

As night is to day, as summer is to winter, as hot is to cold, so yin is to yang. We can only describe what is heavy relative to what is light, yet both have the same aspect of mass. The particular qualities of yin yang pursue this dialectic, each aspect defined by contrast to the characteristics of the other.

Within the body, the front is considered to be yin, while the back of the body is yang. Broadly defined, illnesses that make the patient weak, cold and lethargic are understood to be yin, while illnesses that produce heat, hyperactivity and strong reactions are categorized as yang.

■ A yin or yang aspect can be subdivided into yin or yang.

Although night can be defined by its relationship to day and season by contrast to season, they are always in the act of transforming from one into the other. Thus night is yin and day yang, but what is the relationship of dusk or dawn to midnight or midday? Logically, if yin is in contrast to yang, then within a yin conditioned illness there will be elements that are more yang than others.

While the front of the torso is yin by comparison to the back, the front may be further subdivided. As the upper body is considered to be more yang than the lower, the abdomen is yin in relation to the yang of the chest. A yang illness manifested by heat and hyperactivity may leave the patient weak and listless which are characteristics of yin.

■ Yin and Yang create each other.

Although yin and yang can be distinguished in contrast to each other, they are inter-dependent. We can only be diagnosed as hyperactive when mea-

sured against our periods of inaction. Yin can only be yin because there is yang.

■ Yin and Yang control each other.

To be healthy, yin and yang must form a harmonious balance, but when the quality of one becomes excessive then it will, as a consequence, deplete the quality of the other. When the cup is filled halfway it is either half-full or half-empty, there is a balance of the two qualities. Fill the cup closer to the brim and it becomes less empty or more full. Drain it below the median line, and it becomes less full or more empty. So each quality will naturally expand or contract, deplete or fill in relation to the influence exerted by the other.

■ Yin and Yang transform into each other.

Yin and yang transform each other for good or ill. This change may occur as the body responds to the natural cyclic rhythms of life and bring continued balance and harmony. Or traumatic change may be wrought as the result of rapid depletion in one element thus producing an unwanted excess in the other. All the normal cycles of life have this transformatory rhythm, for exertion must be attended by rest, taut muscles must be relaxed and the emptied stomach refilled. A healthy person maintains these common sense rhythms and tries to resist the pressures and stress that provoke imbalance. Illness manifests itself when the deficiency of one aspect is no longer able to support the excess of the other and the system breaks down. The more extreme this disharmony becomes, the closer to total breakdown we come. Effective intervention must be made to restore each aspect to the appropriate level.

The Substances of the Body

Chinese medicine is predicated upon the principle of the observation and organization of symptoms and visual signs into a diagnostic framework. The substances that form part of the diagnostic framework are familiar from our examination of the processes of the inner alchemy of the body, and are common to all forms and expressions of ch'i kung. For the acupuncturist they describe the processes that may make the body, mind and spirit work, and therefore form the underlying theoretical basis for diagnosis and treatment. Each fundamental substance of life has its yin and yang aspect relative to the others, which works through these relationships to create harmonious balance. When these relationships are hindered or break down illness will result. The five major substances that provide the Chinese with a theory for the internal dynamic of the human organism are blood, 'fluids' and the 'Three Treasures', ch'i, jing and shen.

Ch'i

The Chinese make no conceptual distinction between matter or energy. This makes translations such as 'vital energy' or 'spirit energy' problematic. Although these terms serve well as poetic metaphors and enhance our imaginative conception of ch'i, they still leave us far from understanding how the Chinese perceive it. Ted Kaptchuk, in his illuminating book, *Chinese Medicine: The Web that has no Weaver*, offers one of the most accessible definitions when he says, 'we can perhaps think of ch'i as matter on the verge of becoming energy, or energy on the point of materializing.' Traditionally for the acupuncturist such speculation is irrelevant as the whole focus of their medical perspective is centred on the function of ch'i and its effects on their patients.

From a medical perspective ch'i is important because it powers and moves the body. It is the original source of all growth in the body, but can be replenished and fed in order to grow with the body. It is always in motion, passing through the body in four major directions; ascending, descending, entering and leaving. If we are healthy then this four-way traffic will be in harmony, but if the ch'i flows too strongly in one direction, our homeostasis, the equilibrium of our body functions, will be disturbed. Through the outer protective layer, ch'i also protects the body, resisting external infection and the effects of environment and climate.

Ch'i is also responsible for transforming the energy within food into blood, the fluids of the body such as urine, tears and sweat, and of course, into more ch'i. Without ch'i the body's organs and substances would not be contained. Ch'i is the force that holds them together, keeping the blood running through the arteries, the organs in their proper place and ch'i running through the meridians. Ch'i both holds in our fluids to prevent excessive loss, and also governs and regulates their flow. Finally, ch'i warms the blood and regulates the temperature in all parts of the body.

We have seen in Chapter Two how the different types of ch'i function in the body, each playing its part in the overall pattern of energy movement through the body in a process of checks and balances. Disharmonies of ch'i occur when one or more elements of this pattern become sluggish, blocked and deficient, or alternatively over-active and over-productive. Chinese medicine identifies two broad categories of ch'i disharmonies, each with its own sub-category.

'Deficient ch'i' may affect an organ, hampering or preventing its proper function. Thus if ch'i is deficient in the kidneys we could expect symptoms of incontinence or oedema. If the whole body is deficient then it might present symptoms of listlessness and lethargy, and may be accompanied by depression.

'Collapsed ch'i' is a sub-category of deficient ch'i and results when energy is insufficient to hold the organs and fluids within the body. A disharmony of this kind might result in a prolapsed uterus or haemorrhoids.

'Stagnant ch'i' is the second broad category and describes conditions resulting from the impairment or blockage of the flow of ch'i through the body. If the lungs are full of stagnant ch'i, then the harmonious cycle of breath entering and leaving will become irregular, resulting in coughs and lung malfunction. While stagnation in the meridians will affect the limbs leading to aches and pains in the body.

'Rebellious ch'i' is an expression of stagnant ch'i and indicates that the flow has reversed its direction and is running against its natural course. For example, the natural direction of stomach ch'i is downward. If this is reversed then you might expect a patient to be nauseous and vomit.

Ch'i is a yang substance and thus deficiency results in under-activity, which is considered to be a yin condition. Stagnant ch'i, relative to deficient ch'i, is a yang condition resulting from an excess or accumulation of ch'i in an area of the body.

Blood

Chinese medicine does not conceptualize blood and its processes in the same manner as Western medicine. Although there are many coincidences of view between East and West, the circulation of blood and its functions are expressed in an entirely different way. In Chinese medical theory blood's primary function is to circulate continuously around the body maintaining, nourishing and moistening all its parts. The Chinese do not think that this circulation is confined to blood vessels, arteries and capillaries. It is also thought to circulate through the meridians with the flow of ch'i. Conceptually there is little real distinction between blood vessels or meridians, or the flow of ch'i and the flow of blood. The Chinese map the meridians and blood circulation, but in their diagnosis of conditions they are more concerned by the generality of flow rather than its precise course or direction.

Food is turned into blood through a process of the distillation and refinement of 'essence'. The food is first 'ripened' in the stomach and then passed on to the spleen. In the spleen it is distilled into a refined and purified essence. This is transported by the spleen ch'i up to the lungs. As the essence moves upward through the body, nutritive ch'i begins the process of transforming it into blood. When this 'blood-essence' arrives in the lungs it combines with 'clear' air and finally combines into blood. This blood is then circulated around the body by the co-ordination of heart and chest ch'i.

Chinese medicine describes two major disharmonies of the blood which are described as 'deficient blood' and 'congealed blood'. Deficient blood results from a failure of the blood to bring nourishment to an organ or to the body as a whole. In the case of the heart this may bring about palpitations, while an overall deficiency would bring symptoms such as dizziness, a pallid complexion or dry, flaky skin.

Congealed blood conditions are caused by blockages in circulation, which may mean swelling in the organs or the development of tumours and cysts. Acute, piercing pain can be a symptom of this condition.

Blood is defined as a yin substance and is one of the liquids of the body.

Jing

Jing, or essence, is the underlying substance of all organic life, supporting and nourishing the body. It is the source of development and change. Contained within jing is the 'programme' of our life, unfolding through a process of maturation and regulated by the relative ascendance of its yin or yang qualities in the organs. A cycle of eight-year transitions marks out the course of our physical maturation, describing the relative periods of strength, vitality, sexual potency, fertility, ageing and finally death. Failure to mature, sexual dysfunction, infertility, premature ageing and inherited disorders are all the consequences of disharmonies in jing.

Ch'i is a moving 'external' force, while jing is the inner essence, deep and supportive, moving gradually through time. Compared to each other, ch'i is the yang force while jing is yin. However, jing in relation to blood is the yang active force that produces long-term change. Blood is yin by comparison to jing, because it does not carry the possibility for development or change. The function of blood is to circulate around the body in a continuous, harmonious cycle throughout our lives.

Shen

Shen, or the spirit, is a yang substance that sets mankind apart from other forms of life. It is the original vitality that lies behind both jing and ch'i. The presence of shen is indicated by our human consciousness and is associated with our personality, intellect and powers of discrimination and choice. Befuddled and confused thinking, incoherent speech and insomnia can be manifestations of shen disharmonies. Extreme disharmonies of the spirit can provoke depression and psychological disorders.

Fluids

All the body's liquids, other than blood, are categorized as fluids. This includes sweat, saliva, gastric juices and urine. The fluids bring moisture and some nourishment to the hair, skin, orifices, membranes, flesh, muscles, the inner organs, marrow, joints, bones and our brains. Fluids are divided into *jin* fluids, which are light and clear, and *ke* fluids, which are thicker and heavier. Although considered to be fundamental substances of the body, they are not considered essential, as are the Three Treasures, ch'i, jing and shen. Blood is also considered to be a 'deeper' substance than the fluids, although it is also partly formed by them. The clearest part of the fluid unites with the developing blood and purified food essence on its passage to the lungs and its final transformation. Fluids are distilled from food and are absorbed into and governed by the ch'i of a number of internal organs, the kidneys being the most significant. While ch'i is responsible for the movement of the fluids and governs their function, it is also partly dependent on the fluids nourishing and moistening the organs that regulate its own functions. Fluids are considered to be yin substances and disharmonies display such symptoms as dry lips, skin or eyes.

The five fundamental substances of the body, ch'i, jing, shen, blood and fluids, form the basis of Chinese medical theory. Although they provide the acupuncturist with a conceptual framework on which to base diagnosis, the important factor is how they manifest themselves in individual patients.

The 12 Meridians, the Officials of the Five Elements and the Organs of the Body

The Chinese do not have the same conception of the organs as does Western medicine. Whereas in the West an organ is primarily defined by its shape, structure and physical location, Chinese theory places its emphasis on function first. Thus, within the Chinese theory of the body there is conceptual room for an extra organ that does not have a physical counterpart recognized by Western anatomy. This organ, the 'triple burner' can only be defined by function, the purpose of which can only have meaning within the conceptual context of traditional Chinese medical theory. In this schema an organ can only be discussed in terms of its relationships with the fundamental substances, other organs and parts of the body.

Each organ is linked to one of the 12 primary meridians, the channels that conduct ch'i through the body. The meridians have two channels of energy. One flows close to the skin and is therefore accessible for treatment by an acupuncturist. The other channel flows deeper inside the torso, passing through the organ with which it is associated. Along each of the meridians are the acupuncture points. There are approximately 365 acupuncture points along the 12 meridians. The longest channel, the bladder, has 67 points while the heart and pericardium meridians have only nine each. Each acupuncture point is given a name that describes either its location or the quality it brings to the treatment of an organ with which it is connected.

The Chinese classical medical text, the *Nei Ching*, or *The Yellow Emperor's Classic of Internal Medicine*, makes a comparison between the functions of the organs and the duties and powers of an 'Official' at court. For example, the liver is compared to a general of the Emperor's army and has a role that is associated with planning and the initiation of action, as well as the regulation of body activities and the movement of substances. The heart is awarded the office of 'Lord and Sovereign', ruling over all other organs and governing the vascular system and the blood. All of the Five Elements have two Officials appointed to them, with the exception of Fire, which has four Officials within its influence. Wood is linked with the Officials of the liver and gall bladder, Earth with spleen and stomach, Metal with the lungs and large intestine, and Water with the kidneys and bladder. The four Officials attributed to the Fire Element are the heart, the small intestine, the heart-protector or the pericardium and the triple burner.

the energy channels of the body

thyroid
liver

kidney
stomach
spleen
gall bladder
liver

stomach
gall bladder

spleen
liver
kidney

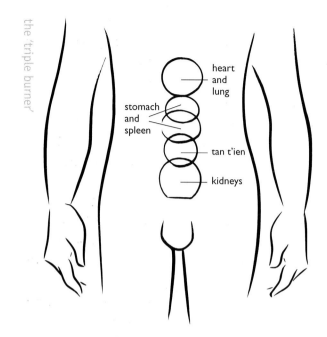

the 'triple burner'

heart and lung

stomach and spleen

tan t'ien

kidneys

It is beyond the scope of this book to discuss in detail the major functions of all the organs. This can be found in many specialist books on the subject. However, a brief look at the role of the triple burner will help to illustrate the Chinese medical emphasis on function rather than form. The triple burner has no physical presence in a Western anatomical sense and cannot be located by an internal examination of the body. Its purpose is to balance the yin yang elements of the body, Water and Fire, and to govern irrigation and the opening of passages within the body. Acting also as a thermostat, the triple burner regulates body temperature in response to changes in climate. The triple burner is sub-divided into three separate burners located in the upper chest, the middle of the body between diaphragm and navel, and the lower abdomen. All three burners should maintain the same temperature to be functioning harmoniously. If one area feels warmer or cooler to the touch than the other, this will indicate an imbalance that may need

treatment. Yang deficiencies in the burners are likely to lead to cold and stillness, which encourages a build-up of fluids. On the other hand, yin deficiencies will lead to the body overheating and dry up the fluids. Spiritually, the triple burner governs the stability of the Fire Element, balancing the two extremes of volatility and impassiveness in our personalities.

All the 'Officials of the Five Elements' must work together, just as the functionaries of the Yellow Emperor's court worked to bring peace and order to the Chinese Empire. If one Official fails in his duty, this places a burden on others, which threatens the stability of all. The Officials are bound together to co-operate and assist each other in the maintenance of what Kaptchuck describes as the 'harmonious land-scape of the body'.

The Causes of Disease

Chinese medical theory recognizes three primary categories of dysfunction from which disease is likely to arise. These are described as internal, external and general or miscellaneous factors. The root causes of internal disease are attributed to the patient's emotions, while external causes result from the effects of climate penetrating the protective layer of ch'i surrounding the body. Miscellaneous factors are the consequence of our lifestyle, such as diet, the time we give to exercise, work and leisure.

Internal Imbalances

Internal disease is said to be the product of our emotional state, be it temporary, episodic or deep-seated conditions that we have carried with us all our lives. These emotional states may have been with us since infancy and gradually built up blockages in the energy channels and dysfunction in the organs. All these emotional states are associated with particular meridian channels or organs within the body and, once diagnosed, may be treated by working on the acupuncture points associated with them.

Five major emotional states are identified with these internal causes of disease; anger, sadness, fear or shock, worry and, interestingly, joy. There are well-understood and easily observable human conditions that are given similar credence for their ill effects on the body by many medical traditions throughout the world. Our own Western psychological research also confirms the importance of emotional well-being to general health and the ability to recover from illness.

The characteristics of these emotional states are described by acupuncturists in ordinary, commonsense language. They are not the product of Western-style medical studies or analysis, but represent the landscape of observed human behaviour that we all share.

Anger includes the spectrum of feelings from mild irritation to furious rage and is said to affect the liver. Chinese medicine concludes that anger will make the ch'i rise up through the body to the head, where it becomes a likely cause of headaches.

Sadness can mean sorrow, loss, grief, regret or remorse. This powerful emotion can have dramatic effects on our physical health, particularly when grieving for the death of a child or dearly loved partner. Longer-term sadness or regret, for past failures in life or for dreams unfulfilled, can also play upon our emotional and physical health.

Fear sends adrenalin flooding through our system, tightens the muscles and sets the heart racing. The extremes of this emotion are usually confined to infrequent episodes for the majority; sudden shock can cause heart attacks and collapse. However, in the course of our daily lives, we are far more likely to be affected by symptoms relating to phobias and anxiety than strictly frightened to death. Chinese medicine expects to see fear reflected in dysfunctions of the Water Element, the kidneys and bladder.

Worry is often associated with dysfunction in the Earth Element. Worry wears us down, breaking the patterns of our sleep, and can lead to obsessive behaviour or pre-occupations that disrupt our lives. It is this emotion that is linked with stomach ulcers, depression and even more critical forms of mental illness.

Joy is the emotion associated with the heart and the Fire Element. It is difficult to imagine such an emotion having a deleterious effect on our health, but an excess or deficit of joy will have its consequences. To be excluded from fun and happiness, particularly over long periods, will bring emotional upset and the possibility of decline in physical health.

From the perspective of our health, it is not that these emotions should always be held in check or eliminated. Fear can sometime be motivating. Grief may need to be expressed to bring comfort. What Chinese medicine advocates is the 'Middle Way', important to both Taoism and Buddhism, a course steered between extremes, always countering excess in one area with the restoration of healthy energy in areas that are deficient. Preserving our sense of proportion and balancing our emotions will go a long way towards encouraging health and longevity.

External Imbalances

External imbalances are brought about by the influence of climatic conditions on the body. In Chinese medicine they are called the 'Six Pernicious Influences' or the 'Six Evils', which are, wind, fire or heat, cold, damp, dryness and 'summer heat'. Internal imbalance may weaken the body's protective ch'i, hampering its effectiveness in repelling the adverse effects of the weather. All of these influences are part of the natural web of life. In themselves there is nothing intrinsically pernicious. They only become an 'evil' when their relationship with the body is unsuitable. The effects of these influences are swift, just as the sudden arrival of sneezing can herald a cold.

Wind is a yang force which brings injury to yin. When it is in combination with other elements, such as heat, it can produce fevers and conditions such as influenza. Strong winds are to be avoided, particularly those that come from the great plains of Central Asia, as these can affect the mind as well as the body and lead to irritation and anger. If your ch'i is weak, then even draughts are dangerous and should be guarded against.

Heat is a yang influence and produces all the common associations of red pallor, perspiration, fever, thirst and paucity of urine. Cold is yin and increases the generation of fluids in the body. In combination with wind it can bring the onset of the common cold.

Illnesses caused by damp are brought about by both living and working in damp atmospheres, and by exposure to humid climates, thunder storms and the like. Damp is a yin influence responsible for an increase in fluids, particularly in the legs and abdomen, and it is associated with urinary and bowel irregularities. Dryness, by comparison, is primarily a yang condition and is expressed by such symptoms as dry skin or a dry throat, thirst and constipation.

'Summer heat' is an influence always associated with exposure to extremely hot weather. Understandably its symptoms include excessive sweating and high fevers, which may lead to exhaustion and dehydration.

The Six Pernicious Influences do not determine ill health or imbalances. They can only, as their name implies, influence events and must be combined with all the other aspects of diagnosis before a treatment is embarked upon.

General or Miscellaneous Influences

General influences act upon us through the effects of our lifestyle, such as the quality of nutrition we get from our diet and our physical and sexual activity. Food is the source from which essence and fluids are distilled and transformed. The quality and nutritional value of our intake is obviously important to the health of our blood, fluids and consequently the vitality of our ch'i.

Physical activity is important to sustain the body's strength and stamina and to harmonize the passage of ch'i around the meridians. Naturally, stress on particular parts of the body resulting from injury or repetitive actions will affect the organs as they attempt to compensate. Where it is impossible to change your lifestyle to ease the stress on localized areas of the body brought about by lifting, or by straining the voice as a consequence of your work, the acupuncturist would seek to create a balance within that takes this into account. Late nights and long hours at work or play will also drain our levels of energy, and exercise is a important element in the replenishment of our vital store of ch'i.

To over-indulge in sexual activity is to be profligate with one's ch'i. Chinese medicine views ejaculation as a pleasure to be savoured rather than wasted. Excessive activity is likely to affect the kidney jing, which causes an overall reduction in vitality, and symptoms such as dizziness and lumbago.

Miscellaneous factors include trauma, burns and bites from insects and animals. Even these sudden, outside interventions are considered in relation to the patient's overall health rather than isolated for specific treatment.

Diagnosis

The effectiveness of the acupuncturist's diagnosis is based upon his or her ability to 'look, hear, touch and smell'. In order to piece together the picture of the patient's health, the signs that are displayed in the patient's voice, complexion and odour and the quality of the skin and pulses must be read with intuitive subtlety. The acupuncturist works hard at developing sensitivity over the course of his or her professional life. Each patient brings a new experience and new expression of symptoms that must be interpreted, remembered and absorbed into practice.

The most important of the diagnostic sensitivities that the acupuncturist must develop is that of touch. Primarily when reading the 'pulses' of the patient. The *Nei Ching* places the reading of the pulse as the foremost diagnostic tool available to the physician. The pulse is felt in three different positions on both wrists and with two different pressures applied. To the skilled practitioner this reveals the relative states of the 12 Officials of the organs and which imbalance may be affecting the patient's health. Twenty eight different qualities of pulse, each indicating that an organ is imbalanced, are described in the Chinese medical classics. These are read by the acupuncturist through the tips of the first three fingers of his hand, which are placed on the patient's wrist. These qualities may be found on their own or combined with others and may be felt in all the 12 pulses, or only in one. For example, a hard, robust pulse indicates fullness and an excess of ch'i, while a soft pulse points to a deficiency of ch'i.

The tongue is considered to be the second pillar of traditional Chinese diagnosis. Through changes of colour, localized conditions, shape and coating, the condition of the inside of the body is revealed. A healthy tongue is pink and moist with no coating, fur or 'moss'. The relative states of its colour from hot red,

through healthy pink to dull and pale, indicate deficiency or excess of yin and yang. A pale tongue may also be caused by a blood deficiency and may point to what in the West would be called anaemia.

Together with judgements that he or she makes about the colour of the patient's face, the sound of their voice and their smell, the acupuncturist begins to process the information that the patient's physical signs have revealed. To complete a diagnosis the acupuncturist must look further into the emotional state of the patient. Patients are asked to describe their own symptoms, preferences or aversions of taste and reactions to changes in climate and season. Equally important is an assessment of the patient's quality of energy at particular times of the day, as each meridian has a time when it is weak or strong through the 24-hour cycle.

The most difficult and subtle of all the diagnostic judgements that the acupuncturist makes is the assessment of the patient's shen, or spirit. For true

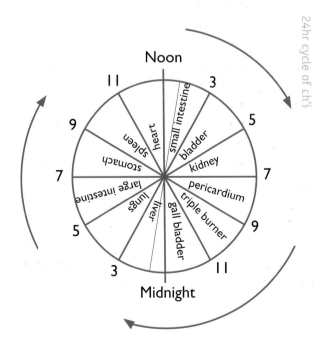

53

Acupuncture

health to be reached, the spirit must thrive, and without spirit there is no life. This assessment requires the development of a rapport and intuitive understanding of the patient beyond that usually expected of a medical consultation. This is the essential quality of empathy that completes the holistic diagnosis on which acupuncture treatment is built.

How Acupuncture Treatment Works

Acupuncture is based on the treatment of approximately 365 points located along the meridian lines, or channels of ch'i running through the body. These channels bring ch'i to the organs and distribute energy through subsidiary channels, much like the blood capillaries, to every part of the body. Together with blood, ch'i powers and sustains the patient's mind, body and spirit and is the fundamental energy of life. By inserting needles into the points, the acupuncturist influences the flow of energy in the meridians to restore depleted energy in the organs and bring the body back into balance. This may be directed towards the physical causes of illness or projected at deeper levels which influence the spiritual well-being of the patient.

A fine needle is inserted into the precise acupuncture point on the meridian that the acupuncturist has decided to treat. This may be far from any area of localized pain or obvious expression of physical symptoms in the patient's body. The acupuncturist chooses the best point on the pathway that will influence the organ that he wishes to treat. Acupuncture needles are inserted to a depth of a few millimetres, depending on the size of the patient and the fleshiness of the skin. Areas of more flesh, such as the buttocks, require greater depths. Insertion of the needles is quick and painless, as the needles are so fine. Once a needle connects with the flow of ch'i in the meridian a momentary tingling sensation

or a dull ache may be felt. The needles are manipulated by the acupuncturist on insertion and either left for some minutes in the patient, or removed quickly, depending on the treatment.

Scrupulous standards of hygiene are met by qualified practitioners of acupuncture. All reusable needles are

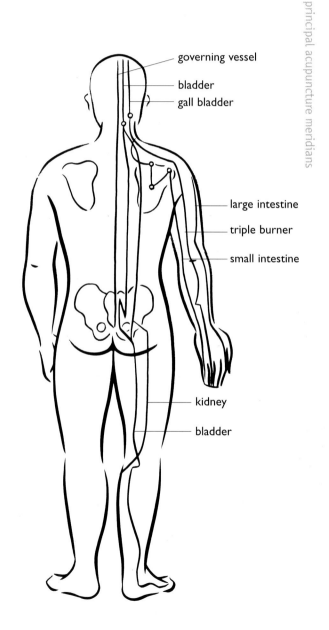

governing vessel
bladder
gall bladder
large intestine
triple burner
small intestine
kidney
bladder

sterilized to hospital standards, which are regulated in the UK by environmental health officers and in the USA by the Occupational Safety and Health Administration. Many acupuncturists use disposable needles, but the preference among the profession is to use the higher quality reusable variety.

Other traditional treatments used by acupuncturists are moxibustion and cupping. Moxibustion consists of burning the leaves of the herb *Artemesia vulgaris latiflora*, commonly called moxa, near to or on the patient's body. The herb is dried and takes on a consistency that has been described as a cross between wool and cardboard. Shaped into a cone, it is placed on an acupuncture point on the body and lit. The moxa cone is left until the patient feels the skin becoming warm and then removed. This process will be repeated until the acupuncturist is satisfied that it has had time to take effect. The purpose of moxibustion is to warm the patient's ch'i. This method is used to treat conditions that exhibit coldness resulting from the climate, or physical symptoms such as a 'frozen shoulder'. Muscular injuries and swollen joints are also responsive to treatment with moxa. Larger areas of the body are treated with a moxa stick. This is lit and passed closely back and forth across the body, gradually warming it to a comfortable temperature.

Cupping is a familiar technique in the West and was used extensively by doctors in the past. Acupuncturists use cupping to disperse locally congested areas caused by damp, wind or cold. A vacuum is created in a glass cup by lighting a taper inside it for a brief moment before it is removed and the cup placed quickly on the skin. Suction holds the cup in place and no discomfort is caused to the patient. Cupping is used most often on the back in the treatment of the common cold, asthma and backache.

Treatment also includes giving advice to the patient on all aspects of their lifestyle that may be influencing their health, and positive measures that can be taken to combat imbalance. This may be advice on diet, recreation or strategies for avoiding stress. Traditionally, the acupuncturist would often prescribe ch'i kung, tai ch'i chuan or meditation to harmonize the system and bring good health and longevity. As with all Oriental practice, the patient has his own part to play in regaining health. Taking appropriate exercise, maintaining a good diet and applying restraint in all things will complement the acupuncture treatment and make it more effective.

Length and frequency of treatment is necessarily affected by the nature of the illness, and whether it is acute or chronic. Three or four treatments for an ailment are common, but more deep-seated illness may need to be treated over a longer period with the

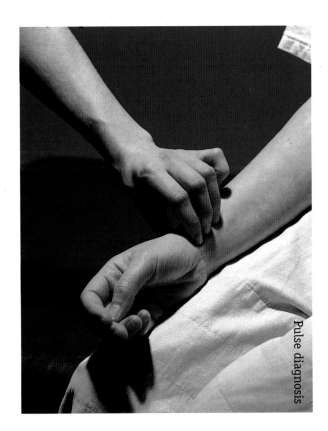

Pulse diagnosis

patient making weekly visits. However, as with all medicine, it is beneficial to attend regular seasonal check-ups to forestall future problems.

The Past into the Future

Acupuncture is an ancient practice with roots extending back over 2,000 years. One of the earliest references to its effectiveness as a healing therapy can be found during the reign of the Emperor Jen Tzung. The emperor became critically ill and was cured by the renowned physician Wang Wei-yi using acupuncture therapy. The grateful emperor was so impressed by his treatment that he founded an imperial institute for teaching and research in acupuncture. Jen Tzung gave

Cupping

acupuncture additional status and prestige when he built a temple dedicated to the memory of the great sage and physician Pien Chueh, installing him as acupuncture's patron saint. Research at the institute must have borne fruit, for in 1026 BCE Wang Wei-yi fashioned the famous 'Brass Man', on which were mapped the meridians and acupuncture points used in therapy. The Brass Man still serves as a master template today.

This tradition of scholarship and high quality training has been maintained into the present. When the Communist regime came to power in 1949 acupuncture at first found little favour from the marxist intellectuals in Beijing. However, it was not consigned to the 'dustbin of history', but instead found official government sanction and support. The price paid for this official sponsorship was the standardization and systemization of practice and training. This system is known as Traditional Chinese Medicine, TCM, and is taught in universities, institutes and colleges throughout the Chinese mainland. It is from these institutes that much of the startling evidence for the analgesic qualities of acupuncture in surgical operations originates.

China's vast population needs fast and effective medicine at a cost that its goverment can afford to meet. TCM is both effective and cheap and does not result in a huge bill for manufactured drugs bought from multi-national pharmaceutical companies. This does not mean China has turned away from Western surgery and pharmaceutical interventions. TCM works alongside its Western counterpart in a successful complementary relationship that has brought benefits to both traditions.

One aspect of the more 'rational' view of acupuncture taken by the Communist-sponsored institutes has been its concentration on the yin yang theory of diagnosis rather than that of the Five Elements, the concept of yin yang as a 'rudimentary dialectic' being more in accord with Maoist thinking than the more spiritually orientated Five Element theory. Today the Five Element theory is more likely to be used in Taiwan, Japan, Korea, South East Asia and the West than in mainland China.

All forms and manifestations of illness and imbalance are responsive to treatment by acupuncture, except those requiring surgical intervention. Traditionally, apart from the setting of bones and the healing of wounds, Chinese medicine has conceived of the body as a holistic entity that would be grossly assaulted by surgery. This approach is still evident within the institutes of Traditional Chinese Medicine where much research is being conducted into the cure of cancer by the employment of acupuncture and ch'i kung. Successes are claimed, but until an equal and open dialogue is conducted between doctors from East and West, we are unlikely to be able to make realistic judgments as to their worth.

Electro-acupuncture is another innovation to an ancient tradition that is used extensively in China to anaesthetize patients during surgical operations. A small machine is connected by wires to acupuncture needles inserted into points in the body. When connected to the power source the machine generates a current that is controlled by a dial. Gradually the output level is increased until the patient feels a tingling sensation at the point or along the meridian. The output is mild and always within comfortable limits. Electro-acupuncture is also employed by acupuncturists when the patient may have a very painful condition.

Auricular, or ear acupuncture, was discovered at approximately the same time by the French acupuncturist Nogier and researchers in China during the 1950s. Their discoveries linked certain points in the ears to the organs of the body. By carefully probing the ear for areas of tenderness, problems in the body can be identified and treated. Needles are inserted into the acupuncture points to harmonize areas of imbalance. Ear acupuncture has been found to be particularly effective in dealing with problems of drug addiction, from smoking all the way to hard drugs such as crack cocaine and heroin.

Acupuncture still enjoys the confidence of great numbers of people in all walks of life within China and Japan, who are as likely to go to the acupuncturist as they are to a doctor or dentist trained in Western medicine. This is also becoming more commonplace in the USA, UK and other Western nations. Acupuncture can offer solutions to conditions as

Inserting a needle

varied as backache, asthma, hay fever, acne, eczema, and joint problems, which patients have found unresolved by conventional Western treatments.

There is undoubtedly a need to temper our Western deterministic attitudes to medicine with more engaged holistic therapies that encourage the patient to take responsibility for their own health. Increasingly, people resort to expensive drugs, plastic surgery and designer-therapies to keep them young, confirming a persistent Western faith in an 'external elixir' that can be taken to resolve all ills. Centuries before our own civilizations in the West began to evolve credible medical theories, the Chinese had already rejected the quest for the Great Pill as a worthwhile endeavour. They discovered that by working with the inner energies of the body, health, vigour, and the youthful condition of the body can be maintained into great age. Acupuncture can offer a challenging alternative to Western medical practice that avoids dependency on over-prescribed antibiotics or other manufactured drugs. Above all, it attempts to heal the whole person, spiritually, psychologically and physically using a three-dimensional attitude to healing that often seems under pressure in Western medical practice. Acupuncture puts the unique qualities of each individual at the centre of its practice, uniting both the physician and the patient in a co-operative act of healing.

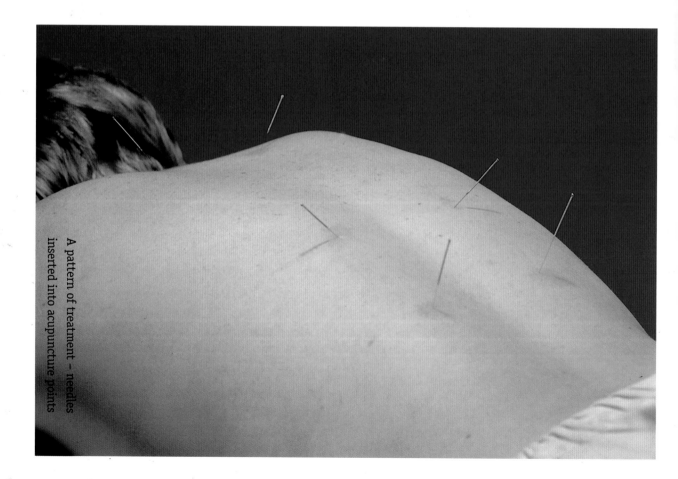

A pattern of treatment – needles inserted into acupuncture points

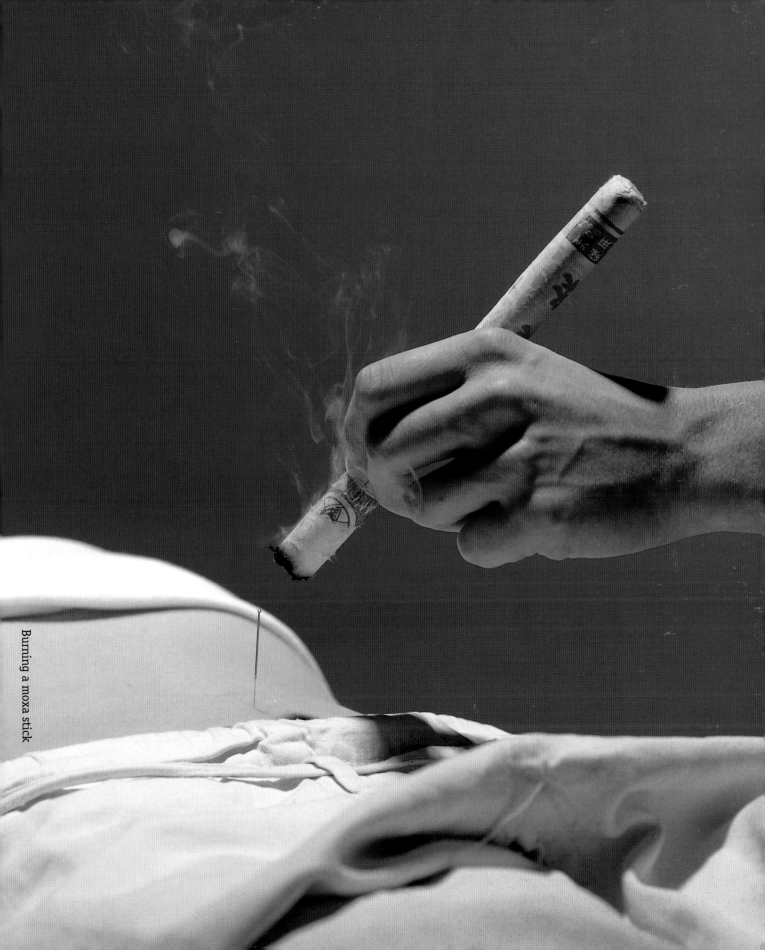

Burning a moxa stick

SHIATSU

Shiatsu could be seen simply as a Japanese version of acupressure. Certainly it shares much of the same method; the manipulation and massage of body and limbs and specific pressure applied to meridian points. Shiatsu is also founded on the same vision of the human body, sustained and energized by ch'i according to the schema of traditional Chinese medicine. In Japan, this energy is called ki. However, as our human experience demonstrates, the differences lie in more than just names, the context is all important. It is the singular Japanese cultural context within which we must explore this healing system that gives shiatsu its unique vision.

Japan has, throughout its history, enjoyed a vibrant indigenous culture. Preserved by geographical isolation from the mainland of Asia, it never became the victim of invasion or effective foreign domination. Yet, across the sea lay the most enduring imperial power the world has so far seen, the Chinese Empire, ruled by the 'Son of Heaven'. Emperors and dynasties might come and go, barbarian Mongol and Manchu may usurp the throne, but the longevity and brilliance of China's culture always sustained continuity and power.

From the earliest times Japan was overwhelmed and seduced by this powerful civilization. Chinese culture, its religions, art, music, philosophy and writing system all made their way across the China Sea to the islands of Japan. There they were adapted and honed to fit the unique patterns of Japanese life. This was a system more tightly regulated and controlled than even the 'Son of Heaven' could boast. It was a system dominated by a ruthless military caste, the samurai, which constructed its power on an elaborate pyramidal structure of family and group obligations and loyalties.

This social solidarity, formed by family ties and the hierarchical obligations of group, is common to all Asian cultures. However, it is in Japan that the systemization of this model into associations around which modern cultural activities are organized is at its most sophisticated. The pursuit of traditional arts, crafts, divination, healing and martial arts have all been preserved through lineages and schools for their own sake, as a means of gaining insightful experience. The process of making a pot or brushing a character or healing a patient becomes a moving meditation through which the potter, calligrapher or healer seek to manage and harness their own vital spirit, or ki, to achieve an enlightened peace.

Since the beginning of the 20th century, Japan has been revitalizing these old traditions and turning them into broader social and cultural movements that have attracted adherents and practitioners in the West. This has led to a peaceful cultural exchange of considerable importance and impact. Judo, karate, the 'way of tea' and Japanese schools of flower arranging have all made their way to the West. What is offered through these 'arts' is an opportunity to achieve physical and moral health through association with others in their practice.

Shiatsu, in this modern context, is therefore not only an effective system of maintaining the health of the body, but for many practitioners it is also a 'do', a spiritual path. In this model the process of treatment is as important to the shiatsu practitioner as it is to the recipient. Together they form a context, a partnership of giving and receiving, where personal as well as physical development may be explored. At the end of a treatment the giver and the receiver have shared an experience which has formed a mutual sense of peace and well-being.

Vital to this process of learning is always the teacher, the 'Way' and the practitioner's lifelong commitment to learning and understanding more. Through an intimate process of learning, where the teacher gradually reveals a spiritual direction alongside practical instruction, the student may serve an apprenticeship in the 'Way', or do of shiatsu. The shiatsu practitioner must seek a practical understanding of treatment and diagnosis, but also a compassionate, holistic understanding of the health and vital spirit of the patient. Only when practitioners have developed these sensitivities and understood them through their own bodies can self-awareness be achieved and true treatment be given.

This treatment is given, according to Japanese cultural tradition on a mat or futon laid on the floor. The receiver lies prone in a comfortable position attended by a shiatsu practitioner kneeling close by. At this point a quiet moment of centred breathing by the practitioner helps to calm and relax the receiver before the gentle placing of a hand on the *hara* (*tan t'ien*) or the lower back conditions the receiver to the shiatsu healer's touch. Physical and psychological harmony is the essence of the techniques. These techniques are given by gentle pressure of hand, thumb or leaning elbow, placed on the acupuncture points known in Japan as tsubos and along the meridian lines familiar to Traditional Chinese Medicine. The rotation of limbs and gentle stretches accompanies the pressure of hand and thumb, revitalizing energy along the meridian lines.

To ensure a comfortable experience for the receiver, the healer must be able to apply shiatsu techniques through the correct positioning of the body, focusing his centre of gravity over hand or thumbs to bring relaxed pressure on the treatment lines. This is characterized by graceful rolling and stretching movements made by the shiatsu healer while working on the receiver's body. Correct, comfortable posture with a consideration to form contributes to the healer's well-being and helps the healer work with the floor, not just upon it.

Unlike methods of massage where the receiver is lying on a couch or treatment table, working on the floor encourages a closer, more interactive process of healing. There is far less sense of a healer giving treatment and much more that of the healer working with you and your body to energize the flow of ki around your body. The floor, serving as a metaphor for the earth itself, supports and grounds both the receiver and the healer, giving a unique quality to shiatsu not shared by other Oriental healing practices.

Shiatsu is not, therefore, simply a Japanese version of Chinese acupressure applied compassionately to give healing and relief to a patient. Shiatsu is this and much more, for it is also a reflective way of cultivating and harmonizing both body and mind. While the giving and receiving of shiatsu does not necessarily require spiritual belief, empathy is certainly crucial to the quality of the experience.

The Origins of Shiatsu

Shiatsu, which translates literally as 'finger pressure', is not an ancient system of healing. Shiatsu is a modern term and was coined in the first half of the 20th century to describe a synthesis of traditional massage techniques and classical Chinese medicine with new sources of medical insight derived from the West.

Although it is a comparatively new system of health maintenance and treatment, the bedrock of its practice lies in the tradition of therapeutic massage called *anma*. This is a venerable system of massage, exercise and breathing techniques dating back to at least the 6th century CE, when a Chinese Buddhist monk introduced *tuina*, tao yin and the theories of Traditional Chinese Medicine to Japan. These Chinese theories and techniques combined with older local traditions, to establish the Japanese practice of anma.

Anma used a combination of tapping, rubbing, squeezing, stroking, and the pushing, pulling and rotation of limbs to achieve its results. Three hundred years ago, during the Edo period, all Japanese doctors were required to study anma to gain an understanding of the human body, the acupressure points and the meridians as understood by Chinese medicine. Anma might be applied by a doctor for its ki-stimulating qualities in combination with acupuncture, moxibustion or medicines in the treatment of a specific condition.

Although anma was a practice frequently employed by Japanese doctors right up to the early 20th century, it was by no means their exclusive preserve. Anma had a firm folk tradition of both self-treatment and of recourse to massage therapists, who would offer treatment for the relaxation and general well-being of their clients. Anma massage therapists of this kind were often blind, and the therapy gave them a valuable means of support and status within Japanese society. As Western medicine began to usurp the pre-eminence of traditional Chinese medicine, acupuncture and other traditional ki-based techniques in the treatment of illness, anma's status as a respected therapeutic treatment declined. By the early 20th century anma was licensed by the Japanese government only for recreational activity and its efficacy as medical diagnosis and treatment denied.

At this time, a number of anma practitioners sought to escape the restrictions imposed on it as therapy and remould the tradition to meet the challenges posed by Western views of the functioning of the body. Prominent among these anma therapists was Tamai Tempaka, who incorporated Western understandings of anatomy and physiology with anma bodywork techniques to form a new therapeutic synthesis. Originally Tempaka described his system as *shiatsu ryoho*, the 'finger pressure way of healing', then as *shiatsu ho*, the 'finger pressure method' until it finally became known simply as shiatsu.

Although Tempaka may be seen as an inspirational figure in this process, he was by no means alone in this drive to re-establish the therapeutic credibility of anma in the 20th century: other healers established their own schools, naming their own systems, each emphasizing different principles of treatment. Gradually shiatsu became accepted as a generic term for describing these combinations of modern Western methods of body manipulation and understanding of bone structure, autonomic system and internal organs with anma and traditional Chinese medicine that worked on the muscles, lymphatic system and the circulation of blood.

Shiatsu has never, therefore, been a uniform system of healing. Many schools were founded by different teachers whose treatment techniques reflected their personal philosophies and motivations. Two of the most influential figures in the acceptance and recognition of shiatsu as a credible modern alternative therapy were Tokojiro Namikoshi and Shizuto Masunaga.

By 1964 the Japanese Ministry of Health officially recognized shiatsu as a therapy as 'a form of manipulation administered by the thumbs, fingers and palms, without any instrument, mechanical or otherwise, to apply pressure to the human skin, to correct internal malfunctioning, promote and maintain health and treat specific diseases.'

Zen Shiatsu

By the 1960s, shiatsu was also beginning to make an impact in the West as the interest in alternatives to purely rational scientific explanations for our health and well-being grew. Eastern philosophy, religion and martial arts began to influence the mainstream of Western culture and gain in popularity and acceptance. Shizuto Masunaga was a pioneer in this process and his teachings have had considerable impact on the development of shiatsu in the West.

Masunaga was much influenced by his studies in Western psychology and Zen, which he synthesized with the practice of shiatsu and traditional Chinese medicine, to create Zen shiatsu. He said that in 'both Zen and shiatsu we are dealing with something that cannot be explained rationally but that should be felt by the living body.' Masunaga's inspiration for this view was the Zen master Zenshi Hakuin, who had emphasized self-anma as important to the development of both mind and body. In this way, as we have discussed above, shiatsu was to be seen not merely as a methodology of treatment but as a pathway to self-realization.

Whereas in the practice of Zen it is the master who sets the koans and poses the challenges of the student's spiritual progress, Masunaga maintained that in 'shiatsu your patient is the master. You can achieve *satori* (enlightenment) by curing diseases and restoring health'. Thus, in the words of Masunaga's pyschology teacher, Professor Koji Sato, shiatsu is 'man to man Zen'.

Masunaga's work not only gave shiatsu a spiritual purpose: through experimentation and refinement he defined many of the elements of modern diagnosis and treatment. He introduced warm up activities known as *makko ho*, to stimulate and activate the flow of ki, improved the hara method of diagnosis and added to the number of meridian lines used in treatment.

How Does Shiatsu Work?

Shiatsu takes a holistic view of the body according to the principles of Oriental medicine. Body and mind are considered as one. What affects the mind will affect the body, and the proper functioning of the body will keep the mind clear and spiritually well. The organs of the body are understood to be sources of subtle magnetic energy, generating the flow of ki along the channels or meridian lines throughout the body. This force binds us together in a cohesive energetic entity which works with and alongside the physiological elements of the body. When imbalances in this flow of energy disrupt the good function of the organs, illness results.

By using therapeutic massage to stimulate the flow of ki along the meridians, shiatsu encourages mind and body to stay healthy and resist disease. This comes not just by receiving treatment, as shiatsu is only part of the process. Proper breathing, exercise and a healthy diet are also part of maintaining the energetic balance, and the patient must take responsibility for his or her own well-being in the longer term.

Shiatsu's purpose is to detect and diagnose the blockages and imbalances in the flow of ki and treat them using a combination of thumb pressure applied to *tsubo* points and the stimulation of the meridians with hands, forearms and elbows, to regenerate our energy.

The shiatsu practitioner begins by using fingers and palms, and all the developed sensitivities of experienced touch, to search along the body's channels, to feel for the subtle changes and temper of blood circulation, muscle tone and energy. Once detected, the shiatsu practitioner will make a diagnosis and work on these areas according to need.

Shiatsu practice divides itself into three strategies of technique, described as 'calming', 'sedation' alternatively termed 'dispersal', and 'tonification'. In a shiatsu session all three strategies are employed to ensure good overall balance to the body, but one strategy will be chosen for its particular efficacy in treating the specific area of imbalance diagnosed.

If the receiver's ki is over-stimulated or agitated, gentle stationary holding of the affected areas with the palm of the hand will pacify and 'calm' the flow of ki. This can be supported with gentle rocking or light pressure applied in a circular movement of the palm. Where there are blockages or concentrations of ki, a combination of stretching, rubbing, shaking or squeezing will disperse the energy and sedate the body. Alternatively, to increase areas of energy or stimulate the circulation of blood, the body is 'tonified' by applying sustained direct pressure to attract the flow of ki along the meridians and to restore balance. Thus our body, seen as one energetic whole animated by an interchange of ki from the internal organs to the surface and back, can be restored and revitalized by working from the outside to affect areas deep within.

The Meridians and the Five Elements

Shiatsu works with the same meridian channels used by Traditional Chinese Medicine and makes its intervention through the massage and stimulation of these channels of ki that run through the body. The passage of ki through these channels is conditioned by the same principles of bi-polarity, the interchange of yin and yang, or in Japanese *in* and *yo*. Within the body all the organs of the body are paired and matched to their correspondence with the Five Elements of Wood, Fire, Metal, Earth and Water. Shiatsu practitioners accept the same Five Element schema of associations and correspondences that is commonly used in Traditional Chinese Medicine to aid their diagnoses of their patients' conditions.

Tsubos

Of the 365 classical acupuncture points located along the 12 major meridians, 60 to 100 are thought to be the most effective in shiatsu practice. These acupressure points, called tsubos in Japanese, are regarded as openings to the channels of ki beneath the surface of the body. They are often described as having the size and shape of the tip of the finger, with a narrower opening to the surface and a broader-based hollow beneath, located in the ki meridian. By using his or her fingertips the shiatsu practitioner can feel these hollows in the ki channels and diagnose their condition.

Where there is an absence of ki, the surrounding tsubos will feel empty and lacking in energy. Correspondingly, in the areas where the ki is blocked

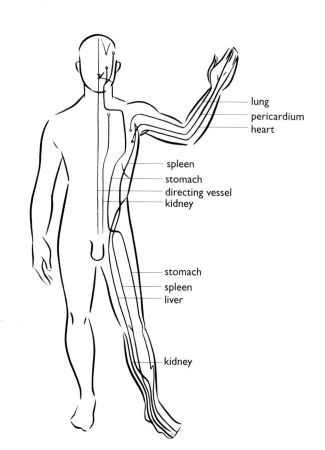

lung
pericardium
heart

spleen
stomach
directing vessel
kidney

stomach
spleen
liver

kidney

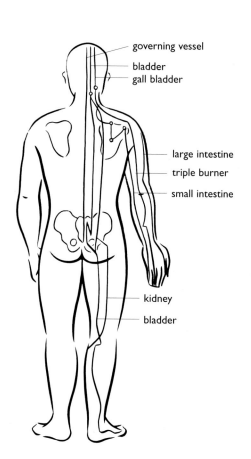

governing vessel
bladder
gall bladder

large intestine
triple burner
small intestine

kidney
bladder

the tsubos will be tense and constricted and are often painful when touched. This sensitivity to touch may indicate disharmony in one or other of the organs. *Yu*, or 'associated points' on the back of the body, and *bo*, or 'alarm points' connect directly to the organs and can assist the practitioner in making a diagnosis by their reaction to pressure. Temperature can also assist this process with areas full of ki tending to feel warm and empty areas cold.

Shiatsu practice is not confined to working solely with fixed tsubo points, for other temporary tsubos will open and close with the constant fluctuations of the flow of ki. The shiatsu practitioner will seek out these hollows and work with them to release tension and constriction.

Kyo and *Jitsu*: Yin and Yang

The terms kyo and jitsu refer to the energetic quality of ki flowing within the meridians. Their relationship matches the constant fluctuation of yin or yang, so that a channel or tsubo can only be described as kyo relative to jitsu in another. Jitsu areas, full of ki and protruding above the surface, are consequently the easiest to detect by touch. They are dispersed or sedated by stretching, squeezing, rubbing or shaking the affected area.

Channels that are kyo, or empty, are much harder to detect and lie deeper within the surface. These areas are treated by tonification. The shiatsu giver patiently holds the affected area, giving time for warmth to penetrate the hollow and restore the imbalance of ki. Poetically, the classical Chinese medical books compare the process of tonification as waiting for a cherished lover patiently, tenderly and without concern for the passing of time.

As kyo and jitsu are relative to each other, each channel will contain areas that are full or empty and can be treated to restore their balance. The shiatsu practitioner will be seeking to discriminate between the channels to find the area with the fullest ki and that with the least energy. By balancing the meridian of the most jitsu with the channel exhibiting the most kyo imbalances, the other channels will tend naturally to restore themselves.

Diagnosis

The philosophical foundation of shiatsu practice is, as we have seen, that of traditional Chinese medicine. The qualified shiatsu practitioner will employ the whole range of diagnostic practice that is common to Oriental medicine wherever the influence and power of Chinese culture has been felt. The shiatsu practitioner will be looking for the same initial diagnostic signs as the acupuncturist. They will ask sensitive questions to seek

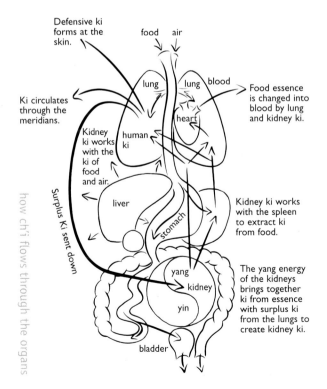

how ch'i flows through the organs

associations with ill health in the patient's lifestyle. The tone of the patient's voice will be carefully 'listened' to for the subtle nuances that might betray emotional stress. The practitioner will also search the face for signs of ki imbalance. Following the vital diagnostic skills of 'asking', 'listening' and 'seeing', must come that of 'touching'. Of course the detection of areas of kyo and jitsu in the course of a treatment will form part of this process. However, the shiatsu practitioner has a unique method of touch diagnosis to employ. This palpation of the belly area is known as 'hara' diagnosis.

Hara Diagnosis

Oriental philosophy locates the source of all the body's strength and energy in the belly area of the body, between the ribcage and the pelvic bone. Ki, the manifestation of this energy, is responsible for the health of our body, mind and spirit. It is circulated by the lungs as 'breath' around the body until it arrives in the hara and is concentrated in the 'one point', the vital centre of the body, called the tanden in Japan. As the hara is the storage centre for the body's ki energy, it is also culturally understood as the centre of the spirit and thus influences and forms the mind. In this world view these elements of mind, body and spirit cannot be addressed separately; each will reflect the state of each other.

The hara is therefore the root of our whole person. Our character and health can be judged through it. A colloquial expression such as *hara o tateru*, or 'upset hara' describes someone who is disturbed or angry, while *hara ga guru*, literally 'to have hara' serves in the same way as the English expression 'to have guts' suggesting bravery and an indomitable spirit. As the hara is the source of all ki energy, then all disease must stem from this area. Touch diagnosis of the hara reveals all imbalances and sickness.

Three contrasting methods of touch diagnosis may be made in shiatsu treatment, according to the particular view of the hara taken by different schools. The simple view divides the hara into an upper and lower region. The upper region, located between the navel and the ribcage, should feel responsive, pliant and energetic. By contrast, the lower region, lying below the navel and including the pubic area, should feel firm and robust. An alternative visualization of the hara divides the region in the same manner as the triple burner into three regions. Here, a healthy diagnosis should reveal a supple and unconstrained response to touch in the upper region, influenced by heart and lung ki. The central region around the navel should be elastic and malleable when touched, while the third region, the area of the tanden and the kidneys, must be firm and strong.

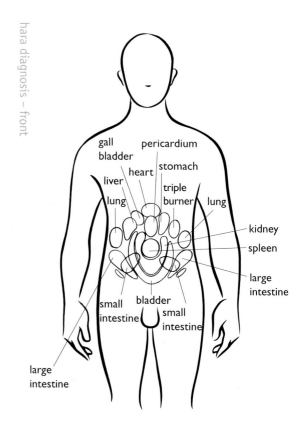

hara diagnosis – front

Masunaga, the originator of Zen shiatsu, interprets the areas of the hara as having even greater depth and complexity. In Masunaga's system, the hara is a map of sensitive areas arranged between ribcage and pelvic bone that correspond directly to the organs. Through the exploration of touch, measuring the kyo and jitsu of these areas, the condition of each organ can be diagnosed. This will tell the practitioner which meridian lines to tonify or sedate.

Hara diagnosis is a very tactile process and depends on how comfortable the receiver feels about being touched in this area of the body. It must always have the patient's consent. The shiatsu practitioner's approach to making a hara diagnosis must be calm, considerate and reassuring for it makes the opening physical connection between the giver and receiver.

Diagnosis is made with the receiver lying face up and the practitioner sitting in *seiza* position (see page 74), with his or her knees folded under, close to the patient. Gently, he or she will place his or her nearest hand on the patient's hara, with the heel of the hand resting below the navel and the fingers extending above it. Time will be allowed for the connection to be accepted by the patient before any exploration is undertaken. When this trust is communicated through the hand, the giver will carefully slide her other hand under the arch of the receiver's back where a reflection of the hara's condition may also be felt. The more arched this lumbar region, the more likely it is that the muscles will be tight and tensed. The hand is then brought from the back to the front, to support the upper hara. When both hands are comfortably placed, the practitioner will gently probe the area above and below the patient's navel with the extended fingers of the near hand.

Although hara diagnosis is an important analytical tool characteristic of shiatsu's sensitivities to the body's fields of energy, the practitioner will not rely solely on this method. As we have already discussed, all the diagnostic techniques available to traditional Chinese medicine will be used together with hara diagnosis, in order to build a complete picture of the patient's state of well-being. To refresh ourselves, these are: *bo shin*, or 'looking'; *bun shin*, 'listening'; *mon shin*, or 'asking questions'; and finally *setsu shin*, or 'cutting through', the manual palpation of the hara.

A Shiatsu Treatment

A shiatsu treatment can take anything from 30 minutes to an hour and a half to complete. Traditionally, the patient lies on a futon or padded surface on the floor, allowing the practitioner to use his or her own body weight and the natural force of gravity to press deeper into the treatment areas. This close, grounded

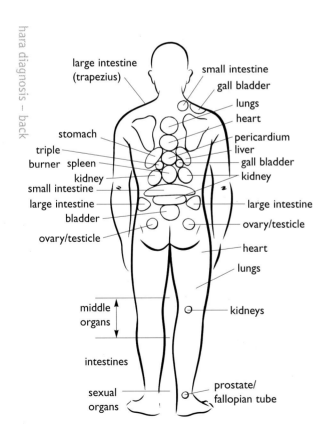

hara diagnosis – back

large intestine (trapezius)
small intestine
gall bladder
lungs
heart
stomach
pericardium
liver
triple burner   spleen
gall bladder
kidney
kidney
small intestine
large intestine
large intestine
bladder
ovary/testicle
ovary/testicle
heart
lungs
middle organs
kidneys
intestines
sexual organs
prostate/ fallopian tube

contact helps the giver and the receiver to feel a mutual sense of connection and support unlike any other massage experience.

Treatment is given to the receiver clothed, preferably in thin, loose clothing of some natural material. Rather than detract from feeling the kyo and jitsu in the receiver's body, this separation of direct contact with the skin enables the practitioner to focus on the fields of ki energy running below the surface. The practitioner works with both hands on the receiver's body, with one hand acting in the yin role, tonifying the kyo in the meridian fields, while the other acts as the yang force, calming the jitsu.

The yin, or supporting, hand remains stationary while the yang, or active, hand explores the energy levels in the meridians. There is a constant exchange of 'messages' flowing between the supporting hand and the active hand, guiding the practitioner to where the imbalances of ki energy may be felt. A skilled practitioner will be able to make these two points of pressure feel as one, as the flow of energy is harmonized between them.

This is a connection felt by both giver and receiver, for as the patient feels the ki flow from one point to another through their own body, so the ki flows through the practitioner, forming a circuit of energetic exchange. Masunaga, the founder of Zen shiatsu and the originator of this two-hand technique, describes this experience as sharing 'life-compassion'. The 'two points felt as one' is both a physical and spiritual metaphor, demonstrating the oneness of the life-force. When we are ill or unhappy our body is disconnected and separated from that life force. We feel the sickness and the pain through our bodies disrupting the equanimity of our mind. When we are well the body is not 'felt' by the mind and there is no separation between mind and body as they act in unconscious unity.

While the yin hand remains still, 'listening' to the ki energy deep in the organs, the yang hand slides fluidly along the meridians, pausing only to apply a steady, constant pressure at tsubo points along the channels. Generally the kyo areas will be tonified and strengthened first, drawing off the excess jitsu energy from blocked tsubos and gorged channels. The practitioner will use a range of techniques, applying pressure to the tsubos with thumbs, fingers, forearms and elbows. Stretches may also be employed to open up and increase the flow of ki through the meridians.

It is important both for the comfort and well-being of the receiver and the effectiveness of the treatment that the practitioner approach the giving of shiatsu with empathy and compassion. Without the ability to respond to others and to have a genuine desire to heal, it is unlikely that the practitioner will be able to develop the vital intuition necessary for good holistic treatment. Human warmth and the ability to understand and connect with the patient's condition is as important to the treatment as is the quality of the physical technique employed. Indeed, without this quality of mind governing the practitioner's hands, the treatment would be crude and invasive.

When the giving of shiatsu is approached as a do,

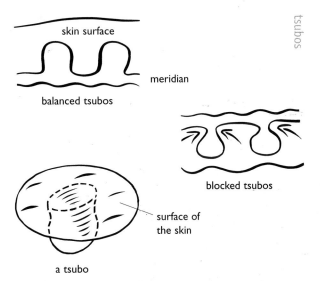

skin surface

meridian

balanced tsubos

blocked tsubos

surface of the skin

a tsubo

tsubos

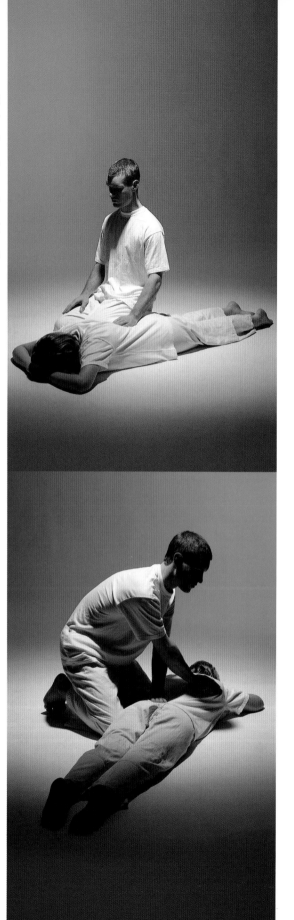

Sitting in seiza and making first contact

Stretching the upper and lower spine

or a spiritual Way pursued through the discipline of practice, then the perfection of form becomes the foundation on which understanding is built. The mind is disciplined and trained by the body through a single-minded devotion to perfecting technique to fit its purpose. This long absorption in the process of learning the Way provides lessons which can only be experienced physically, and comprehended intuitively. In this way the practitioner comes to a treatment with the same disciplines of form as the martial artist when performing a *kata*, or sequence of techniques. The martial artist seeks to reach the state of mushin, or 'no mind', a mental platform that makes no prejudgments and holds no preconceptions. It is this open mind that comes fresh to each new moment, recognizing its uniqueness and difference from the moment before. The objective is to transcend skill to achieve *mugamae*, or 'no-posture', the physical reflection of mushin where the body responds intuitively and acts appropriately to any stimulus. Not surprisingly, therefore, the techniques of shiatsu do share the same principles of balance, movement and the application of the limbs as the *kihon waza* (basic technique) of any Japanese martial art.

The first and most fundamental aspect of good martial arts technique is the ability to co-ordinate breathing with the body in action. This co-ordination must also extend to reading an opponent's intentions from the rhythm of their breathing and match one's own accordingly. The shiatsu practitioner takes the same starting point, tuning into the patient's breathing pattern to synchronize her techniques with the exhalation of breath.

Good posture goes hand in hand with effective breathing. The practitioner must be able to manoeuvre comfortably around the patient lying on the floor. This demands moving extensively on the knees and requires good balance and a relaxed body. To do this the practitioner centres his or her own hara and centre of gravity between a wide base of knees and feet, ideally keeping three points of contact with the floor. All movement is made from the hara or lower abdomen. The upper body is imagined as feeling light, and the lower heavy and grounded, as if the earth has anchored you to its surface. Ki is transmitted from the earth, through the tanden and along the underside of the limbs. The practitioner concentrates on the 'one point' within the tanden, summoning the breath and directing this ki through their hands to the patient.

It is this attention to form and the physical and mental disciplines of a 'Way' that prevent shiatsu from being characterized as just another massage treatment. For the practitioner, the process of shiatsu treatment is as important as the outcome for the patient. In fact, they cannot exist without each other; for it is by honouring the process through a dedication to both its spiritual and healing purposes that empathy is developed. When the practitioner's heart is in his or her hands the patient will receive the most effective and sympathetic treatment.

What Can Shiatsu Heal?

Although it is clear that a shiatsu treatment is underpinned by the practitioner's commitment to the 'Way', it must ultimately be judged by its healing outcomes. A 'Way' that fits no purpose provides no answers to any of life's questions and is devoid of any meaning. Form is only important to the Japanese archer because it contains the secrets of how to hit the target. If the archer consistently misses the target, then the form must be incorrect. The struggle with form is to arrive at the moment when the arrow releases itself from the bow and finds its own way to the target. It is the same for shiatsu; without the evidence of healing then

Working down the spine in the lunge position

Working down the leg

Moving to the head and palming the shoulder blades

Connecting with the hara

there would be no meaning to shiatsu.

Fortunately for shiatsu, there is qualitative case study evidence to suggest that treatments do bring positive benefits to the receiver. The main thrust of shiatsu treatment is preventative. It is an intervention designed to encourage the flow of ki around the body. A balanced flow of ki sustains good health. Shiatsu stimulates blood circulation and the lymphatic systems, helping the body to clear itself of lactic acid and other unwanted toxins. The stimulation of the internal organs, endocrine and autonomic systems encourages them to function healthily. Investigations have indicated that applying pressure to the tsubos releases the body's natural pain killers; endorphins and enkephalins. By receiving regular treatments the body is toned, toxins are cleared and energy flow is evened, so that our mind can work with our body's fullest attention.

Shiatsu can also be effective in treating specific ailments and conditions. Practitioners' case notes and studies demonstrate many successful interventions to help patients with a variety of conditions. These vary from strains, chronic back pain, stress and anxiety to the relief of asthma and bronchitis. Shiatsu makes its diagnoses according to the theoretical principles of classical Chinese medicine. It is not surprising therefore that it will treat the same tsubos for the same conditions as the acupuncturist, but with thumb and finger pressure, palming and stretching rather than the insertion of needles.

The sensitivity in the practitioner's hands and body can modify and adapt shiatsu technique to relieve almost all conditions. However, while shiatsu may be able relieve many conditions it cannot cure a tumour or heal a diseased tooth. It will stimulate and revitalize the body's energy, bringing a balance to body and mind that will help you fight the cancer. With a toothache, more immediate pain relief may be brought. The tooth can be anaesthetised by squeezing the deltoid muscle at the top of the shoulder for pain in the upper jaw or by firmly squeezing the pectoralis major muscle, found close to the front of the armpit. However, you will still need to get the tooth filled. When the shiatsu practitioner offers a specific treatment focused on a particular ailment, it is to generate the healing process through the stimulation of ki in that area, alerting and mobilizing the body's natural defences. It is through this holistic process that shiatsu provides the best circumstances for the body to heal itself.

There are of course contra-indications to the use of shiatsu, such as in the case of infections that may be spread around the body. The diagnostic process should alert the practitioner to any situations where treatment needs to be modified or avoided altogether. It is therefore essential that you provide a complete picture of your health to the practitioner before embarking on any treatment process.

Shiatsu, as befits a holistic philosophy of life, is an energetic system of health care which looks at the state of the receiver's mind as well as the body. The practitioner is dedicated to the purpose of healing the whole person, requiring experience, patience, empathy and compassion. Although it can take many successful interventions to treat acute illness and bring relief to pain and stress in the body, its greatest benefits come from regular treatment. Therefore, it requires a commitment to treatment and a willingness from the receiver to take a reasonably long-term view of its effects on any particular condition. Immediate benefits will come from the toning of the body and the easing of tightness and strain in the muscle groups, energizing the body. An energetic body will naturally make you feel alert and alive, stimulating the mind and renewing its capacity to deal with stress and the vicissitudes of everyday life. The more frequently you receive treatment, the more likely it is that you will become

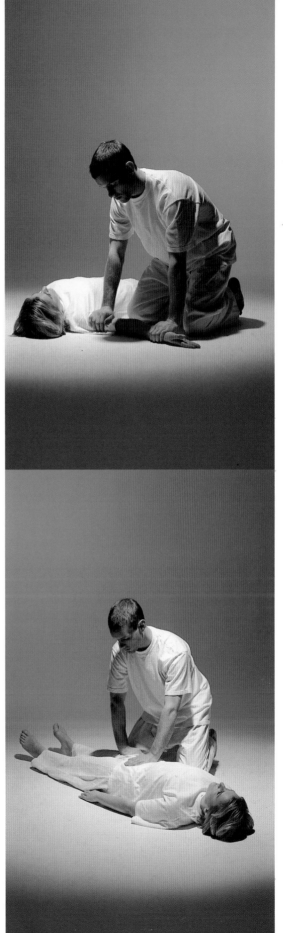

Palming the arms

Palming near the leg

attuned to your own body and how to care for it. An essential part of this body maintenance programme will be the self-treatment routines and exercises that the practitioner will teach you.

As with any other health professional, the more familiar the shiatsu practitioner becomes with your particular condition and personality, the more likely it is that he will be able to help you. Equally, your confidence in the practitioner is vital. The openness with which you receive the treatment and the likelihood of your heeding their advice depend on this confidence. Shiatsu can be given to you without your belief or commitment, but it will probably not be such a redeeming experience without your co-operation. When empathy flows both ways, true healing of mind and body can be attempted.

Practising shiatsu can also be a discipline, a do or Way pursued for the illumination of the spirit and the development of a moral mind. Receiving shiatsu, learning shiatsu for the pleasure of treating family and friends, and becoming a practitioner oneself, are all steps along this continuum. This is not the kind of health system in which the receiver is left on the outside by professionals guarding secrets. Shiatsu may require three or more years of professional training to become a practitioner, but it is open to all. Many practitioners will also be teachers, with their own schools, or affiliated to larger institutions, and will be actively recruiting students. Short courses and support groups encourage participation and can be the first steps on the road to more active involvement. By bringing healing to others we begin the long and difficult process of healing ourselves. Ultimately, the best way to encourage an insightful and compassionate mind within a healthy body is by practising shiatsu as a do, or Way, to give as well as receive.

Stretching the spine

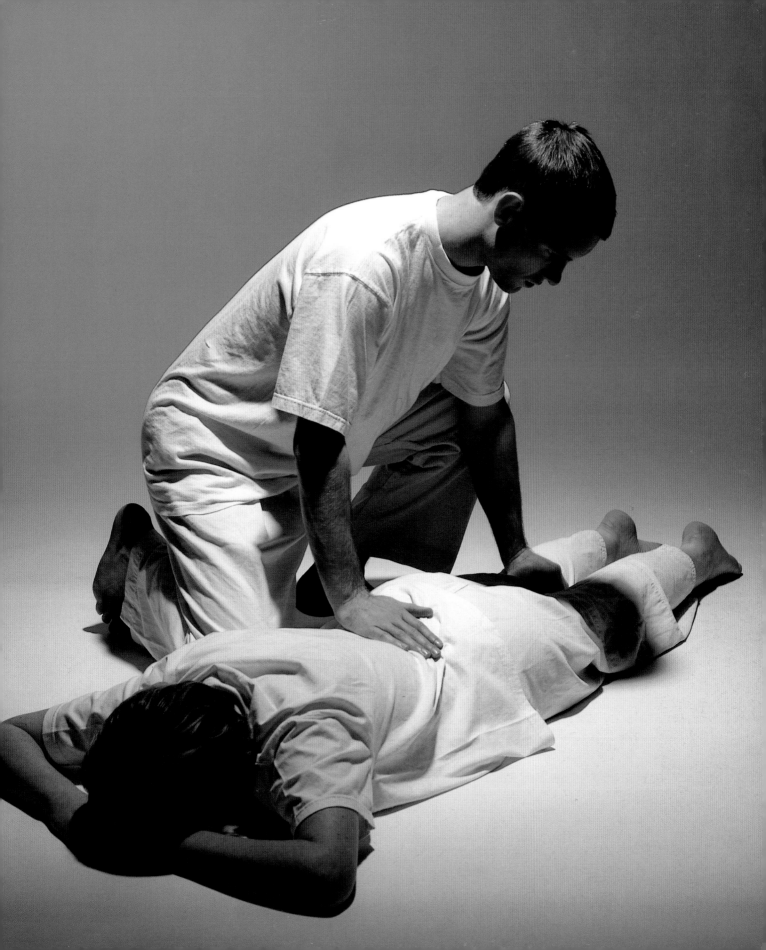

Do-in is the Japanese name for the ancient Taoist practice of tao yin, or the 'gentle approach to the way'; a ch'i kung exercise intended to promote general health and to treat specific conditions. Early Taoist practice of tao yin included physical exercises to improve the flow of ch'i, or ki, through the meridian channels and therapeutic touch. Centres of pain or discomfort in the body can be anaesthetized by the gentle application of holding, or pressing with the hands. Taoist practitioners recognized this natural phenomenon and incorporated self-massage and touch into the tao yin practice.

Do-in represents the Japanese tradition of Taoist ch'i kung from which all the health applications of ch'i energy work, such as acupuncture, shiatsu and oriental yoga, derive. Do-in exercises stimulate the flow of ki around the body, develop breath control and stretch tendons and muscles to produce a flexible, soft, healthy body. Acupressure points, or tsubos, are pressed to tonify or disperse kyo or jitsu, full or empty areas of ki, and restore balance to the energy channels, and are the basis for shiatsu techniques for self-treatment. Indeed, shiatsu practitioners often teach forms of do-in exercise to their patients as a means of maintaining the effects of their treatments.

Do-in, as a Japanese variant of ch'i kung, is not primarily concerned with the maintenance of health and vitality for its own sake. Like ch'i kung, it shares the same long-term spiritual end: the transformation of the spirit through inner alchemical change of the body. Do-in not only provides a 'gentle approach' to the daily exercises needed by the practitioner's body, but also a 'Way', or do, of spiritual practice. Michio Kushi has brought do-in to the West as a developed and system-ized practice which he calls the 'Tao of Shin Sen', or *Shin-sen Do*, 'the Way of Spiritual Free Man'.

Although shin-sen do energy work has been adapted and refined from the legacy provided by Hindu, Taoist, Buddhist and Shinto practice, it has eschewed secrecy or mystic initiation in its transmission. Do-in, in the guise of shin-sen do, is a modern cognate do form, open to all. Kushi sensei's philosophy, principles and methods are described comprehensively in published works and he and his followers conduct lectures and workshops advo-cating the shin-sen do system. In the religious or mystic tradition of Taoist ch'i kung, the practitioner forms an apprentice to master relationship with his teacher. Shin-sen do does not require this absolute level of commit-ment to training with a guru or master sage. The performance and understanding required for the spiritual process of do-in are naturally enhanced and clarified by learning from a teacher and demand serious commit-ment. However, the open practice of do-in is encouraged at any level where it may benefit health and well-being.

Shin-sen do has a traditional Neo-Confucianist ele-ment to its practice that is overlaid by its modern advo-cacy of world peace as an ultimate goal of spiritual practice. Kushi offers the regeneration of the self as a means of countering and eventually overcoming the degenerative effects that current lifestyles and political conflict have had on the social body. Like Chu Hsi, Kushi

sensei advocates changing ourselves in order to begin to influence and change those around us and thus estab-lish universal harmony and peace. Shin-sen do is ch'i kung framed by a philosophy of idealistic optimism.

Unlike other forms of spiritual energy work, do-in can be practised entirely on your own, without the necessity of special equipment or a practice hall. All the exercises that form the course of daily ritual can be per-formed in a clear, comfortable space in your home. Do-in exercises can take very little time to perform and have been designed to fit the busy schedules of the Tokyo office worker, not the Taoist mystic. Essentially, do-in exercises are performed in two daily sessions, preferably in the morning and evening. These exercises work on all the meridians of the body to stabilize the flow of ki (ch'i) and prevent the onset of illness.

Do-in and the 'Way of Eating'

Kushi sensei's shin-sen do advocates a holistic pro-gramme of mental and spiritual training, founded on a macrobiotic way of life. To practise Kushi's shin-sen do comprehensively, a macrobiotic diet is encouraged as an important foundation to the daily round of physical and spiritual practice. This concern for the importance of natural food also extends to a principled way of prepar-ing, serving and eating food. The serving and the arrangement of the meal should be gracefully and sim-ply performed, emphasizing an aesthetic in harmony with natural order and beauty. Dietary restraint and modest behaviour are also prescribed.

Kushi sensei considers it impossible to achieve the physical, psychological and spiritual condition necessary to benefit from shin-sen do without the adoption of a macrobiotic diet. To leave one part out of a holistic ener-gy work system would create an imbalance and negate the positive effects of other elements of do-in practice.

The principal basis of the do-in macrobiotic diet is the eating of whole cereal grains. Except in areas of extreme cold, such as high mountain areas or the polar regions, a vegetarian diet is considered the best prescription for healthy eating. In preference, food should always be chosen from the produce of the region where you live. Kushi bases this do-in principle on the concept that 'soil is equal to blood' and therefore local produce is particularly fitted to supply you with the nutrition suited to your needs. This is the natural way to harmonize your diet and the physical rhythm of your life with the cyclic change of the seasons particular to the area where you live. Organic food free of artificial ingredients, chemicals, genetic interference or industrial processing should be chosen, as the ki within the soil has given it unadulterated potency.

Whole cereal grains, pulses and other vegetables retain life and goodness and should be fresh up to the moment of cooking. Following the principles of yin and yang (in and yo), the meal should be prepared, cooked and the ingredients chosen to balance complementary and opposing elements, thus fire is matched to water, carbohydrate to minerals, high to low temperatures, salt to oil and so on. This macrobiotic diet provides a natural store of energy which, together with the breath, can be converted by the body into ki energy.

The Principles of Breathing

Breathing is the most vital function of our lives and sustains a continuous interaction between ourselves and our environment. Through our breathing we take in the ki of the universe to revitalize and replenish the pre-natal ki with which we are born. The pattern of our breathing reflects the inflating

centrifugal purpose of yin and the deflating centripetal function of yang. Balancing our breath is not solely a matter of keeping an even constant. We need to vary its depth and frequency to match the physical demands of movement or stillness that we make of our bodies. The rhythm of our breathing affects the pace and function of organs, respiratory and circulation systems, the alert functioning of the brain and ultimately our spiritual well-being. It is vital therefore, as with all ki (ch'i) energy systems, to focus on the development of breathing patterns that amplify the generation of ki through the intake of air, and are suited to the physical or spiritual condition we wish to encourage.

Calm, measured, deep breathing will slow the heartbeat and settle down the metabolism. As our metabolism slows, it produces a serene, peaceful yin state which will assist the clarity of our minds and open our spiritual consciousness. If we are breathing fast and shallow, the opposite yang effects will occur, speeding up our metabolism to make our perceptions more partial and excitable. To ensure the development of physical, mental and spiritual harmony, we must learn how to vary the strength of breathing to suit our purpose.

If we wish to produce the calm inner tranquillity suitable for meditation then we take long, slow, quiet breaths through the nose. The out-breath should be extended three times longer than the in-breath. This is termed 'The Breathing of Selflessness'. If we need to react urgently to stress or challenge and launch our body into movement then we can employ 'The Breathing of Action'. This time we inhale and exhale through our partially open mouth, taking long, deep and strong breaths. In all, do-in describes five standard ways of breathing and five special methods of breathing that are taught to practitioners and used in 'the daily way of life'.

The Daily Way of Life

According to the philosophy of Kushi's shin-sen do, our physical and mental welfare and our spiritual happiness are dependent on an ordered day. This daily round is a balance of activity and reflection, marking the passage of time with do-in exercise, prayer and the mindful appreciation of food, work and social contact. Kushi outlines ten aspects, important to the development of a harmonious day. These are:

■ To rise before dawn.
Traditionally, in China and Japan, the time of *Cho-Tei*, 'The Morning Court', when all important state decisions were made. A do-in exercise is performed to greet the dawn and absorb the powerful energy of this beginning to the day.

■ To cleanse both ourselves and our surroundings.
The maintenance of personal hygiene and a well-cared-for, clean home, is an obvious standard for healthy living. However, cleanliness is embedded in the culture of Japan, where the influence of the Shinto religion attaches great importance to rituals of purification. A clean body and home shows them both respect and demonstrates a clean mind and pure heart.

■ The performance of do-in exercises.
A variety of exercises utilizing breathing and voice techniques are performed in the morning to sustain and stimulate the flow and energy charge of ki and prepare us for the day.

■ Prayer.
Shin-sen do practitioners are encouraged to pray and give thanks to the spirits of our ancestors, all living beings and to the universal spirit, or god, that animates all phenomena.

■ Respect and give thanks for what you eat.
At each meal the practitioner should reflect and give thanks for food and the natural environment from where it has come.

■ To start our daily work with a positive attitude.
Do-in practitioners should approach each day's work with a relaxed mind and enjoy it for its own sake, charging themselves with positive energy. Equally, this positive attitude should be extended to our colleagues with whom we should work harmoniously and co-operatively.

■ To take responsibility for the society within which we live.
Our positive attitudes and our moral behaviour are part of the fabric of social life. We must contribute to the well-being of society by seeing it as our personal responsibility to ameliorate suffering and work for peace.

■ To reflect and give appreciation for the day.
Before or after the evening meal the practitioner should evaluate whether he or she lived up to the standards they have set themself. No day should pass without a conscious appreciation of the day's activities.

■ To study the 'Way of Life'.
The training of a samurai was not complete without the study of philosophy, the humanities and the arts. Our physical side is incomplete without cultivating the mind, which disciplines and civilizes our behaviour. The samurai described this concept as, *bun-bu ryo-do*, 'the sword and the pen are one'. Each day the practitioner should balance the activity of the day with quiet study, writing or meditation to deepen their understanding.

■ To complete the day with a period of self-reflection.
The final act the practitioner is expected to undertake before sleep is a review of all the day's activities. Each

aspect of conduct should be measured against the standards of their do-in practice to complete a checklist of their life-enhancing development. All aspects receive equal weight. A review of your daily diet is as important as your treatment of colleagues or the love and gratitude you show for the wonder of creation. Spiritual progress can only be realized by paying attention to the development of the mind, the body and the capacity for moral compassion. When the review is complete and a mental note for extra effort is made, the day is completed by the simple act of washing the body and cleaning the teeth. Normal act of hygiene that it may be, to the do-in practitioner it is a final act of purification.

The Techniques of Shin-sen Do-in

The techniques of do-in have been developed, modified and sometimes simplified from exercises familiar from ancient times to the present. Unlike other health systems we have reviewed, do-in is a self-exercise system and does not include techniques for treating others. Although the exercises are aimed at the physical improvement of health and general mental well-being, do-in exercises include techniques for developing spiritual awareness.

All do-in techniques are of short duration and can be performed at home, either standing, sitting, kneeling or by lying on a floor or a hard mattress. No props or special equipment are required. However, harmony with your surroundings and the environment is the key to do-in practice. Consequently, care should be taken in choosing the time of day and the place to accord with the spirit of each set of exercises. Shin-sen do-in philosophy regards humans as only manifestations of ki rather than having a physical or material existence of their own. To be in harmony with place and setting is to recognize our connection with what Kushi calls,

'the infinite dimension of vibration and energy in the ocean of the infinite universe'.

Do-in techniques are divided into four major categories of practice designed to meet the requirement of an holistic daily plan for physical, mental and spiritual development. These categories are named, 'Special Exercises', 'Daily Spiritual Exercises', 'Daily Exercises' and 'General Exercises'.

Daily Spiritual Exercises

Daily Spiritual Exercises are practised when the sun is rising and performed either alone or in the warm company of friends or family. They include techniques for the development of breathing and good posture, prayer, still moments, purification rituals and vibrational sound chanting. All these exercises are intended to give a positive charge of ki through the body to awaken and energize the physical self and stimulate the mind. This alert and active body-mind gives a positive focus to thoughts and brings clarity to our spiritual perceptions.

Daily Exercises

Daily Exercises are sub-divided into four categories: *so-cho-shu-ho*, or morning exercises; *kin-sei-shu-ho*, or evening exercises; *kei-raku-cho-sei*, meridian exercises and 'additional exercises' used for stimulating breath or relaxing the body for sleep.

Morning exercises can be performed soon after waking and getting out of bed. They are designed to progress through ten steps to bring body and mind into a balanced energetic condition and include processes for stimulating the circulation of blood and body fluids and the flow of ki through the meridian channels. Morning exercises aim to release stress and tension in the muscles and joints so that you may begin the day with a relaxed and comfortable body.

Evening exercises have ancient energy work origins and aim to restore levels of ki, rejuvenate the body and increase longevity. While morning exercises are designed to fit the whole person for the active day, the evening exercises aim to calm and pacify over-stimulated minds, slow metabolism and bring us back to a state of composed balance. These exercises are performed either before going to bed or earlier in the evening before the practitioner has eaten. They are performed as a sequence of 20 steps with one technique flowing into another.

Although all do-in exercises have some relationship to the stimulation of ki, the meridian exercises are specifically directed to un-blocking and releasing the accumulation of stagnant ki in the energy channels. The scope of this book prevents detailed examination of all the do-in techniques we are reviewing here. However, for the purposes of examining how do-in works directly on the meridian channels we have illustrated this particular set of techniques, which are simple to perform, take little time and can be practised easily at home, providing you are reasonably flexible. Remember if you do try techniques at home, approach them calmly and progressively to avoid discomfort or injury.

Kei-raku-cho-sei: Meridian Exercises

There are six exercises which act on the 12 major meridian channels. The meridian exercises, unlike the more flowing do-in morning and evening exercises, involve holding your posture at the extreme range of its movement for the passage of two slow breaths.

■ Exercise for the lung and large intestine meridians.
Stand with your hands behind your back with palms facing out and your thumbs interlocked. Keep the feet slightly more than shoulder width apart. From this posture, lift the chin and drop your head back to stare at the ceiling, simultaneously raising your arms gently behind you. Next bend the body forward to your maximum extension, keeping the thumbs locked and arms stretched up behind your back. Hold this position for the duration of two slow, relaxed, deep breaths. Switch the position of the interlocking thumbs from bottom to top to be able to detect which side of the meridians is more congested and blocked by feeling greater tension or discomfort in the left or the right.

■ Exercise for the spleen-pancreas and stomach meridians. Begin this exercise in seiza, or natural right posture, with your knees folded under you and the right big toe crossed over the left. Raise your arms slowly over your head, with fingers interlocking. Gradually lower the body and arms backwards as far as you are able towards the floor. The further you stretch back the more the spleen-pancreas and stomach meridians, which run centrally up the body, will be extended, and the whole area of the spleen, stomach and pancreas will be stimulated. Again, this posture is maintained for two slow, deep breaths.

■ Exercise for the heart and small intestine meridians. Sitting with legs open and knees pressed towards the floor, the soles of the feet are held together with your hands around the toes. Slowly bend forward until your forehead touches your thumbs. Holding this posture breathe in deeply for the passage of two breaths. This is a familiar exercise taught by many shiatsu practitioners to their patients for self-treatment.

■ Exercise for the heart governor and triple burner meridians.

The starting position for this exercise is more difficult to perform if you have not developed the flexibility required to sit in the lotus position. From sitting in the lotus position with legs crossed and the feet tucked in, cross your arms and press each knee down with opposite hand. Slowly bend forward to the floor and hold for two breaths. This stimulates the central and spinal regions of the body activating the heart governor and triple burner meridians.

■ Exercise for the liver and gall bladder meridians.
Sit on the floor with your legs extended wide in front of you and the backs of your knees held down to the floor. Slowly slide both your arms with your hands and fingers extended, down one leg to bend forward and grasp your foot. Always try to bend as far forward as you comfortably can, so that your forehead touches your knee. Breathe in deeply for two breaths and slowly unfold. Repeat this process again on the opposite side.

■ Exercise for the kidney and bladder meridians. Exercising the kidney and bladder meridians involves simply sitting on your bottom with legs outstretched and slowly bending forward to grasp your upturned toes with the head touching the knees. Once more the posture is maintained for two slow intakes of breath.

General Exercises

General exercises are more specifically directed to cover all parts of the body and to treat and un-block stagnant areas of ki. These techniques can be broadly described as techniques for self-massage using the hands and fingers. Co-ordinating these self-massage techniques with different breathing exercises, the vital flow of energy can be controlled and directed to bring self-healing to the body. Again, these techniques are performed as a continuous flowing exercise, conducted primarily from a sitting or kneeling position.

Kushi sensei's shin-sen do-in provides a clear and regulated path for working individually with ki energy, well-suited to our times. Although comparatively little-known outside of Japan, it is one of the number of systems that is opening up the experience of ch'i kung, or energy work, to the West. As a means of stimulating and activating ki, it is intended to increase health and well-being, extend your lifespan and provide the whole mind and body required for gaining spiritual peace.

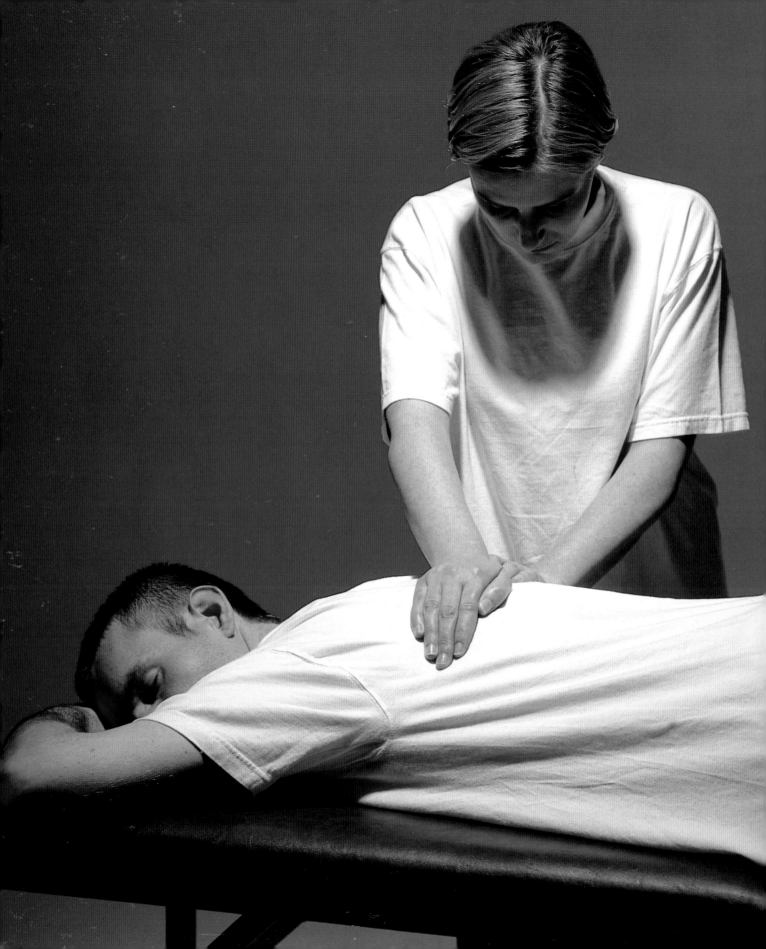

Reiki, pronounced 'ray key', is a simple Japanese word that locks a complexity of meanings within the two characters with which it is brushed. The *kanji*, or character for rei can be translated as 'universal spirit' or 'aura': the subtle force that works on the cosmic scale. Ki is the internal life energy that animates and empowers our life, health and well-being that we have become familiar with throughout this book. Together they can be translated as 'universal life energy'.

This universal life energy is conceived by the founding 'grand masters' of reiki as being a benevolent, all-pervading, absolute force, which can override negativity and bring health and vitality to body, mind and spirit. Reiki is a loving power, a spiritual entity that is given a physical dimension in life and the substance of matter. Different cultural and spiritual traditions might translate this as original wisdom, the absolute infinite, the great spirit or god. Reiki's great strength lies in this ambiguity of meaning, for although 'universal life energy' is understood to be an 'intelligent' force which 'knows' how to heal you, there are no tests of belief or dogmas to uphold. Whether you believe this force has the consciousness of god, explain it as some neutral elemental power or have no concept for it at all, this energy acts within you, with or without your belief.

This spiritual dimension to reiki may make it one of the most difficult of the healing disciplines informed by the principles of ki for a sceptical mind to find credible. It may also be the reason, paradoxically, that it has gained in profile and popularity during the last decade of the 20th century. When disillusionment with the achievements of science and reason are continually generated by powerlessness in the face of pollution, poverty and uncertainty, reiki speaks a simple truth. It is simply that holding is good for you. We have all felt that power. It is a universal cultural folk belief in the simple restorative power of a cuddle or hug when we are distressed; the soothing of pain by holding the affected area. Often these acts of holding are generated by love, as when the parent holds a hurt child, or by compassion and the compulsion to soothe the hurt of others. Legitimately, we can direct that compassion to ourselves when we hold our own bodies to anaesthetize pain. Reiki is merely a systemization of this simple, observable truth.

Reiki practitioners believe that universal life energy can be accessed as a force for healing by the simple act of touch: the laying on of hands. The reiki practitioner claims no particular gifts or personal reservoirs of spiritual power, but merely acts as a conduit through which this subtle energy runs to the receiver. Ki is not stimulated, tonified or unblocked by massage or moxibustion, it is merely exchanged and channelled through the hands of the practitioner to the receiver directly from its source; the universal life energy itself. This procedure is not given or received, it is shared. As ki is channelled through the practitioner to the receiver it does not discriminate between them. Both will receive healing and restored energy throughout the course of its passage from one to the other. Whatever the respective mood or illness of practitioner and patient, negativity and sickness do not pass between them. The practitioner is not drained to fill the patient. The transmission of ki acts independently, suffusing both with its energy in equal measure.

The Reiki Story

The story of the foundation of reiki by Dr Mikao Usui is told by a Reiki Master directly to his or her students. Although the story has appeared in several books on the subject of reiki, the oral transmission of Dr Usui's quest and enlightenment is an essential rite of passage. The intimacy of this transmission and the relationship it begins to establish between master, student and the purpose of reiki, is an important element in the student's path to understanding. It is intended to welcome the student into the reiki family and reveal its compassionate heart.

Dr Mikao Usui was the dean of a Christian theological seminary in Kyoto, Japan, towards the end of the last century. This was at a fertile conjunction in time when many creative Japanese were struggling with the reconciliation of the best elements of their own culture with new ideas from the West. One day Dr Usui was asked a probing question by some of his students, for which he was not prepared. He was asked if he believed literally in the Bible story and specifically the parts that described Christ's mission of healing and the miracles he performed. When Usui confirmed his belief in Christ's ability to heal the sick he was challenged further. If he believed in this power and that Jesus had conferred this power on his disciples then surely Dr Usui would be able to demonstrate his own power to heal. This was a challenge which profoundly affected Usui, for although he felt confirmed by his faith and was certain this power to heal existed, he knew he could not perform any act of healing himself.

He felt that he could not, with any honour, shrug this challenge off, as it went to the heart of his faith. Accordingly he resolved to resign his position and seek the answers in a Christian country, the USA, through the study of the scriptures. When he had answers he would return and teach again.

Usui entered the University of Chicago and studied philosophy and theology for seven years. Despite gaining a doctorate and a profound knowledge of the Bible, he was not able to understand how Christ performed his miracles or how this power could be transferred to others. This lack of specific answers led him to broaden his search and compare the story of Buddha's acts of healing and how these acts were interpreted in Indian and Tibetan Buddhist commentaries.

It is at this point that the story, as related by different masters, diverges. Some say that Dr Usui went on to travel and study in Northern India and Tibet. There he is said to have learnt Sanskrit and made a thorough interrogation of the sutras within the monasteries where they had been recorded. Whether Dr Usui gained insight into the Buddhist teaching in the USA, or in Tibet, or both, what is certain is that he felt that the sutras confirmed his quest. This healing power did exist and there was an intellectual case for that belief.

All versions of the story agree that he returned from his studies to Japan and entered a Zen monastery in Kyoto, hoping to penetrate the secrets he felt lay within the Buddhist texts. After many more years of study and *zazen* meditation, he felt he had the beginning of an answer when he came across a reference in an ancient sutra, written in Sanskrit, to certain symbols and phrases that could provide the key to Buddha's manual system of healing.

Armed with this knowledge he decided to undertake a 21-day period of fasting and meditation on Mount Kuriyama. His aim was to prepare an open mind and spirit so that he would be able to understand the meaning of the symbols. During this period he fasted, chanted, prayed and meditated until, on the very last day, he was granted a vision where the original symbols and their meanings were revealed to him. Charged by his enlightened state, he returned to the monastery to discuss how best to put this new understanding of healing to useful purpose. After much debate the monks and he decided that, as the poor, and particularly the beggars and cripples of the slums could not afford doctors or acupuncturists, his healing mission should be to them.

For the next three years Usui worked in the slums, bringing the healing gift of reiki to the poor. Although he enjoyed much success in healing the physical ailments of his patients, he became profoundly disillusioned by what he saw as their ingratitude and contempt for the spiritual change which he believed to be essential to true health. Despite his cures, many of his patients chose to continue their lives of begging and petty crime rather than use their restored health to get jobs. He concluded that reiki should not be given without an exchange. If the patient gave nothing in return they would accord it no value and treat it lightly. Usui knew that without spiritual healing, his reiki treatments would be unworthy of the vision which had moved him so profoundly on Mount Kuriyama. Accordingly, Dr Usui set down the Five Spiritual Principles of Reiki that should underpin the work of healing. These are:

> Just for today, let go of anger.
> Just for today, let go of worry.
> Just for today, count your blessings and
>   honour your parents, teachers and neighbours.
> Just for today, live honestly.
> Just for today, be kind to all living things.

Dr Usui left the slums and began a new mission to those who would appreciate both his treatments and his teaching. From this point forward Dr Usui gave no further treatments or training without payment. Indeed, the training of practitioners today is accompanied by the exchange of significant fees at the passing of each reiki degree. Although this may at first glance seem to have a mercenary aspect, in the context of Japanese schools of spiritual and martial disciplines it has many precedents. High fees are still charged for the passing of 'dan' grades that mark progress in the 'Way', be it a martial art or Japanese flower arranging. The higher the 'dan' grade, the heftier the payment. The fee represents an acknowledgement by the student of the worth of what he has been taught and a demonstration of gratitude involving some personal sacrifice.

Usui then embarked on a pilgrimage of healing around Japan and taught a small number of disciples to the level of reiki mastery, including a retired naval officer, Dr Chijuro Hayashi. Hayashi was named by Usui as his successor and, after the death of his mentor, went on to establish the first reiki clinic in Tokyo. The healing work conducted by Hayashi and his students at the clinic established the reputation of reiki in Japan. It is doubtful, however, whether Usui's System of Natural Healing, as it is called, would have made its translation to the West without the intervention of a remarkable woman.

The reiki tradition as it is practised today has been preserved and passed on by the efforts of Hawayo Takata, a Japanese American born in Hawaii to emigrant sugar cane farmers. Widowed at an early age and seriously ill with a life-threatening condition, Takata went to Japan to see her family and make peace with her spirit. While in Tokyo she was led by an inner message to seek treatment at Hayashi's reiki clinic. Takata was healed, and convinced by this transforming experience that she should become a student and make her own contribution to reiki. Hayashi recognized the diligence and devotion of Takata when he initiated her as a Reiki Master in 1938.

With Hayashi's blessing, Takata returned to Hawaii where she began to practise and teach reiki, bringing it to the wider community of the West and ensuring its survival. After the death of Hayashi, Takata assumed the leadership of the reiki tradition and during the 1970s began to initiate Reiki Masters in her own turn. When she died in 1980 Takata had trained 21 masters whose own students all trace their lineage in the system back to her. Today the family inheritor and O Sensei, or great teacher, of the Usui System of Natural Healing is Phyllis Lei Furomoto, Takata's granddaughter.

Initiation and Lineage

However simple the physical act of channelling reiki may be, the process by which one is trained to become a practitioner is not merely the product of learning hand positions, symbols or charts. Learning reiki is a matter of the direct oral transmission of its principles and practice through a ritual of empowerment and initiation. The practitioner is opened and connected to the universal life energy by the teacher, who in turn was initiated by their own teacher in an unbroken line of transmission back to the founder, Dr Mikao Usui. It is a practice not unlike the consecration of Christian priests whose authority is understood to stem back directly to Saint Peter, the first

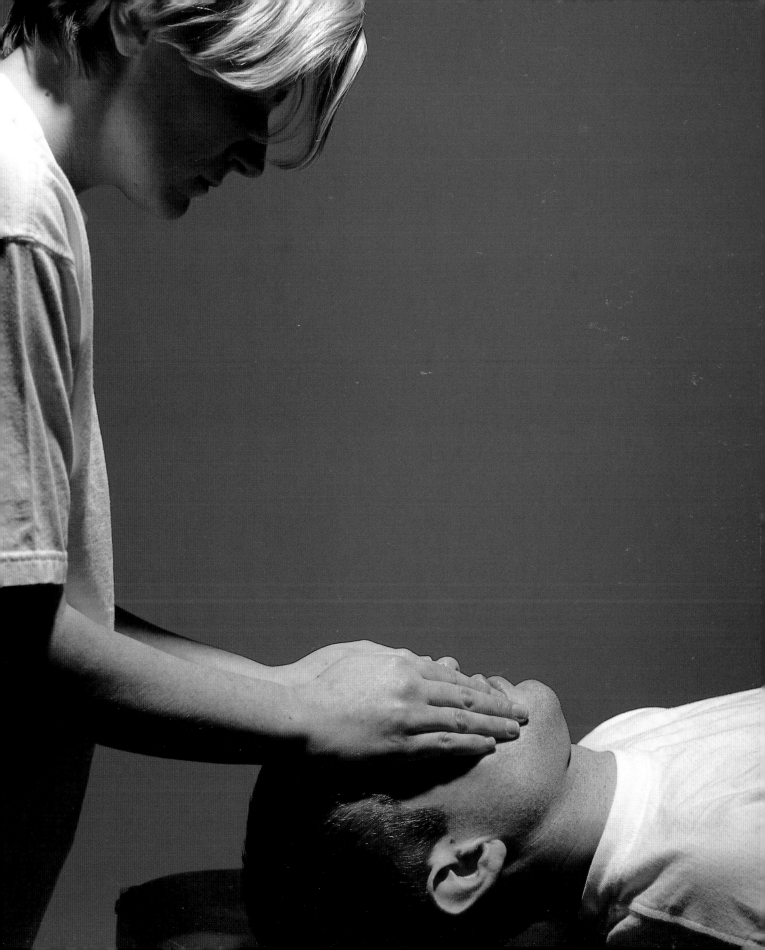

bishop of the faith. Although, as a Christian himself, Dr Usui may have had this model in mind, the direct oral transmission of knowledge and enlightened understanding is part of the culture of Eastern social and religious tradition within which reiki is set.

Reiki sets three degrees of initiation for practitioners. An apprenticeship passes through first and second degrees to reiki mastership, when the practitioner becomes empowered to teach and initiate others.

How Reiki Initiation Works

Reiki practitioners believe that we are born with the inherent ability to access the energy of reiki. Over time we have lost this ability and our system has become blocked. The initiations and attunements performed by a Reiki Master open up a channel to this energy and release a continuous flow. From the moment the attunement is performed, the student is connected, and able to summon this ki energy and channel it to others. The Sanskrit symbols are a formula, or mantra, which empowers the Reiki Master to gain access to this universal life energy and open a path to others.

First Degree (*Shoden*)

Initiation into the first degree usually takes place over a weekend or a number of evening sessions. Its purpose is to welcome the student into the reiki family and to empower them to take their first step as a practitioner and provide hands on healing to others. Reiki energy, faithful to its North Indian and Tibetan inspiration, is conceived as operating through the nadi, or energy channels, and chakras; the centres of life energy. This is in contradistinction to the map of meridian lines and tsubos more familiar to the traditional explanation of how ki flows through the body in China and Japan.

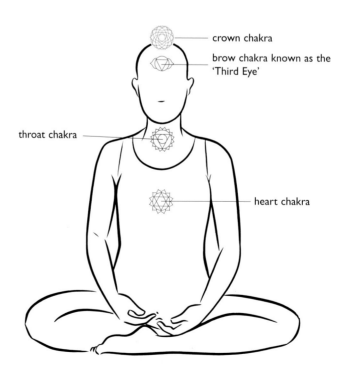

crown chakra

brow chakra known as the 'Third Eye'

throat chakra

heart chakra

Second Degree (*Okuden*)

Second degree is generally undertaken by a practitioner who has gained some confidence in practising reiki. This initiation bestows more attunements and introduces the student to three visual symbols which must be committed to memory. The practitioner is taught to use these symbols to enhance the power of treatments and develop the ability to transmit healing at a distance from the recipient. With second degree initiation the practitioner is given the power to attempt the healing of emotional and mental suffering.

Reiki Mastership

It is not necessary to become a Reiki Master in order to practise reiki successfully. Reiki Mastership involves a long apprenticeship working with a Reiki Master, who will be encouraging the student to develop the depth of commitment and conviction necessary for this step. The practitioner must develop spiritual insight and the qualities of empathy and compassion necessary to reiki as a living vocation. Only when the practitioner can demonstrate these qualities to the satisfaction of the Reiki Master will he or she be initiated into this level. The exchange or fee paid at this level is considerable and acts as a further deterrent to the uncommitted or insincere. Reiki Mastership gives the authority to teach and to pass on attunements, and everything must be done to establish that those initiated are worthy of Dr Usui's legacy.

Reiki Treatment

A reiki treatment is usually carried out on a massage couch with the client lying fully clothed, initially in a prone position. It is important that the client should feel comfortable and relaxed and if they feel cold or

The first degree makes four attunements.

■ The heart chakra.
This centre attunes the physical heart and the thymus, said to be the body's spiritual heart. Attunement promotes unconditional love and compassion.

■ The throat chakra.
The throat chakra is associated with the thyroid gland. The spiritual opening of the throat chakra on the etheric level establishes trust and empathetic communication.

■ The third eye.
This regulates the pituitary gland, identified with intuition and higher levels of consciousness. It works on the hypothalamus, which regulates body temperature and moods. The attunement of this chakra establishes the intuition and deeper understanding which allows the practitioner to connect to reiki.

■ The crown chakra.
This is associated with the pineal gland, sometimes described as 'the receiver of light'. The crown centre gives the practitioner higher energy and spiritual consciousness.

exposed a practitioner may offer them the comfort of a blanket. Reiki practitioners believe that clothing is no impediment to the power of this subtle energy reaching the client.

Reiki is a hands-on treatment and involves gently touching the client with about 15 combinations of hand positions on their head and body. These hand positions are held in a gentle, resting position and given ample time for the reiki energy to channel itself through the practitioner to the client. Generally, these positions are held for at least five minutes before the practitioner moves on to another.

Unlike acupuncture or shiatsu, the reiki practitioner makes no specific attempt to diagnose or control the process. A reiki treatment is governed by the intuitive contact that the practitioner makes with the client through touch. Reiki practitioners say that it is

the innate intelligence of reiki itself that dictates how long to hold a position on the client's body. When sufficient ki energy has passed to that area the practitioner will feel the need to move.

Reiki is a completely non-invasive therapy and applies no forceful pressure to the body and no manipulation of limbs. In this manner it is completely safe and unthreatening. Just how it works is of course a matter of debate and particularly for the scientifically minded a matter of incredulity. Some may see it as therapy for those fooled by mystique and magic. However, most practitioners are very sane individuals who are willing to confess that they also first approached reiki with some doubt. The confirmation that it works has been provided for them by the effect on their own lives and health and the testimony of their clients.

What can be said is that the experience of reiki seems to instil a meditative state of almost complete relaxation, to the point where the client may easily drift off into sleep. Usually at least three treatments are recommended on consecutive days, as experience has shown practitioners that clients may feel some headaches, nausea or other non-threatening side effects after the first or second session. This is considered to be the consequence of clearing out the negative influences within the body. The final session brings harmony and balance back to the body and a feeling of well-being which lasts for about 48 hours. As this is essentially a preventative therapy, self-treatment and regular sessions with a practitioner are likely to produce the best long-term effects.

To attempt any scientific explanation without long-term research would be futile. Reiki, alongside many complementary health therapies, posits a challenge to Western medical orthodoxies, and is usually explained away by suggesting that it may have a placebo affect. Some practitioners put forward the view that it is the correspondence of the chakras, covered by the hands in treatment, to the glands of the endocrine system

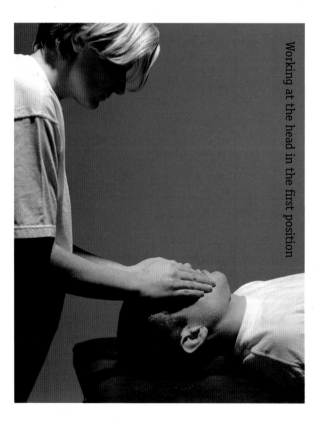

Working at the head in the first position

that provide an explanation of its effectiveness. The endocrine system regulates the secretion of hormones, which in turn drive our metabolism, rate of physical growth, reproductive functions, personality and mood. Our ability to resist disease and cope with stress relies on the good function of the endocrine system, which must be maintained to avoid ill health. Reiki works through these chakra and gland centres, harmonizing and balancing the energy flows and creating the optimum conditions for well-being.

Emotional conditions are particularly responsive to reiki treatment and it is in this area that the medical profession have allowed it some recognition. Reiki has proved itself very effective in supporting and comforting patients with anxieties and fears, particularly the terminally ill. Cancer and AIDS patients have testified to the peace and serenity reiki treatments impart, which give them the strength to face their condition. Indeed, reiki has played a vital role in bolstering the spirit of the individual to fight life-threatening conditions and overcome them.

The Reiki Community

Although reiki does not describe itself as a 'do', or Way dedicated to spiritual and moral improvement, it is clear that it meets many of the necessary criteria. Reiki practitioners see the pursuit of healing and its practice as a spiritual endeavour, putting them in direct contact with a force for good. The disciplines of treatment and the quality of respect and compassion shown to clients form a life-changing methodology. Values are altered or reinforced and the practitioner works to reach that condition of open mindfulness which is the essence of the upright warrior for life. Reiki is also a co-operative activity where a number of practitioners may jointly place hands on a recipient

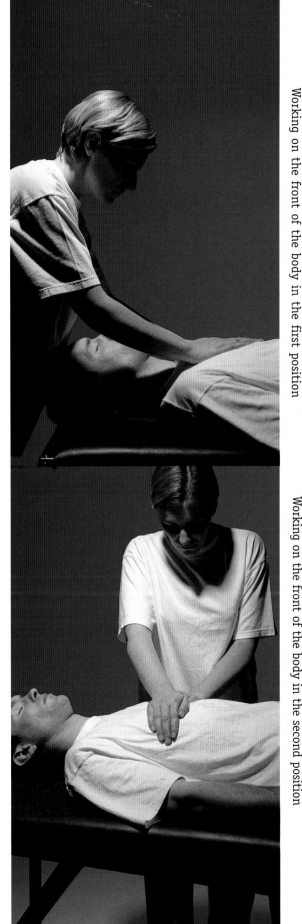

Working on the front of the body in the first position

Working on the front of the body in the second position

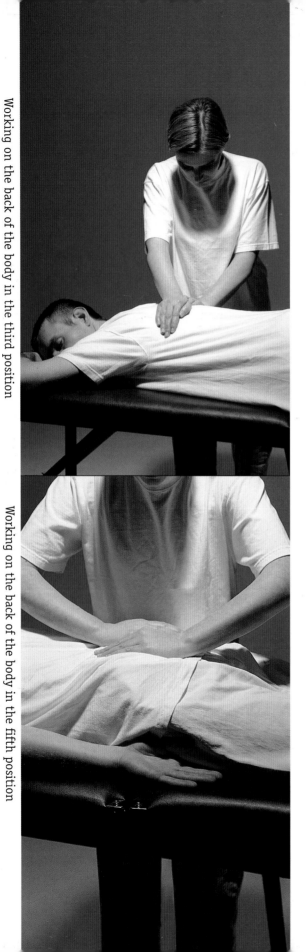

Working on the back of the body in the third position

Working on the back of the body in the fifth position

to increase the power of treatment. Distance healing, where the practitioner visualizes the recipient of a treatment while separated from them physically, also lends itself to co-operative practice and reinforces the sense of collective responsibility and endeavour.

The experience of a reiki treatment is the recruiting ground for this therapy and draws many people to the desire to practise, often initially on themselves and for close family. Indeed, this is how Hawayo Takata suggested reiki should be approached. The positive changes made by reiki in one's own life give the practitioner the desire to seek a deeper understanding of this most subtle of energies by healing others.

With any serious spiritual and mental discipline the student must have confidence in the integrity and wisdom of the teacher. There are now many Reiki Masters. The Reiki Alliance, set up in 1983 by Phyllis Furomoto to preserve the *Usui Shiki Ryoho*, or System of Natural Healing, numbers over 800 masters. Other Reiki Masters who received initiation from Takata have founded parallel organizations, which in their turn have initiated more masters. This is a natural consequence of time and human organization. However, if you become interested in learning reiki or receiving treatment, always politely check the lineage of a Reiki Master to establish that they have clear links back to Hawayo Takata. Beware also of fast-track training programmes that take you from first degree to mastership in a couple of weekends. As with all legitimate 'Ways', the dedication to a process which unfolds and reveals itself over time is the only way to discipline the self and empty the ego. As Dr Usui found, what comes easily is rarely valued, and you must be prepared to make an exchange beyond the financial to enter into the true spirit of reiki practice.

Self-healing position

ENERGY, FORM AND SPIRIT

There is always an uneasy tension in our minds when we associate serious study of the martial arts with the concept of a life-long spiritual quest. For the great majority of us in the West, despite street violence, murders and the sudden devastating attacks of terrorists, we lead peaceful lives in the assurance of a consensus for public order. In these circumstances, training in any martial art might seem to be unnecessary, potentially quite dangerous and, from the viewpoint of a peace loving society, psychologically questionable.

Civilized societies throughout history have opted largely to disarm their civilian populations, with or without their consent, and place the defence of public order into a professional category of armed and organized warriors. The power that this has historically placed in the hands of the warrior, and his ability to abuse it, has necessarily been a major consideration for all civilizations. History has all too often been written in the blood of these abuses across pages that testify to our attempts to curb them. Time seems to teach a very slow lesson, for the problems of bridling aggression and resolving human conflict seem as intractable now as when Buddha, Lao Tze and Confucius first set down their thoughts on the Way.

Each of these great inspirational figures put man and his individual responsibility at the centre of this tension between the legitimacy of a martial act and the requirement to lead a compassionate, spiritually fulfilled life. The East has not been alone in this quandary. Our own Western Classical and Christian traditions have wrestled with the issue. Can a man or woman of peaceful spirit ever justifiably act violently in defence of their own self or on the part of others? This is a question we may all have to ask ourselves at certain moments in our lives. It is likely that this moment will be a critical one requiring an urgent response, which we will be ill-prepared to make both mentally and physically. In these circumstances it is all too likely that the judgments we make and the action we take will not match the best moral standards that a just and harmonious society would expect of us.

The upright Confucian scholar and the Taoist sage lived in times when war and the depredations of bandits were close and commonplace events, and fear of violence was the preoccupation of the powerless. In those times the just and upright man may have needed to protect himself and to spring to the defence of the weak and the oppressed. If he were not to be brutalized by the process of learning martial skills to defend himself, then the process must not only be dedicated to technical perfection but also to training the mind. It is not just the quick mind that can take advantage of an enemy, but the moral mind that uses violence only as a last resort and always in proportion to the circumstances. As war and violence seem to be part of the nature of man, then the foundation of a harmonious society depends on changing the nature of man himself. If, in training for combat, man can be led through a process that teaches him physical

restraint, ethical principle, idealism and spiritual discipline, perhaps he may be able to control his violent nature. The hot, aggressive yang emotions are curbed by the cool, still serenity of yin.

This ideal of the 'martial spirit', that the warrior should be trained for the affirmation of life and not its destruction, has been long in gestation. These philosophical ideals were not shared by all, neither were all martial arts exponents who were seeking spiritual ends pacifists. The ethics of martial restraint have marched forward with the times, and as the civil world has become more disarmed so the concept of self defence has grown broader. Modern authentic martial arts almost universally claim their underlying purpose to be the training of an 'open heart in an open mind'. The ideal of the warrior is one who has been confronted by his own violence of spirit, competitiveness and hot temper and who has learnt to control and turn them into more productive energies. This is more than finding a harmless outlet for aggression in sport or games, nor is it the sublimation of this powerful energy into competition at work or business. It is an attempt to defeat the ego and all attachments to pride and conceit. It is the belief that through the long and dedicated process of unifying the body and the mind, the spirit will attain the natural openness and spontaneity that represents the Tao within us. As Sun Tzu wrote in his *Art of War*, over 2,000 years ago: 'To subdue the enemy's troops without fighting is the supreme excellence.'

The term martial art is a poor translation for the modern Chinese *wushu* or its Japanese equivalent, budo. *Wu* or *bu*, which we translate as 'martial' has a more complex etymological root. The Chinese character wu is a combination of two elements, the upper part standing for 'halberd' (a blade mounted on a pole). The bottom radical means 'stop', literally to 'stop the halberd', which can be interpreted as the 'cessation of arms', or more generally the prevention of violence and acts of aggression. The word *shu* stands for art, as a body of knowledge, principles and techniques pursued for the perfection of the human spirit. In Japanese this word is do, the Way, and is a direct translation of the Chinese word, Tao. Thus the highest aspiration of the martial arts is that they should be the 'arts of peace' pursued through a way of harmony with the universal spirit. The key to unlocking this spirit is to understand with our bodies and our minds the universality of ch'i, the energy that gives us life, and to respect and sustain it in ourselves and in others.

Centuries ago, such idealistic concepts were a luxury that the violence of the times could not afford to many. To be able to make moral decisions about the appropriate escalation of response to attack not only requires moral maturity but also a high command of skill. It is harder to disarm or subdue an aggressor with minimum harm than it is to defend yourself with an equally aggressive counter-attack. Few had the time, will or opportunity to pursue their martial skills to this level of perfection, for such moral purpose, save the hermit sage or the monk.

It was one such monk who provided the inspiration for the transformation of fighting skills into martial arts, charged with spiritual purpose. His name was Bodhidharma, or Tamo in Chinese, a Buddhist monk who travelled a long journey of both the body and the spirit from his home in India to the Shaolin Temple, in Henan Province, China. The evidence for and against the historical accuracy of the stories woven around Bodhidharma's life is always a matter of scholarly dispute. However, his status as the patron saint of the martial arts and the story of his life provide such a powerful creation myth, that it cannot be left untold.

The Shaolin Temple had been founded by another Indian Buddhist monk, Batuo, in 495 CE with the support and patronage of the emperor. Shaolin was a monastery of great distinction and power, as it was built on one of the five sacred mountains of China. Once a year it was the custom of the Chinese emperors to pray for the peace and prosperity of the empire atop one of the five mountains. Shaolin rested on the most central of the five and was often visited by emperors, generals and high officials.

When Bodhidharma arrived at Shaolin in 527 CE, he found a monastic community, ostensibly committed to the pursuit of enlightenment through meditation, study and chant. However, it was clear to him that the monks of Shaolin were physically and mentally inadequate to the task. Bodhidharma set a determined and ferocious example for the *Ch'an* (Zen) tradition which he established at Shaolin, meditating for long hours in austere seclusion. It was clear to him that if the monks were to have any chance of piercing the truth, then they must be given the physical stamina to meet the challenge of meditation. In true practical Ch'an fashion, he set about devising a training system that would improve the health and physical stamina of the monks under his tutelage. He introduced a system of physical exercises known as the Eighteen Lohan Hands, which he reinforced with an internal exercise system based on tendon and sinew stretching. Although this system was not a martial art of itself, the ch'i kung exercises and callisthenics that Bodhidharma introduced to the monks of Shaolin provided the inspiration for the schools of martial arts that were to follow.

Internal and External Martial Arts

Shaolin became a centre of development in the martial arts, as both monks and lay students began to evolve Bodhidharma's exercises into the boxing system known as *Shaolin Ch'uan-fa*. Ch'uan-fa, or techniques of the fist, emphasized punches, strikes and kicks rather than grappling and throwing, but did include the use of weapons, despite Buddhist prescriptions against killing. Before the arrival of Bodhidharma, martial skills were entirely the preserve of warriors and were valued for their effectiveness in combat alone. Shaolin set a different course for the martial arts by using the discipline of vigorous training as a powerful form of moving meditation to complement the stillness of the Ch'an trance. Sets of punches, kicks evasions and blocks were arranged into moving sequences, or forms, that developed the monks' senses and perfected their technique. Through attention to the detail and perfection of the form, the mind can be wrested from attachment and extraneous thought until it loses itself in the process of action. The body is then free to act intuitively and openly, guided by the subconscious, 'no-mind', from which enlightenment springs.

Although Shaolin fighting skills utilized the internal ch'i kung tendon stretching exercises initiated by Bodhidharma to give them force and power, the training system was essentially external. The Shaolin warrior trained very hard, spending long hours toughening the hands punching sandbags and breaking bricks, and building overall strength and stamina, which the Chinese call li. Shaolin ch'uan-fa is fast and swift in form and depends on tough stance training and stretching routines to build up ch'i in the muscles of the body. Only after this toughening and external ch'i-building process is complete will the student begin to relax and turn his attention to the inside organs of the body. As this training starts from the outside and works in, it is characterized as a 'hard' or 'external' martial art. However, a completely new approach to martial arts training was to emerge in the 13th century CE, founded by the Taoist priest, Chang San Feng and called t'ai ch'i ch'uan, Great Ultimate Fist.

This system broke with the 'hard' Shaolin ch'uan-fa approach to training and emphasized 'soft' forms and gentle rhythmic exercises that drew their power from the internal alchemy of ch'i kung. Out went the lifting of weights and the pounding of sandbags to be replaced by a focus on breath control, the internal development of ch'i and techniques of visualization. T'ai chi ch'uan relies on the process of channelling ch'i energy along the meridians of the body to the muscles, rather than building strength through weight training or endless push-ups. Instead a subtle internal process of stretching and tensing the tendons massages the internal organs and encourages the vital flow of ch'i around the body. The slow-flowing movements of the forms open the body and relax the muscles and tendons to create great flexibility and dynamism in the torso, hips and limbs. From these relaxed postures a whip-like energy can generate a blow of intense, focused power.

No system of training would be complete if it did not conform to the principles of yin yang. As li is the external strength of the body, so jin is the body's internal strength. Both li and jin are ultimately required for the complete harmony of form that can sustain action, and wise students will cultivate both. Thus, students of the soft or internal martial arts move from slow, relaxed training forms, to faster and more vigorous training after an adequate apprenticeship. Technical skill must be locked into every movement and gesture before these 'soft' forms can be integrated with the mind and true power generated.

In China, it was not uncommon to train in both the external and internal systems, beginning when young with the harder, Shaolin-influenced ch'uan-fa styles and progressing with age and wisdom to the softer strategies embedded in t'ai chi, pa kua and hsing-i. While both internal and external ch'uan-fa carry within themselves the seeds of the other, this division of emphasis and intention has grown more distinct over the centuries.

During the long years of Manchu rule from 1644 to 1911, the government discouraged military training among the civilian population. As an alien ruling class presiding over a populous and volatile nation, they had no wish to see their military power opposed. The Chinese people nevertheless continued their training in private, some in secret societies pledged to overthrow the Manchus, while others trained for more pacific ends. These private schools, divorced as they were from military practice, began to turn the emphasis of training away from combat for battle, to that of individual combat, unarmed forms, athletic demonstration and the maintenance of health. During this period the internal martial arts flourished and new systems such as pa kua and hsing-i were developed alongside the increasingly popular t'ai chi ch'uan. Although the soft styles produced experts capable of beating the most effective of Shaolin stylists, increasingly teachers began to look towards the healing and spiritual aspects of their systems rather than self-defence.

While the practice of t'ai chi ch'uan had a greater following in the north of China, Shaolin ch'uan-fa predominated in the south. The Southern Shaolin Temple, in Fujian province, became a focus for resistance to the Manchu oppressors and was burnt down by imperial troops and the monks scattered. This diaspora led to Shaolin experts settling in many places across South East Asia and America, where they began quietly to pass on their skills.

Shaolin found its vindication when Dr Sun Yat Sen's revolutionaries overthrew the Manchu dynasty in 1911. Many of his Kuomintang party activists were lay Shaolin ch'uan-fa students and the skills of Chinese wushu were revived as a national art or *kuoshu*. This support fostered the growth of larger martial arts organizations such as the Ching Woo Athletic Association, which had extensive branches across China, bringing the benefits of training to even wider audiences.

Today the martial arts receive official support from the Communist government. Wushu, including both internal and external systems of ch'uan-fa is practised in public gymnasia and sports centres and is studied in specialist training schools and universities. While the regime has not encouraged the spiritual aspects of the martial arts, it has seen their value as a dynamic system of physical culture of benefit to both mind and body. This prompted the development of standardized forms suitable for competitive performance, marking a further orientation of the martial arts towards athletic sport at the expense of self-defence.

Despite the growth and development of martial arts as sports, the great majority of practitioners of the internal arts practise for the preservation of their health and the development of their vital energy. Early in the morning in the parks, temples and gardens of Chinese cities and towns this can be witnessed, as people gather in their hundreds to practise the graceful movements of t'ai chi. Opening their energies and attuning themselves to their surroundings, they await the transfer of ch'i permeating down from the trees as they slowly dance out their solo forms. It is an image both beautiful and mysterious, communicating an older and deeper wisdom that is taught by the body to the mind and then passed to the spirit. This is the mystery of the internal martial arts to which we turn next in our encounter with ch'i.

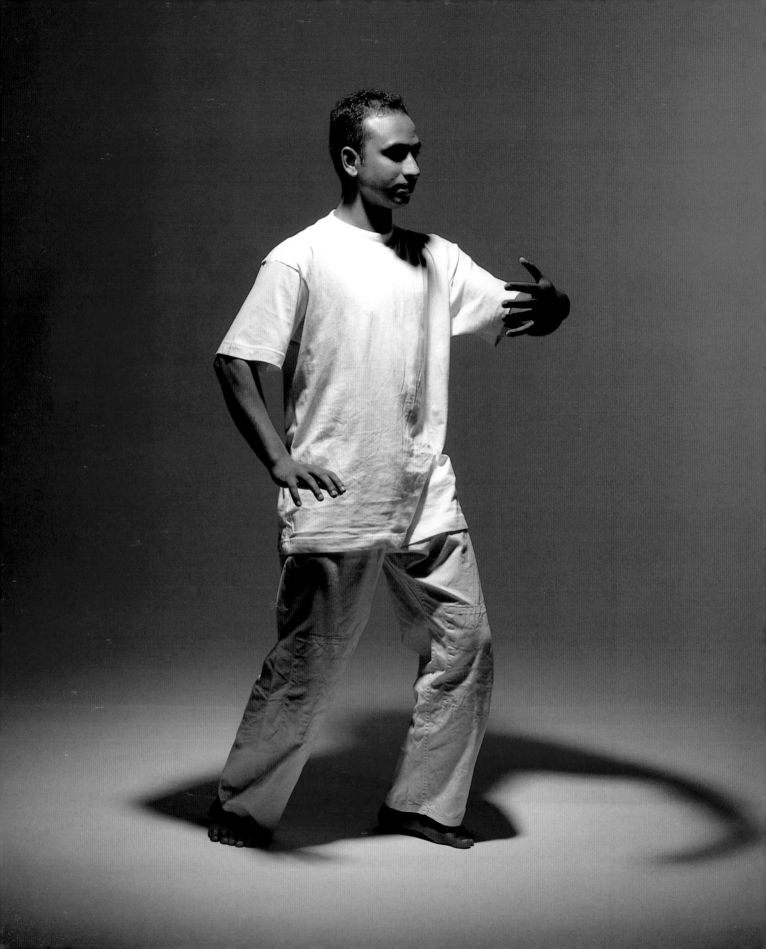

T'ai chi ch'uan undoubtedly wears the most familiar face of all the Chinese martial arts that have taken root in the West. T'ai chi's appreciation of nature and place in performance, coupled with the slow, timeless grace of its forms, give it a strange, ethereal beauty. Combine this aesthetic with its qualities as exercise and its accessibility, then you have an 'art' that reaches beyond the 'martial'. An art open to everyone that is at once both ordinary and profound.

T'ai chi has managed to bridge the boundary of imagination between those attracted to it as a martial art and those who eschew any association with combat or violence. Virtually alone of all the martial arts it is possible to practise t'ai chi with little or no reference to its history as a system of self-defence. Indeed for the great majority of practitioners who gather in the early morning beneath the trees to weave this intricate dance of the spirit, fighting would be the last of their considerations. Multi-layered and multi-faceted, t'ai chi has transcended its origins as a subtle and devastating method of combat taught in seclusion to the few, to become the 'people's' ch'i kung, openly promoted throughout the world as a way of health and beauty that can stimulate the mind and heal the spirit.

While many have little concern for the martial aspects of t'ai chi, there is a strong counter argument articulated by more traditional teachers and their students who see this as a negation of the intention in each form. Like playing golf without a ball, you may believe you have developed a perfect swing and follow through, but until you come to hit a ball you will never know if your technique is truly fit for the purpose. If the intention is not in the form, then the form is empty and without meaning and you may just as well make random gestures in the air. From this perspective, the focus on the combat meaning in each form gives impetus to the generation of internal power and the knowledge of where to direct it. The purpose in this case directs the form and leads the practitioner to an insightful understanding of each movement.

Whatever level you approach t'ai chi from, or from whichever perspective, it seems to have a unique quality that enables it to match the competing expectations and needs of its adherents. This is a singularly unique quality in any system of physical culture, martial or otherwise, and is the product of a long period of gestation, adaptation and experiment that can be traced back through the centuries to a Taoist temple on the Wutang Shan mountain.

The Roots of T'ai Chi Ch'uan

Tradition ascribes the creation of t'ai chi ch'uan to the 13th century Taoist priest, Chang San Feng (Zhang San Feng). He began his martial arts training with the monks of Shaolin, learning the forceful external art for which it was so famous. Training was intensive and hard, with much time devoted to the physical strengthening of the body through the striking of poles and sand-filled bags and the manipulation of weights. Although Shaolin was a Buddhist institution it attracted many lay disciples from China's other great traditions, Taoism and Confucianism, who came to develop their skills of ch'uan-fa and their knowledge of ch'i kung.

Having satisfied himself that he had come as far with Shaolin ch'uan-fa as he could, Chang San Feng moved on to the Purple Summit Temple, a Taoist monastery sited upon Wutang mountain. Here he continued his martial and spiritual training atop the summit of one of the most sacred mountains of the Taoist faith, suspended between earth and heaven. It is said that one day Chang San Feng stopped to watch a fight between a snake and crane, and was struck by the natural power and flexibility of their movements. This inspired him to reinvent his ch'uan-fa into a softer style, emphasizing breath control and the channelling of ch'i. Chang San Feng abandoned the hard, external toughening of Shaolin for the inner training methods integral to ch'i kung practice, substituting the principle of jin for that of li. His style was first known as *Wutang Lohan Ch'uan-fa*, or Wutang 32-pattern Long Fist, and was to be developed by his successors into t'ai chi ch'uan-fa. As the first teacher to be recorded as having turned to this softer, internal approach, he is considered the founding father of all the internal Chinese martial arts.

Wutang Long Fist continued to be practised at Purple Summit Mountain by Taoist priests and devotees, influencing the development of other forms of the internal martial arts and laying the foundation of the schools of t'ai chi ch'uan that were to emerge in the 18th and 19th centuries. Today three major schools of t'ai chi ch'uan are practised by the majority of t'ai chi adherents worldwide. Each of these schools is represented within a family tradition passed down through a line of masters from one generation to the next and jealously guarded from outsiders. These secular traditions are identified by the family or clan names of their founding patriarchs, the Chen, Yang and the Wu.

Authority and credibility within the Chinese and the Japanese martial arts is gained by being able to claim a teaching lineage that goes back in a direct line of transmission to the founder of the school. If the line is broken, then the authenticity and integrity of what is taught can be subject to serious doubt. While this question of lineage may not guarantee the competence of the teacher, it is much more likely that it will be closer to the source if it has been passed on directly from a master to his successor, specially groomed and chosen for the task. Each style of t'ai chi is therefore closely identified with a family, or clan, who have stamped their own character on the forms. Thus the Chen style is more martial in character and has a close stylistic affinity with the fighting stances of Shaolin boxing. While the most widely practised style of t'ai chi ch'uan, founded by Yang Lu Chan (1799–1872) places greater emphasis on soft, graceful movement in the pursuit of health. For anyone coming to t'ai chi for the first time, these differences may be too subtle to identify and of little import. All styles contain a clear, identifiable core of principle and practice that transcends their differences, to release the energy and vitality of the spirit.

The Principles of T'ai Chi

T'ai chi, or 'grand ultimate', is the cosmos as it is expressed in the t'ai chi symbol, which represents the two facets of the one unity that are yin and yang. Within the gentle rhythmic patterns shown on the outside, the t'ai chi exponent conceals an armoury of open and closed fist punches, kicks, throws and locking movements. It is a complex system of self-defence techniques which, when used at pace, can effectively counter any aggression. T'ai chi overcomes the hard with the soft, opposes force by yielding and defeats external force with internal force. If an opponent uses yang force then the t'ai chi exponent will use yielding yin to deflect it and will oppose a yin move with a yang riposte. According to this principle, a straight line opposes the circular and a circular movement opposes the straight. Consequently, a circular kick is countered by a straight push or a straight punch by a circular deflection. The t'ai chi practitioner flows in sinuous patterns, weaving in and out of an aggressor's kicks and strikes. Sometimes he or she twists swiftly like the snake away from the attacker's path only to dart back with the sharp strike of the crane's bill. Stillness confronts motion and aggressive intention is out-paced by initiative. This yin yang principle runs through all the fundamentals of t'ai chi movement, techniques, energy development and theory.

T'ai chi ch'uan could also be described as 'yin yang boxing' and to be complete, must balance the martial yang with the complementary yin aspect of health. Without the practice of t'ai chi as a way of health, generating the internal power of the practitioner, the forms become empty gestures. For unlike Shaolin boxing the t'ai chi exponent has no developed arm or leg muscles to deliver the power of a strike or push, but must rely on the ability to store and release the explosive power of ch'i. All of the sets of strikes, blocks, kicks and seizing movements that comprise t'ai chi forms are designed to stimulate the flow of chi along the meridians and massage the internal organs. As the t'ai chi exponent makes each flowing action of the set, a gentle stretching and toning of the tendons takes place, opening up the flow along the associated meridian and into the organs. The gentle continuity of movement relaxes the body and allows the free passage of blood and ch'i to boost the energy and vitality of the body.

The movements of the t'ai chi practitioner are also defined by a set of principles and maxims. Each school of t'ai chi organizes and describes them in their own way, but they all work to a familiar pattern. The first and most important principle the practitioner must learn to keep is to maintain a state of complete relaxation. All tension and restraint must be emptied from the mind and body. The student of t'ai chi learns this principle slowly, through strict attention to posture and perfecting the movements of the form. By relaxing completely and centring the mind on the tan t'ien, weight is sent to the feet. The shoulders must be sunk and the elbows dropped naturally to allow ch'i to rise up and circulate throughout the body. If the elbows are bent, this will raise the shoulders and hold ch'i high in the body, weakening posture and unbalancing the body and making the top heavy and the bottom light. To counter this the head and body must be aligned with the sacrum, the back held straight and the chest drawn in to allow ch'i to sink to the tan t'ien.

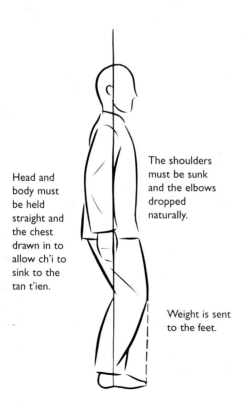

Head and body must be held straight and the chest drawn in to allow ch'i to sink to the tan t'ien.

The shoulders must be sunk and the elbows dropped naturally.

Weight is sent to the feet.

The waist provides the foundation for all bodily action and is the source of true power in action. It must provide a flexible axis from which each t'ai chi movement can be executed with swiftness and strength, or with measured pace and intrinsic power. If movement originates from the waist and is connected, then the whole body works together. Waist, arms and legs must move together as one. If one part moves independently of the other it will disrupt the continuity of movement and the flow of ch'i. Both centrifugal and centripetal force is generated through the waist, and can be used to generate the whiplash energy of *fajing*, an explosive emission of ch'i.

The waist rests on the legs and must rely on the feet to maintain a solid, rooted base. This is achieved by simultaneously pushing the legs towards each other and down against the earth, while the feet hold the legs on a firm base by curling the toes and clawing the ground. Energy and momentum are locked into the coiled power of this posture and can be unleashed with tremendous focus and force in combination with the torsion of the waist.

To be able to move dynamically, we must be able to shift our weight from one foot to the other and distinguish where our balance rests. Throughout the t'ai chi forms, except for rare moments, the weight of the body will be distributed unevenly. The flow from one leg to another must be smooth and continuous, avoiding any inclination to over-extend the body.

Centrally important to the entire practice of t'ai chi is the development of internal force, or jing. As the t'ai chi exponent moves through the techniques of the form, the tendons that connect bones to muscle are gently flexed. Ch'i is attracted by this flexing and flows through the intricate web of connecting tissue to make the whole body flexible and strong. This elasticity is the key to internal power. The t'ai chi exponent does not stand in the way of a powerful force but gives way like the willow bending in the wind and springing back when the energy of the force is played out. Through the internal power of jing, the t'ai chi practitioner balances the forces of yin and yang by being both soft and gentle, then hard and powerful.

While other systems of exercise and physical culture champion the maxim that there is no gain without pain, t'ai chi denies it. Aerobic exercise, running and rowing may be enjoyable and useful in themselves, but they leave the body tired and the lungs heaving for breath. Rather than take this extreme path that uses up energy, t'ai chi takes the opposite direction. The t'ai chi exponent looks for the stillness in movement, slowing down each movement of the body to the point where it can barely be discerned. By this means the breath becomes long and deep and ch'i sinks to the lower energy field to replenish the vitality of body and mind.

The Practice of T'ai Chi

The art of t'ai chi has four elements: the practice of solo exercises, where each stance and movement represents a fighting action; pushing hands; free form sparring and ultimately self defence. For the majority of practitioners of the art, it is the first two elements that will form the basis of their practice. Some will want to go further and test their skills and reactions in the dynamic context of a free sparring session. It is to be hoped very few will ever have to use t'ai chi ch'uan to defend themselves.

For the student of t'ai chi these judgments about where to place the emphasis of their practice are made along the way. Whereas they may have taken up t'ai chi for health reasons alone, they find that the martial aspect provides a more practical demonstration of the use of internal power. Certainly it would be impossible

Bend the bow, shoot the tiger

Round deflect punch

truly to understand the energy within strikes and blocks, or the art of seizing and locking the joints without working with a partner in a moving exchange of technique.

T'ai chi ch'uan provides a progression through all these elements, each confirming and complementing the others. If the t'ai chi exponent is unable to uproot or push back a partner with internal force, can the movements of the solo exercises have any physical integrity? Will they be doing the practitioner any good at all? It is not that the student is concerned with how to use and apply what has been learnt in real fight, but that the movements are, to use the martial arts researcher Professor Friman's words, 'martially inspired'. To visualize and imagine the purpose and function of the form fills each action with intention and energy without which the health benefits cannot be gained.

The Forms of T'ai Chi Ch'uan

Solo exercises form the basis of all practice. The student of t'ai chi is introduced to stances and postures on which he will build the moving form. Shoulders are relaxed and dropped slightly forward, the knees are bent to align with the toes and the spine is held straight. Between the crown of the head and the acupuncture point kidney one, located on the sole of the foot, a straight line is formed. The feet claw and root the student to the ground, simultaneously activating the upward flow of ch'i through the acupuncture point. When this posture becomes integrated with movement, the agile and graceful actions of the form can take shape.

Many of the stances that the practitioner takes imitate the actions and characteristics of animals. They serve not only as physical forms to imitate, but their names provide poetic metaphors to describe action and intention. Names such as 'Crane Cools its Wings' or

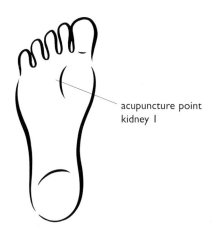

acupuncture point kidney 1

'Snake Spits Venom' suggest that we should have the elegant stability of the crane and the lightning strike of the snake. The hands held with fingers open in the gesture of a claw flex the tendons and draw down the flow of ch'i along the associated meridians. In self defence, these ch'i-charged fingers can be as strong as steel and can be used both for seizing an opponent and for delivering a powerful, knife-like strike.

Each school of t'ai chi ch'uan has its variations on these sets of movements which can consist of as many as 78 or more movements, although many modern styles have shorter forms. The practitioner moves through these sets in a prescribed sequence, shifting forwards and back and side to side, making the evasive patterns and manoeuvres of imaginary combat. From the beginning to the end the practitioner strives to realize the interplay of yin and yang within the seamless movement of the form, never allowing distractions to interrupt the flow.

Pushing hands is another exercise used to condition the t'ai chi exponent to the ebb and flow of yin-yang and to grasp the tactical application of the phenomenon. Two partners stand opposite each other in a stable posture making contact at the wrist, with the hand held in the warding off position known as *peng*. As one partner pushes towards the other in a straight line, the second responds with a deflecting curving push to the side of his body. Both hips and torso are turned in unison with the action of the hand to achieve the gentle, elastic power of the movement. When the deflection is completed, the roles are reversed and the second partner pushes back in a straight line towards the first. This combination of straight push and curving deflection is repeated by each partner in a continuous rolling exchange. Each partner is attempting to read the power and the direction of their partner's movements in order to lead or direct their opponent's balance beyond the point of correction.

Adherence to the partner is essential for grasping and the application of a pull or push down, or joint lock. The 'sticking hands' exercise is designed to equip the t'ai chi exponent with the sensitivity to movement that is required for the task. One person will place a hand upon the top of their partner's hand, which is then moved freely in any direction. The first person must follow their partner's hand movements without breaking contact throughout the course of the exercise.

Increasingly popular at t'ai chi events in both China and in the West, is the exercise known as uprooting.

Here one opponent takes up a rooted posture while the other tries to push them backwards with internal force. This is accomplished by sensing a moment of weakness in the opponent's posture and pushing upward and backwards to send them reeling. Experienced practitioners can yield to and absorb their opponent's push and remain in a relaxed, rooted posture to withstand a very powerful force. This exercise can also form part of a pushing hands routine.

By practising the different solo and partner forms, the t'ai chi exponent develops a unity of perception in body and mind, which can react instinctively to meet physical challenge or emotional crisis with calm equanimity.

T'ai Chi and Health

T'ai chi is the most popular form of ch'i kung practised in the world today. For many practitioners the association with the disciplined search for spiritual release through the inner alchemy of the body is not their primary concern. The appeal of t'ai chi lies in its ability

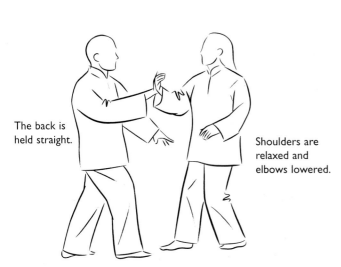

The back is held straight.

Shoulders are relaxed and elbows lowered.

pushing hands

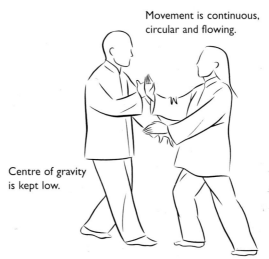

Movement is continuous, circular and flowing.

Centre of gravity is kept low.

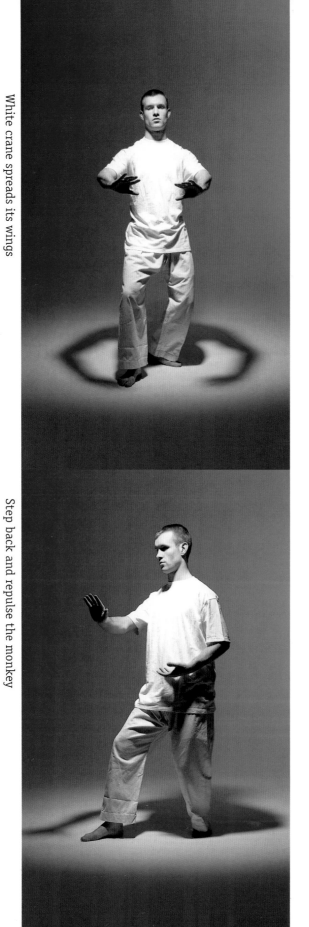

White crane spreads its wings

Step back and repulse the monkey

to bridge the motivational divide between the adept on a quest for enlightenment and those who have humbler aspirations concerned with general health and well-being. It is in this way that martial arts in China and Japan have also crossed another chasm from training for war to training for peace. By using the disciplines of combat as their inspiration the martial arts attempt to replicate the qualities that their practice engenders, but without this leading to aggressive or violent consequences. Self-defence is reinterpreted in a civil rather than a military context. No longer is it merely the self-defence of the body from external attack by an aggressor, it is also the defence of the body from ill-health and the mind from stress and anxiety. The body and the mind become a new internal battleground where the long-term goal is to conquer the ego and forge the spirit.

With such ambitious outcomes the practice of any martial art would seem a very forbidding undertaking from the outside. Yet we can see from the evidence of our eyes that many hundreds of thousands of people from all walks of life and of all ages and size gather in the parks and open spaces of China's cities to practise t'ai chi daily. In the early morning as the ch'i rises from the earth and filters through the trees they informally assemble to enjoy the inner stillness of the forms before facing the oncoming rush of the day. Some will perform the sets under the guidance of a teacher, others will come together in lively, gossiping knots of friends, while the lone figure seeks out contemplative isolation beneath a favourite tree.

T'ai chi's open face invites you in, rather than imposing constraints or restricting opportunities to practise. Once you have learned a form or set, you can practise it anywhere: in the local park, in your garden or where there is room inside your house. Although a teacher is a necessary starting point and a continuous requirement for those concerned to go deeply into the art, t'ai chi practice is something you can work with totally alone, driven by your own expectations and challenges. Most importantly, it is a discipline that does not require a high level of fitness at its starting point. The slow, gentle forms allow access to those with a very basic level of fitness or to those left worn down after serious illness. Gradually the flexing, tensing and massaging of tendons, meridians and internal organs will open the blocked channels and restore the even flow of ch'i. All that is required for the slow but inexorable increase in vitality, strength and stamina that t'ai chi provides is patience and application.

There are no quick-fix ways to the benefits of t'ai chi or any other martial art. A weekend course or a few sessions at a health centre provide a wonderful introduction, but they cannot substitute for long-term committed practice. The self defence of body, mind and spirit requires constant attention and application and is not something that can be taken up then neglected. T'ai chi offers a pathway to effective preventative health care for as long as you care to travel it, but it cannot be given to you as a cure.

T'ai chi practice serves long-term fitness goals admirably, providing a low-intensity physical programme that improves the circulation of blood, aids respiration, adds to muscular strength and develops the flexibility of bones and joints. Each solo t'ai chi set can take 30 or more minutes to perform, thus meeting the standards set for minimum daily exercise suggested by the World Health Organization to help prevent heart disease. American research conducted at Johns Hopkins School of Medicine in Baltimore to study the effects of exercise on blood pressure for older adults found surprising results for the effectiveness of t'ai chi. When they matched a group practising an aerobic exercise regime to a group practising t'ai chi over a period of 12 weeks, they found that the drop in blood pressure levels were almost equal between the

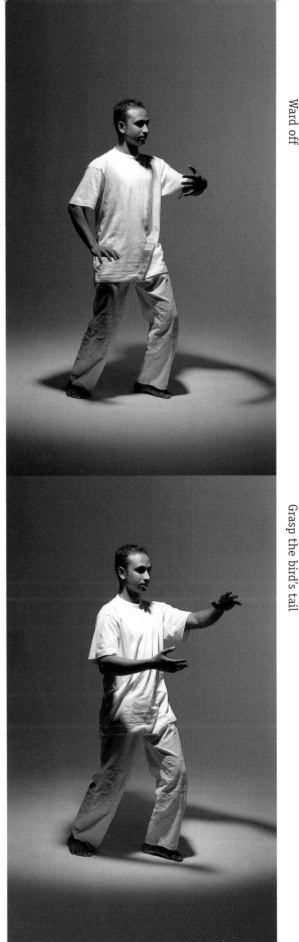

Ward off

Grasp the bird's tail

two groups. Despite the higher level of physical intensity and effort required by the aerobic group, they were not able to produce significantly higher benefits to their health.

Unlike many other sports and fitness activities, t'ai chi also has the positive benefit of not contributing to your ill health. There is no jarring of knee joints and ankles, all too familiar to the urban jogger pounding the streets. You will not break your leg or pull a hamstring throwing yourself into an over-enthusiastic football tackle. There is nothing to fall off, crash into, or get hit by, and t'ai chi provides one of the safest and most effective systems of physical culture ever devised.

When practice is finished the charge of ch'i generated will leave you fresh, glowing and benignly happy. Once the improvements to your health have sunk in, then it is likely that this will stimulate you to take care of yourself in other areas of your life. After practising for some while, junk food, late nights and excessive indulgence may seem less attractive and not nearly as interesting or necessary as you once thought.

Most importantly for any discipline that takes the long view, t'ai chi has the depth to sustain interest and motivation over a lifetime. The subtlety of t'ai chi forms require constant adjustment and attention to the precision of the practitioner's movement. These skills are not easily learnt and they provide a spur to take interest in the challenge of continuous personal improvement in skill. This struggle can be as exciting as in any sport, but here the challenge is presented in your own mind and body and you face the toughest competitor of all, your own will and ego.

Although there is always a challenge provided by the struggle to improve the depth and quality of your skills, t'ai chi is not an austere discipline only to be practised by the serious. It is totally absorbing, and serves to heal the mind by providing a tranquil, still space in which to end the clamour of restless thought. As you train your body, you train your mind, and as you train your mind, your body learns to move with mindful intention. The two are locked in the consciousness of the present, undistracted by the moment before or the next moment to come. Listening to this, the dialogue between the spirit and the breath, the body opens to the flow of ch'i and flushes the mind clean of stress and anxiety.

The Chinese say that 'what is accomplished by the mind is made known by the hand', thus the improvement of skills is not to be sought for its own sake, but as a physical demonstration of mental and spiritual progress. Ultimately, the focus for your training is the achievement of the three spiritual goals of emptiness, effortlessness and spontaneity. This means the ability to reflect the peace of the great void within you, to move and act appropriately without conscious determination in any situation, and to interact with life without prejudgment or the imposition of ego-led conditions. The dedicated practitioner seeks to connect the Tao, the source of the universe, through the active agency of ch'i, to the core of one's identity and walk the virtuous path of the realized person (*chen jen*). This is the true way to defend the body, mind and spirit.

PA KUA CH'UAN: EIGHT TRIGRAMS PALM

Pa kua ch'uan, or 'Eight Trigrams Palm', is one of the most refined and captivating expressions of the internal principle to be found in the Chinese martial arts. Although it is not as well known in the West as other styles of Chinese wu shu, or martial arts, it is becoming increasingly popular as Western practitioners of t'ai chi seek to deepen their experience and understanding of the soft arts. In China, master teachers of wu shu view pa kua as one of a trinity of martial arts that exemplify the internal principles of ch'i kung through differing facets. Often these three internal arts are seen as providing a progression of experience in the development of ch'i and internal force that can be linked to the maturation of the individual.

In this hierarchical model, the student begins with the art of hsing i, progresses to pa kua and completes their development by training in what is considered to be the most subtle of the soft arts, t'ai chi ch'uan. Thus hsing i, with its use of explosive force and linear attacks is most suited to the young. T'ai chi, on the other hand, is the style best suited to those who have learnt the patience and wisdom that comes with age and can and must rely on skill and subtlety rather than strength. In this schema, pa kua represents the middle years, when, as Confucius said: 'A person at 40 will not be diverted'. It is during middle age that the martial artist begins to accept that the strength and power that he or she may have relied upon is truly a delusion. Realizing that much of what passes for skill, particularly in competitive bouts and displays, is founded on the 'outside' showy aspects of their art, the mature practitioner begins to look for deeper meaning. At this point the understanding grows that to 'do nothing', by observing the Taoist principle of wu wei (non-action or non-interference), is to work with the natural order and not against it. To be spontaneous and natural brings the individual into harmony with the universe and gives the spiritual peace that is the desired outcome of the martial artist's journey.

The Origins of Pa Kua

The origins of pa kua as a fighting system are uncertain. However, is likely that it shares its beginnings with t'ai chi, in the practices of Taoist adepts living in the remote mountain eyries they favoured for their closeness to the heavens. In the late 18th century Tung Hui-ch'uan, who is said to have learnt the art from a Taoist priest in Kiangsu province, brought pa kua from obscurity to public attention. Upon his arrival in Beijing (Peking), he issued an open challenge to practitioners of all the martial arts schools to stand against him in competition. In a series of boxing contests he fought against prominent martial artists of many different styles and established the reputation of pa kua by defeating all comers. One of these encounters is legendary and accounts for the

close connection between hsing i and pa kua in terms of practice and allegiance.

It is said that Tung Hui-ch'uan met the renowned hsing i master Kuo Yun-shen in an epic three-day struggle. For the first two days of the contest neither had the advantage, but on the last day Tung Hui-ch'uan launched a whirlwind of exchanges that left Kuo Yun-shen with no effective riposte. It was in the spirit of the internal martial arts that Kuo Yun-shen showed no bitterness in his defeat and Tung Hui-ch'uan displayed no contempt for a beaten rival. Indeed, each recognized the validity of the other's skills and power and they resolved that from then on students of each school, pa kua and hsing i, would train in both systems. To this day it is common that a Chinese master of the martial arts will teach these two systems in tandem as complementary aspects of the internal principle.

Pa Kua and the *I Ching*

The theory and practice of pa kua is based on the philosophy of change represented by the endless interplay between yin and yang described in the ancient source of wisdom and lore the *I Ching*, or *Book of Changes*. Although legend ascribes the authorship of this book to Confucius, modern scholarship asserts that it is a compilation of many ancient texts, with its oldest passages dating from around 800 BCE and the latest from 200 CE. Despite the unlikelihood of any involvement by Confucius in its writing, it is undeniably Confucian in its outlook and general philosophy. Essentially, the book concerns itself with the establishment of social and cosmic order and the harmony of human relationships, which can be assisted by divination. The book is a repository of oracular knowledge couched in poetic descriptions that do not easily reveal their profundity.

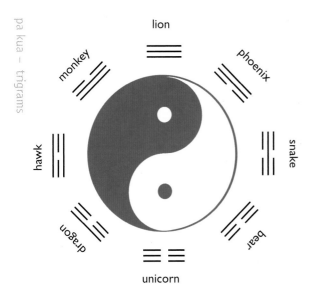

the 'creative' associated with heaven and the attribute of strength. *K'un*, the 'receptive', a combination of three broken yin lines, is yielding and is associated with the earth. The trigrams are also associated with parts of the body and therefore have equal importance in the divination of the body's health and vitality.

By studying the philosophical and perceptual meanings that underlie the pattern of the eight trigrams, the pa kua student brings insight to practice, thus enabling him to perceive and anticipate change and divine an appropriate response to meet it, in both combat and life.

The Eight Trigrams

Name	Attribute	Imagery	Parts of the body
Ch'ien, Creative	Strong	Heaven	Head & heart
K'an, Abysmal	Dangerous	Water	Liver & throat
Ken, Stillness	Resting	Mountain	Back, hands & feet
Chen, Arousing	Movement	Thunder	Kidneys & ears
Sun, Gentle	Penetrating	Wind	Intestines
Li, Clinging	Brilliance	Fire	Heart & spirit
K'un, Receptive	Yielding	Earth	Spleen & stomach
Tui, Joyous	Joyful	Lake	Lungs & chest

It is not known for certain how this system of divination came to its complete fruition in the *I Ching*. Originally it was thought that the oracle was limited in its answers to a simple 'yes' or 'no'. This was symbolized by a single unbroken yang line (—), for 'yes' and a single broken yin line (– –) for 'no'. As the oracle grew more sophisticated, additional combinations of lines were added to form units of three lines, the trigram (≡) and then a combination of two trigrams to form the 64 hexagrams, which make up the *kua*, or diagrams of the *I Ching*. By casting yarrow stalks or coins whose length or face represent a yin or yang line, a hexagram can be constructed and then consulted in the *I Ching* for an indication of the consequences of a particular course of action.

The classical arrangement of the *I Ching* trigrams was in the form of a circle surrounding the t'ai chi, yin yang symbol. These combinations of three lines were set down in eight permutations of yin and yang lines and ascribed particular qualities and imagery. Thus *ch'ien*, a combination of three unbroken yang lines, is

The Practice of Pa Kua

The basis of all movement in pa kua is circular and evasive. The practitioner walks a circle from six to 12 feet in diameter, using the bent knees of the 'lotus step'. As his circular walk carries him across each of the trigrams imagined on the ground beneath him, he pauses to perform a short sequence of manoeuvres and actions of the hands and legs. Spinning in a small circle, the practitioner marks the physical character of

Lion

Unicorn

each of the kua in a bewildering, fluid display of swift changes of hand and body positions, diving movements and sudden shifts of direction.

From the outside these actions seem to have little reference to martial actions. Nevertheless, embedded within the elegant, almost surreal beauty of the forms lie a complex pattern of strikes and grasps made with an open palm, the so called 'palm changes' of pa kua. They comprise a set of eight forms that express the characteristics of animals and are associated with each of the kua: the lion, unicorn, snake, hawk, dragon, bear, phoenix and monkey.

In a fighting context these circular movements are used to evade a direct confrontation with an opponent's kicks or blows by deflection or change of direction. Constantly circling, the pa kua specialist seeks to close in and step firmly and deeply around his opponent, to trip, sweep or throw him to the ground. The practitioner always seeks to enter from the outside of his opponent's guard or leading hand, so that he will be unable to use his other hand effectively. This angle of approach will also give the pa kua exponent access to his opponent's back, side and other exposed and vulnerable areas of the body. The speed and suddenness of the manoeuvres draw the opponent into a maelstrom of arms and legs which make it impossible to discern from which direction the next strike will come. Since the time of Tung Hui-ch'uan, pa kua has proved itself in countless exchanges and contests and is considered one of the most devastating and effective fighting systems in the world.

However, the reputation of pa kua does not rest on its fighting qualities alone, for when the exponent walks the circle it has more profound lessons to impart. As you walk the pa kua circle, you walk the circle of the heavens. The cycle of change is reflected in the movements of pa kua, and demonstrates the constantly shifting interchange of yin and yang through the body. Adaptability and the open, spontaneous mind, capable of dealing with the myriad complexities and difficulties of life are taught through the body to the mind. Once the practitioner has learnt to deal with the rigour and unceasing changes of pa kua, then there is nothing in life that should daunt him. Walking the circle the practitioner develops his or her perception of the physical and psychological processes at work in the body and how to organize and direct them. In this way the practitioner seeks to increase both self-awareness and spiritual insight as his body and mind are tuned to the natural harmony and rhythm of the universe.

As with all martial arts, the key to this command of the self is the command of the breath and the vital flow of ch'i. Evenness of action and breathing are harmonized by sinking breath to the tan t'ien. This allows the practitioner to continue normal, unpressured breathing while engaged in the most strenuous exercise. The neck and the chin are held straight in line with the sacrum with the shoulders relaxed, thus easing the flow of ch'i along the Governing and Conception channels. An important element of this command of the body and the flow of ch'i is the principle of *nei-kuo*, *wai-ch'eng*, or 'internally bound, externally stretched'. The internal binding refers to the feeling generated by the muscles and tendons that connect the upper torso to the tan t'ien, the source of ch'i and the body's centre of gravity. External stretching is produced by the movements of the palm changes that flex the tendons by keeping both the arms and the shoulders down.

Breath is directed mentally down to the tan t'ien and up through the lungs, expanding the ribs and exerting a downward pull on the diaphragm. This presses down on the tan t'ien, producing a bound or wrapped sensation in the muscles and connective tissue that surround it. The body maintains a low centre

Snake

Hawk

Dragon

Bear

of gravity by bending the knees and adopting an almost sitting posture. When connected to movement around both the external circle and the smaller circle of the form, this feeling of internal binding and external stretching is created. In a practical sense this internal binding directs you down, rooting you to the earth, thereby counterbalancing the energy directed outwards to the centre of the circle by your arms. As it sinks the body, so it sinks the mind into the tan t'ien to create a feeling of alert relaxation and calm.

The underlying purpose of these martial forms is the cultivation of energy by stimulating the flow of ch'i, through the stretching of tendons, the deepening of breath and the relaxation of the body and mind. If this harmony can be held together under the stress provided by training, then this quality of body and mind can become integral to the self and adapt to any circumstance. Command of the breath is bound to the command of the mind and liberates the spirit. Walking the circle, the pa kua student sets out on the journey of self-discovery through meditation in movement towards a union with the Tao.

武

氣

Phoenix

Monkey

The origins of hsing i are lost in the ancient past. History only picks up its trail when it records that between 1637 and 1661 Chi Lung-feng, from the city of Shanghai, met a mysterious boxer who taught him the secrets of this art. He, in his turn, passed the art on to two of his students, General Ts'ao Chi-wu of Shansi and Ma Hsueh-li of Honan. From these two students the lineage descended as the Shansi and Honan schools. Further splitting in the line of the Shansi school came after the time of the master teacher Kuo Yun-shen, when it sub-divided into three branches in Hopei province.

Tradition accords hsing i a more romantic origin, claiming it was founded by the legendary Yueh Fei, a general of the Sung dynasty. He is said to have been a man of great fullness of ch'i and character and a great martial artist and military strategist. Under his banner, the southern Sung army won great victories and reconquered much of the ground they had lost in Northern China. Whatever the true origins of hsing i, there is no doubt that it is an effective martial art, which has been forged and tested in real combat.

Whereas both t'ai chi and pa kua can be described

P'i: splitting: corresponds to the element Metal

Tsuan: drilling: corresponds to the element Water

as circular in the patterns and expressions of their forms, the direction and intention of hsing i is linear. It is not only linear, but moves constantly forward towards an opponent, meeting force directly with force. One may question, when all the external shape and character of the techniques bear such close relationship to the harder Shaolin boxing styles, why it is judged to be a soft, internal style at all. The answer lies not so much in the nature of the techniques themselves, but in the principles that direct them. These principles become clearer when we examine the meanings that underlie the terms *hsing*, or 'form' and *i*, or 'intention/will'. Hsing refers to the outside manifestation of reality in our person and actions or in the physical shape of form. I is the idea or intention that motivates and drives the external form. It is the hsing i practitioner's task to go beyond form and see the will or intention in a person or action and be able to react spontaneously to events.

This concept is shaped in practice through the representation of animals in its forms. The student of hsing i is not trying to imitate the actions and behaviour of animals, but to give shape to the idea that lies behind them. For example, the monkey form is intended to develop an upright posture and calmness of mind, while the snake form suggests continuous, flowing movement and alert responsiveness in the body. As the hsing i practitioner reads the intention in the forms he gives shape to, he learns to read the idea behind form in the posture and presence of his opponents. With this skill the practitioner is able to anticipate the moment when his opponent will give shape to an attack, and act to forestall and defeat him before it is fully under way. This action is not a counter move, but a pre-emptive strike which, as Hsun Tzu says, 'begins after the enemy does, but arrives before him.'

This learning must proceed through a series of experiential stages. At the beginner level the student will see only the form and will be so preoccupied with imitating the external shape of it that it will be empty and devoid of meaning. Soon consistent training will develop physical confidence so that the student will show form, but still no meaning, or i, within it. Gradually, as the student comes to maturity in the art, he will be able to integrate both hsing and i into performance until he loses form altogether. From the outside he presents no visible sign of his skills or intention to fight. Now the student has penetrated the idea of will and is able to possess both meaning and form without showing it to the opponent. Ultimately, at the highest levels of experience and mastery, the practitioner passes into the state where hsing and i are transcended. Now the practitioner can react with freshness and spontaneity to match the shifting circumstances of each moment without conscious effort or mental command. He has reached what is called by the Taoists 'no-form, no-meaning' and has turned the circle back to rediscover his own pre-natal nature with no gap between impulse and action.

Hsing I and the Five Elements

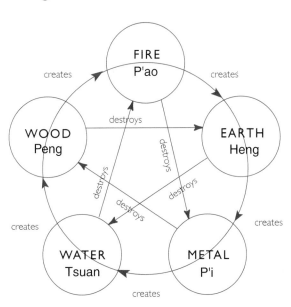

Peng: crushing: corresponds to the element Wood

P'ao: pounding: coresponds to the element Fire

The strategy of hsing i combat is contained in its five basic forms, named the *wu hsing*, and correlated to the Five Elements of Metal, Water, Wood, Fire, and Earth. Each of these elements has a destructive and creative cycle, so, for example, whereas Wood generates Fire it also destroys Earth, is created by Water and is in its turn destroyed by Metal. The Five Fists of hsing i were originally arranged in the order of the creative cycle from Metal to Earth, and this is still preferred by the orthodox line, although some styles now place Wood before Water. Each 'fist' or form corresponds to an element, its associated organs and a dynamic quality of ch'i. The table below sets out the sequence.

As each of the Five Fists are performed, they open up the pathways of ch'i and strengthen the organs to which they correspond. Hsing i invigorates the muscles and tendons by expansion and contraction, stimulates the flow of blood and ch'i, and enables fast, effortless movement. Each 'fist' has the vital quality to generate the other, so that *peng* will lead to *p'ao* and on to become *heng*. As each fist form has its place in the creative cycle, so it has its place in the destructive cycle. Thus heng (Earth) overcomes *tsuan* (Water), which overcomes p'ao (Fire), which defeats *p'i* (Metal) and goes on to destroy peng (Wood), where the cycle begins again with peng defeating heng.

In addition to these five basic fist forms, hsing i includes in its curriculum a further 12 forms based on the characteristics of animals, two of which are mythical. These are the dragon, tiger, monkey, horse, iguana, cock, hawk, snake, eagle, bear, swallow and the legendary t'ai bird (phoenix), which in some schools is replaced with the ostrich. All hsing i techniques are based on a solid foothold and obey the fundamental tactic of 'rise, drill, fall, overturn' comparable to the pattern in t'ai chi of 'ward off, roll-back, press and push'. Hsing i techniques are released with incredible force, using the explosive power of fajing. Ch'i is pulled up from the ground through the legs and transferred to the upper body by twisting the hips. This energy is moved on to the left or right shoulder where, with the full weight of the body behind, it is sent down the arm and out to strike through the knuckles at the split second of contact. The fist forms of hsing i roll forward like the unfolding of a great wave, relentlessly rising and falling as they move straight to the opponent.

Hsing i is an internal martial art that develops great flexibility and strength in the body. To perform the art well, one must develop physical poise and an aesthetic appreciation of the forms. Like all the internal martial arts, it offers learning without end, for there will never be a time when it is completely mastered. As the hsing i practitioner progresses from hsing to i, new insights reveal new weaknesses that previously remained unnoticed or were brushed aside. Faults that are detected in the posture or in the power behind a strike remind us that perfect form can only be found when the body and mind are one. This is the struggle that the hsing i student embarks upon, the spiritual quest for perfection of the self through the perfection of form.

Fist	Element	Organs	Ch'i action
P'i Splitting	Metal	Lungs & large intestine	Like the rise and fall of the axe splitting wood
Tsuan Drilling	Water	Kidneys & bladder	Flows in smooth curves
Peng Crushing	Wood	Gall bladder & liver	Simultaneous expansion and contraction
P'ao Pounding	Fire	Heart & pericardium	Fires suddenly like a bullet from a gun
Heng Crossing	Earth	Stomach & spleen	Strikes forward with rounded energy

神

THE HARMONIOUS SPIRIT

The Spirit of Budo

As we have seen, the Chinese internal martial arts have been formed as much by the spiritual intentions of their founders as their practical utility in combat. By contrast, the Japanese arts long maintained a more practical engagement with ch'i. While Shaolin and t'ai chi ch'uan were being developed in Buddhist and Taoist monasteries by monks and priests, the development of Japanese martial arts was largely in the hands of a professional warrior class, the samurai. Although Japan can lay claim to its own complement of fighting monks, their skills were more often employed in fighting rival monasteries or ambitious samurai warlords than they were dedicated to spiritual enlightenment.

Before the establishment of the Tokugawa bakufu, or military government, in 1603 endless civil wars were the major preoccupation of the samurai and their martial arts skills were honed for deadly practical purpose. Nevertheless, ch'i, or ki as it is called in Japan, was as important to the fighting man as it was to the Buddhist monk or the Taoist priest, for here was the key to the command of breath and vital energy that could deliver the fatal stroke and preserve their lives.

The source of the warrior's power was thought to reside in the lower abdominal area, or the belly, which the Japanese call the hara. In common with the Chinese and other Oriental cultures, the Japanese believed the hara to be the centre of physical and spiritual energy. Both these energies are focused in the tanden (tan t'ien in Chinese), sometimes called the 'one point' and located two inches below the navel. The Japanese samurai came to realize, as did their counterparts in China, that the tanden was a source of great internal power, activated by the breath and manifested as ki.

The fury and temper of battle soon exhausted those who relied only on external power and, if you were to survive, there was an imperative to act decisively and cut down your opponent with one stroke. Consequently, the samurai had a pressing need to develop the skill of centralizing energy in the hara to unleash the full potential of body, mind and spirit behind each cut of his sword. This art of body and mind integration was called *haragei*, the 'art of the belly', and was cultivated as an essential element of a skilled warrior's training. As the samurai developed his skills with the sword and bow, he learned also to develop the power of his breath, or *kokyu*. Mind, body and breath are focused into the *kiai*, a resonant shout emitted from deep in the well of the hara.

It is impossible adequately to translate the term kiai into English. Eytmologically it combines ki, or vital energy, with *ai*, meaning integration. Japanese-English dictionaries describe it as a yell or shout which is intended to overpower or mesmerize the opponent with the force of willpower. When the swordsman accompanies his cut with a kiai, he demonstrates with absolute conviction the intention that it will be overwhelmingly

decisive. It is an explosive vocal emission of synergistic energy, timed to coincide with the climax of a movement or technique. At this instant the entire strength of the body is focused and unified into one moment of decisiveness that cleaves through fear, doubt and hesitation to defeat an enemy with the full force of the warrior's ki.

While the development of ki was an important practical asset to a fighting man, it was always acknowledged that engagement with this force had a spiritual power that could lead to insightful action. The exploration of ki as a spiritual force in the training of the samurai grew in importance as Japan's turbulent history of internecine conflict and civil wars was brought to a close by the powerful Tokugawa clan in the early 17th century.

When Tokugawa Iyeasu defeated his rivals and established himself as the supreme military overlord, or Shogun, of Japan, he unwittingly began to foster the social climate and conditions that transformed the 'arts of war' into 'arts of peace'. The Tokugawa family instituted a military government that, through a combination of ruthless force, bribery and political shrewdness, managed to curb the ambitions of the great landowners and emasculate their ability to mount rebellion. These clan leaders, the *daimyo*, were expected to maintain expensive households in the capital where they lodged their children and wives under the watchful eyes of Tokugawa troops. Every year by the force of decree, they were required to share attendance at the Shogun's court with visits to their own castles and estates, thus curtailing opportunities to gather forces and intrigue for alliances. By this means the Tokugawa shoguns managed to bring about an unparalleled period of peace and social order, undisturbed by major political intrigue and civil war.

The ability of the Tokugawa regime to maintain this internal political and social stability was arguably powerfully reinforced by Japan's voluntary exclusion from the main current of international trade and foreign adventure. In the early 17th century, the Tokugawa Shogun (military ruler of Japan), fearful of the influence of Christianity, expelled the Spanish and Portuguese missionaries and began systematically to suppress the faith amongst his own people. From their reading of political events in other parts of the East, the Tokugawa authorities reasoned that Christianity was a Trojan horse which, once accepted, would open up the country to religious conflict and the possibility of foreign invasion from Portugal or Spain. As the history of the West's dealings in the East unfolded around them in China, the Philippines and other parts of South East Asia, the Japanese government's analysis proved to be remarkably perceptive. In order to avoid this contagion, the Tokugawa rulers hermetically sealed their own borders, preventing any travel abroad or contact with foreign traders for any of their citizens. Such foreign trade that was judged essential was maintained through one trading post on the island of Deshima, within Nagasaki bay. On Deshima, Dutch traders held a monopoly concession for trade between Japan and the markets of both East and West, allowing the Shogunate not only to regulate foreign economic influence, but also to control the exchange of information and ideas.

As a political strategy it proved, despite strains and tensions, extremely successful right up to the 1850s. Between the accession of the first Tokugawa Shogun in 1603 and the enforced opening of the country to foreign trade by Commodore Perry's American naval expedition in 1853, Japan remained free from war with foreign powers. This 'seclusion policy' turned Japanese society in on its self, reinforcing the pursuit of its distinct cultural, spiritual and aesthetic traditions in isolation from outside influences.

From the standpoint of the samurai warrior caste, this peaceful society became problematic. A warrior's social and economic position was founded on the principle of the monopoly of might. Only the samurai were licensed to bear arms and given the power of life and death over all others. The justification for this awful authority was that the samurai maintained order and defended the people from civil strife and foreign conquest. With both these threats diminished, the martial virtues lost much of their practical utility and the samurai's raison d'être became less credible. The samurai elite now had more pressing need for the skills of administration and commerce than the sword and spear. Yet this martial training had been the backbone of the caste's political dominance and could not be entirely abandoned. Successive rulers recognized the dangers of this position and exhorted their feudal retainers to continue to train with the same intensity and martial spirit that their ancestors displayed. However, although a strong tradition of practical military skill was maintained by some samurai, others began to transform the martial arts into paths for self-discovery and spiritual illumination.

Many teachers of the martial arts began to see that the disciplines of martial training, which emphasized equanimity of mind and body, steadfastness and strength of purpose, were important social and spiritual virtues. The struggle for mastery of martial skills could be seen as analogous to the struggle of life itself, and provide valuable insights for the development of the character and spirit. The new enemy was the ego, which must be cut down to establish the harmony of mind, body and spirit. Slowly but inexorably the schools of martial arts, or *bujutsu*, began to stress the importance of aesthetic form and movement above that of combat reality, and to recast their arts as spiritual 'Ways' or budo.

The word 'do' is used to describe a 'Way' or path to spiritual understanding and self-realization. As there will be no end to the challenges and moral dilemmas presented by life to even the most enlightened of minds, so it must be recognized that there is no end to this path. To commit oneself to the 'Way' is to commit to a lifetime of study and practice, constantly measuring the character and the spirit against the ideals that have been set. A do seeks to cultivate the mind, body and spirit for the benefit of both the individual and society. The Way is pursued in the belief that the enlightened mind cannot be created in isolation from the body and that only by disciplining the physical body can we open the spirit. Spiritual progress can be measured by the precision and aesthetic principle demonstrated in the physical form. Command of the physical form is therefore an expression of one's command of the self.

The two Japanese martial arts that we examine next in our energetic journey are better defined as modern martial ways, inspired by martial forms, but dedicated to spiritual and aesthetic purpose. They have been chosen to represent two aspects of the modern reality of the martial arts and are not intended to deny the internal or spiritual orientation of other Japanese martial arts. Neither *aikido* nor *iaido* are pursued principally for their practical application or effectiveness in combat. Each in its own way sets out to cultivate the individual who is both in harmony with his own body and mind and can engage with others in that same spirit. This ideal state is achieved through the development of mushin, no-mind, where the ego-led mind is let go and true consciousness is realized in the spontaneous congruence of thought and action. Like their Chinese internal martial art counterparts they aim at the same goal; harmony with the universe and the liberation of the human spirit.

AIKIDO

Aikido: The Way of Harmony with the Spirit

Aikido, unlike the Chinese martial arts we have examined, is an art conceived and realized in the 20th century by the genius of one man, Morihei Ueshiba (1883–1969 CE).

Although aikido techniques were inspired by the Daito Ryu school of *aiki jujutsu* and used to devastating practical purpose for combat in the samurai past, Ueshiba completely transformed their character and intention. Daito Ryu aiki jujutsu forms a body of fighting techniques designed to break limbs, incapacitate function and throw people down with great severity. Although Ueshiba had trained long and hard under the headmaster of the Daito school, Sokaku Takeda, he was a man of deep spiritual yearning. He could not reconcile himself to the ferocity of intent that lay behind these aiki jujutsu locks and throws. Through the years preceding the Second World War, he began to give these fighting techniques a different cast, softening their application and emphasizing circularity and evasion.

This new approach drew many adherents, particularly when Ueshiba was able ceaselessly to demonstrate against challengers from other martial arts schools that his softer approach was no less effective in subduing and defeating them. Indeed, at times it seemed that Ueshiba had developed powers of evasion and placement beyond those of a mere mortal and that he could beat an opponent without the need to touch them. On one such occasion in 1925, he was visited by a naval officer who enjoyed a great reputation for his skills in *kendo*, the Japanese form of fencing. A disagreement ensued about the nature of the martial arts that infuriated the officer and provoked Ueshiba to challenge him to prove his point by striking him down. Taking up a solid wooden training sword, the naval officer set about his task with what he considered to be irresistible intensity. To his dismay, however hard or fast he cut or quickly he turned, Ueshiba always remained effortlessly outside of his reach. Eventually, exhausted by his efforts and dispirited by his failure to land a blow, he sank to his knees and conceded defeat.

Ueshiba was deeply affected by his achievement and, leaving the naval officer to recover on the *dojo* (training hall) floor, he walked out into his garden. There he was to have a visionary experience which made him realize that the true way of the warrior was to 'manifest divine love' by cultivating a spirit 'that embraces and nurtures all things'. From that moment on, Ueshiba dedicated himself to creating a martial art that would guide others to this insightful reconciliation of intention and action by expressing itself as a way of peace. When Japan went to war, engaging in the futile struggle against the allied powers, Ueshiba retreated to his country home in Ayabe. Here, far from the political intrigue and the arrogant fanaticism of the war party in Tokyo, he quietly farmed and trained. Practising both the skills of agriculture and the martial arts, he perfected a new art for the new era of peace that was to emerge from the long dark tunnel of war: aikido, the way (do) of harmony (ai) with the spirit (ki).

Ai: Harmony

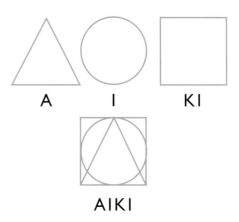

Ai is the Japanese character that expresses the philosophy behind Ueshiba's new definition of the martial arts as 'ways for peace'. It is translated as 'harmony' or 'affinity' and, in the sense in which it is used by the aikido practitioner, it bears a close relationship to the Taoist concept of wu wei, or non-interference. Both terms stress the importance of recognizing that man and nature cannot be separated. They form an indissoluble union sharing the same life force and energy, or ki, the substance of the universe. Understanding and tuning the mind to the great rhythms at work within nature leads to a realization of how these forces work upon the self. The essence of this message is that true peace of the spirit can only be sustained when the mind and body work with the flow of natural events and not in opposition to them.

To accept this concept on a purely intellectual level as the product of bookish learning is not enough. Aikido, in common with all the systems of energy work we have reviewed, insists that we must perceive it in our bodies as well as our minds. Ai is a psychophysical reality that is felt as well as thought and must inform both our conscious and unconscious actions. Aikido offers the practitioner a way of gaining this insightful experience through the disciplines of martial arts training. When the aikido practitioner enters the training hall and interacts with others, this becomes a representation in microcosm of the cosmic inter-relationship of yin and yang.

In a physical sense the aikido practitioner begins to learn this lesson through the practice of technique. All aikido moves and manoeuvres accord with the principle of circularity that is manifested in the cyclic movement of matter and energy within nature itself. Thus, in common with t'ai chi, force is never opposed to force, but always evaded or deflected. The aikido practitioner, or *aikidoka* seeks to harmonize his or her body and actions with the movements of the opponent, circling away from an attack rather than confronting it, in order to blend with and redirect aggressive force towards a harmonious reconciliation. When attacked, the aikido practitioner pivots, leading the opponent around him or herself, or enters quickly into the attacker's undefended space to control and unbalance him. Confounded by spiralling movements and evasion, the attacker's force is dissipated and he is led to a point where he can be controlled with a joint lock, or thrown to the ground.

Ai is also a reflection of aikido's moral precepts that forbid the practitioner from initiating violence or defending himself with inappropriate force or brutality. Instead he or she adopts an entirely defensive initiative, making no move until an attack is launched. Only then will the *aikidoka* move swiftly to control and suppress the aggressive action before it has barely begun. This mental and physical initiative requires the practitioner to be able to read the opponent's aggressive intentions from his posture and sense the direction of his mind. It is an instinctive, defensive initiative that can only be mastered by dedication to practice and years of experience.

The Practice of Aikido

The principle of circular motion is at the centre of all aikido movement and technique. It is used to take advantage of an opponent's physical strength and momentum to defeat him by evasion and the deflection of oncoming force. The aikidoka becomes the centre of a centripetal or centrifugal force that either sucks in an opponent and sends him spiralling to the ground or repels him like a spinning top colliding with a skittle. There are few straight lines in this practice. The movements of arms, legs and the upper body describe arcs and circles in all dimensions as if the aikidoka was at the centre of a rapidly moving sphere. This gives an aikido practice the quality of a dynamic ballet as the practitioners weave and pirouette around the training hall in their flowing traditional training uniforms.

Technically, aikido limits its forms to those that control and immobilize an opponent or cause him or her to be unbalanced and fall to the ground. Although some strikes with the back of the fist or knuckles, may be used to attack vital points on the body, they are more often used as 'blinding actions'. Blows delivered towards the eyes are designed to confuse an opponent before seizing and immobilizing him with a lock on the wrist, elbow or shoulder and pinning him face down to the ground. Unlike Chinese ch'uan-fa, there are no kicks or punches employed to defeat an opponent. Instead, the aikidoka relies totally on the ability to seize or throw the opponent with the minimum of injury or pain. Rather than generating the twisting power of the hips to deliver a punch, the aikidoka uses this torsion and the forward movement of the whole body to check the opponent and knock him over.

Many locks in the martial arts oppose the natural direction of movement in the joints of the limbs and seek to apply pressure to break or dislocate them.

Aikido joint locks work on the contrary principle and are applied in the direction of the joint's natural range of movement. The practitioner twists or turns the joint to the point where it can move no more. Pressure is applied until the opponent feels pain and is compelled to the ground and immobilized. Joint locks are also employed to unbalance and throw an opponent, who must necessarily cast himself in the direction of the force applied, to escape the pain of the lock. In this way an aikido throw is more akin to a projection, with the application of the lock guiding the opponent to throw himself over his twisted wrist or turned elbow. This movement in the natural direction of the joint gives the aikidoka great command over the severity of the pressure applied, allowing the incremental application of pain rather than the delivery of traumatic stress. As the joint has not been unnaturally forced, the pain quickly subsides when the lock is released. Not only are aikido joint locks crushingly effective, but they also allow the practitioner to exercise moral and ethical restraint to cause only as much pain as will guarantee a submission. Ethics and principle are therefore not only a matter of belief but are embedded in aikido technique and strategies of application. Philosophy and action are harmonized to become one unified principle, to be used to diffuse violence and bring about a safe and compassionate conclusion for both attacker and defender.

The aikido practitioner does not learn these techniques in isolation from the context. Each joint lock or projection is learnt by working with a partner in a staged scenario of attack and defence. These pre-arranged sequences are a familiar part of all learning in the martial arts and in Japan are called kata. Both partners take on the alternating role of defender and attacker, so that they can experience how it feels to apply the technique and its consequences. Without feeling the pain and the point at which the lock becomes active, the aikidoka would not be able to make the necessary judgments of control when subduing the opponent.

Although aikido techniques have the potential of great power, the tenor of its practice is relaxed and co-operative. As each aikidoka lends his or her body for their partner to practise a technique on, there is a duty to take care and apply techniques with caution. To understand how to blend with a partner's movements and lead them in the direction you wish to take them requires sensitivity to touch, timing and an understanding of body mechanics. This understanding is acquired by doing and cannot be learnt from videos or books. Naturally, a close, co-operative training relationship of this kind necessitates the building of trust and confidence between aikido partners. This is the social outcome of the principle of ai, or harmony.

Practice is undertaken within the dojo, or training hall, as mats are required to protect practitioners from injury when falling or being taken to the ground. Unlike t'ai chi and other forms of the Chinese martial arts, there is little opportunity to practise outside save for the use of weapons such as sword or staff. Practitioners conform to strict codes of discipline and high standards of etiquette that are a traditional feature of the cultures of the East. The relationship between teacher and student is an important one founded on mutual respect. Respect is owed to the teacher for the commitment made to passing on his or her skills and insight, and to the student for the resolve and enthusiasm demonstrated in practice. This spirit of mannered behaviour and quiet discipline is reinforced by the wearing of white training uniforms and the traditional divided skirt-like trousers, the *hakama*, which gives the dojo something of the atmosphere of a Buddhist monastery. Although there is both an ascetic and deeply spiritual quality to training, the spirit of the aikido dojo is always one of open-hearted, joyful engagement.

Ki in Aikido

In common with all the arts and disciplines we have reviewed, aikido draws its power from ki, the vital energy of the spirit. The ability to tap into this force not only contributes to our health and well-being, but gives us the power to heal and resolve conflict and is the mark of our spiritual progress. Thus a development of the ability to harness the flow of ki and direct it to effective purpose is an essential requirement of aikido practice. Once again, this process cannot be learnt through books or comprehended by the intellect, it has to be understood by the body through training.

Three principles are locked into the fundamental structure of aikido that, over the course of time, develop the practitioner's ability to comprehend, summon and command the flow of ki in his own body and lead the ki of his opponents. These are the control of the tanden (tan t'ien), or hara, the maintenance of central alignment and the use of breath power.

The tanden, located approximately two inches below the navel, is considered to be the psycho-physical centre of the body and the focal point of ki. It is therefore thought of as being both the spiritual seat of the self and the point from which our vital energy is driven. In aikido and other Japanese martial arts the tanden is also called the 'one point' and corresponds to the body's centre of gravity. By physically keeping posture low and grounded and by visualizing the mind resting in the one point, the aikidoka learns to use the body as one. No reliance is placed on the strength of the arms or upper torso alone to execute technique, as this can lead to instability and the wasting of power. Instead the tanden leads the body, providing a stable centre charged with ki that infuses the whole body with energy and momentum. The aikidoka centres his mind in the tanden and encourages the development of breath power by deep abdominal breathing through a variety of exercises and, in this way, can act with the full capacity of the lungs at his command.

By seating our mental focus in the tanden we are able to maintain the central alignment of the body. This is crucial to our capacity to use our breath and the full power of the tanden seated between the hips. Without an upright posture, the shoulders relaxed and the hips centrally aligned with the torso, we cannot command the power of the body as one unit. When the body is centred, so is the mind, projecting our energy before us. The aikidoka trains to perfect this good posture so that it becomes a habitual factor of his or her life.

Kokyu ryoku, or breath power, is the force that drives the body and replenishes our prenatal store of ki. Aikidoka are trained to draw breath deep down into the hara or abdominal area, and to exhale powerfully with a fullness of ki when throwing or pinning down an opponent. The practitioner strives to make this abdominal breathing natural and even throughout his aikido practice, whatever the tempo of training. Eventually, this ability to generate breath power becomes an instinctive and automatic factor of life, allowing him to remain calm and centred in the most extreme circumstances of physical stress or emotional crisis.

Kokyu ryoku is also the ability to achieve a conjunction of the aikidoka's breath with that of an opponent. It allows the practitioner to regulate and time the pace of his breathing and his body reflexes so that he can launch himself across space and arrive alongside his opponent in exactly the right position to overcome him.

The Way of *Aiki*

The two characters of ai (harmony) and ki (spirit energy), when joined together form the unified concept of 'aiki'. Aiki is the physical realization in the body and the breath of 'mushin', or 'no mind'. It is a state of imperturbable composure where the mind remains alert, prescient and impregnable to distraction or fear. When the state of aiki is realized, the practitioner displays no malicious intention and makes no prejudgments about events. Body and mind have become one and remain open and reflexive to events, able to deal instinctively and appropriately with any challenge.

The physical training of the aikidoka in the dojo is the necessary foundation for this pyscho-physical condition. As the aikidoka struggles to achieve a strong, yet relaxed physical posture he must also learn to concentrate his mind into his movements and actions. At first he will be awkward and ungainly as his mind is confused by the complexities of the techniques and he over-directs the actions of the body. Gradually, after much time and effort, he learns to 'just do' rather than think his way through the process until mind and body become totally absorbed in the required action. The physical challenges that the individual faces in the dojo and his ability to meet them become a paradigm for the dangers and vicissitudes he faces in all areas of his life. As he is able to unite body and mind to defeat an opponent, he is taught how to activate the full potential of his energy. This is the true purpose of aikido training and it is intended to foster the individual's ability to integrate the quality of aiki into his character and actions in the world outside the dojo as much as within it. By teaching the body, the mind is conditioned and refined, and is able to see more clearly how anger, impatience, aggression and fear only confound clarity of thought and action. The aikidoka seeks to avoid confrontation and conflict and gain the confidence to lead others to harmony and collaboration. This is aikido as the art of peace and human reconciliation.

Despite its gentle face, aikido is a martial art that is both physically and mentally challenging. As aikido sets ethical limits on its responses to attack, the techniques are often subtle and complex and take much time to master. After all, it is much easier to kick or punch an aggressor than to seize, immobilize and leave them unhurt. Like the Chinese internal martial arts, aikido demands patience and maturity to acquire the skills and consciousness necessary to perform it well.

Physical challenge is explicit in its technique, which requires the practitioner to take many falls from daunting heights and at great speed. However, aikido sets out to be a learning for life. All its physical challenges can be overcome by its compassionate training methods. Learning to fall without hurting oneself is a skill that engenders great physical confidence and is surprisingly easy to accomplish. With the acquisition of self-defensive skills this confidence can be extended into relationships with others, in the knowledge that the practitioner can protect himself without resorting to disproportionate coercion. Alertness, vitality and composure will help us make a success of relationships at work and in our personal lives. On the most functional of levels, aikido will also stimulate the flow of blood and ki, encourage and develop a flexible, fit body, and contribute to our equanimity of mind. All these qualities can result from aikido training. They are the mark of the Japanese concept of do, or the 'Way', a lifetime commitment to perseverance and determined effort in the interests of self-awareness and the forging of the humane spirit.

Shomenuchi irmi nage: entering throw, breaking uke's balance

Shomenuchi irmi nage: entering throw, throwing uke down

Kote gaeshi: wrist turn, nage deflects uke's punch and breaks his balance

Kote gaeshi

Shomenuchi irmi nage: entering throw, uke takes the
fall (ukemi)

Kote gaeshi: wrist turn, nage turns uke back over his
wrist

Kote gaeshi: wrist turn, uke falls to the floor

Kyoku ho exercise: using the tanden, nage
lifts uke and throws him down

Iaido is the spiritual way of drawing and cutting instantly with the sword. It derives from the practical combative skills of *iaijutsu*, when the samurai would draw his sword quickly and cut down his opponent the moment he was attacked. These skills were of more use in the context of a private duel or in response to an assassination attempt than on the battlefield, when the sword was already drawn.

In an imaginative sense it bears comparison to the skills required of a gunslinger in the American West of the 19th century. Indeed, this cross-reference has been portrayed eloquently in the 'Western' movies of Sergio Leone, where the lone wanderer of Kurosawa's samurai films is recast as the gunfighter with no name. In both situations the warrior or gunfighter must seize the initiative and be able instantly to read the intention of the opponent to 'beat him to the draw'. Great technical dexterity is obviously required in order to draw the weapon speedily and use it decisively. This needs to be coupled with an alert mental state that is able to respond intuitively and calmly in the presence of danger without the distractions of fear, confusion or doubt. There, however, the resemblance ends, for although the combat initiative needed by the samurai and the gunfighter bear comparison, only the samurai came to understand that spiritual lessons could be drawn from the acquisition of this skill.

Takuan (1573–1645), the Rinzai sect Zen priest taught that the best way for a samurai to face a foe in combat was to give up any expectation of his own survival. He wrote that the warrior must place his mind 'on top of concerns for life or death'. This does not imply that the warrior should not care, or adopt a position of neutrality in the face of death for either himself or his opponent. On the contrary, this is a positive state of high spiritual perfection that transcends concerns about individual mortality. Takuan based his teachings on swordsmanship on the Taoist concepts of *munen*, or 'no-thought', which finds its realization in mushin, or 'no-mind'. Munen is a state of mind where the swordsman no longer has any thoughts about life or death. When *munen* is achieved, the body will act without any disturbance from the mind and is able to perform spontaneously, without any intentional effort to initiate and maintain it. Mushin is this state in action. Here yin and yang are one, for there are no thoughts about what is good or bad, profit and loss, or life and death: there is only the oneness of the universe. To achieve this state of spiritual peace and transcendence the swordsman must overcome the ego and understand that 'life and death are one'.

The Meaning of Iaido

The word iaido is formed from three characters, 'i', 'ai' and 'do', which describe the philosophical foundation upon which practice rests. The meaning of the first character 'i' is complex and multi-layered. At its simplest it means to 'reside' or 'be in' a place so naturally that the individual is able to adapt to or 'fit' that place as an individual. In the body this state is the natural flow of movement the swordsman undertakes in fulfilment of the form, inspired by a purposeful will. 'Ai' is the character for 'harmony' and represents the coming together of things that rightfully fit together. Ai is also a responsive state of body and mind which is able to adapt to meet any circumstances, however difficult or contrary to expectations. Thus the swordsman who has developed this ability fits naturally into place and is able to harmonize his own thoughts and actions with his physical and social environment. Ai is the harmony that results from synchronizing individual ki with the flow of ki in the universe. 'Do' is of course the path of meditation and reflection in action that the swordsman follows to achieve enlightenment and moral wisdom.

Modern iaido has continued into the present the idea that through the practice of swordsmanship the mind can be 'spiritually forged', to cultivate *heijo shin*, the 'constant, stable spirit'. To attain this true stability or peace of mind the swordsman must have command of the full potential of the intellect, control the emotions and act with integrity and compassion. The iaido swordsman seeks this peaceful, unified condition through training with the sword. By a commitment made to a lifetime of training, the iaido swordsman seeks spiritual insight through the disciplined attempt to achieve the perfect expression of form. Each technical problem or dissatisfaction with personal performance can be described as a 'physical koan' which, although manifested in the co-ordination of the body with the sword, can only be solved in the mind. What stands between the student of iaido and the goal of heijo shin is the ego-led self that is too easily diverted from training by softer options or preoccupied with the showy development of skill for its own sake.

This is *shugyo*, or 'severe' training, where the student of iaido is expected to bear the difficulties of training without resentment or rancour, to find solutions to the technical and moral problems encountered in training, and above all to train diligently and unremittingly. Intellectually, the swordsman must grasp the meaning of the form both spiritually and technically. A high state of mental concentration must be maintained to block out distractions and keep the body alert and active through hours of rigorous practice. By these efforts the iaido practitioner harmonizes the flow of ki through both body and mind and is able to unlock *kiryoku*, or moral energy, the vital force that is the expression of the energized self.

The Practice of Iaido

The practice of iaido is unlike any of the other martial arts we have described so far. While aikido and the internal Chinese martial arts we have surveyed still retain a practical component of self-defence, iaido is completely without modern defensive or offensive application. Unless the wearing of swords were to become fashionable once again, the iaido practitioner knows that the sword will never be wielded to cut down an opponent. The sword has become a tool in the practice of the Way. It is not now wielded with any conscious intention to kill others, but only to subdue the will. As the swordsman's eyes follow the swift passage of the blade through the air he intends to cut down the ego-led self which stands between him and heijo shin, the constant, peaceful mind.

Practically, iaido involves drawing the Japanese *katana*, a long, curved sword, from its scabbard, then making defensive and cutting actions with the naked blade before gracefully resheathing it in the scabbard. This is carried out in traditional Japanese attire in a monastic atmosphere of quiet calm, according to elaborate and precise ritual. Beauty, grace and the aesthetic realization of form is as much an aspect of its performance as the accuracy of a cut or the efficient drawing of the sword from the scabbard. For it is from good form that the even, natural flow that gives life to beautiful movement is grown.

Iaido is performed either standing or in the formal kneeling-sitting postures traditional to Japan which are called seiza and *tate hiza*. In seiza the practitioner folds both legs under and sits back on the heels, while in tate hiza a semi-crouched posture with only the left leg folded under is adopted. Many iaido techniques assume that the practitioner will be attacked whilst kneeling formally in seiza in the imaginary setting of a great lord's castle. Assassination attempts were the constant concern of the lord's retainers and it was their duty to prevent them. All iaido techniques are taught by the swordsman following prescribed sets of movements involving drawing and cutting with the sword in response to visualized scenarios of attack and defence. These equate with the forms of t'ai chi and pa kua, which also follow prescribed sequences of attack and defence. In Japan these forms are called kata.

Each iaido kata follows four distinct phases that must be seamlessly co-ordinated before there is any hope of aspiring to the perfect expression of the form. These are *nukitsuke*, the draw, *kiritsuke*, the cut, *chiburi*, the cleaning of the blade and finally, *noto*, the return of the sword to its scabbard. The four phases mark different positions in the passage from realizing that an attack is imminent and dealing with it, to the swordsman's return to quiet, unperturbable calm when he has cleaned and sheathed his sword.

Mae, the first form or kata of the Muso Jikiden Eishin Ryu school of iaido illustrates the sequence and purpose of each phase in this way. The swordsman sits serenely in seiza with his palms resting on the thighs. Breathing deeply but evenly he awaits the intention of an attack. Perceiving the moment of decision, the swordsman rises slowly to his feet and draws his

sword. At the moment the tip of the sword reaches the end of the scabbard the right foot is moved out and forward as the sword springs forth to make a perfect horizontal cut. Pushing forward in this kneeling posture, he cuts straight down with the sword. After a brief pause, the swordsman rises to his feet. Simultaneously, he makes a sweeping cut over his head and down to stop and hold the blade poised above the floor. This is chiburi and the action represents the flicking of excess blood from the blade before resheathing it. The final act of the drama arrives when the swordsman has assured himself that he is in no more danger. Smoothly, he slides the length of the blade back into the scabbard, slowly sinking down once again into a kneeling position until the sword is fully returned with the final faint click of the handguard pressed against the scabbard's mouth. Of course, in all this sequence of action the opponent is not present. The practitioner is engaged in a battle for control of his mind and body, fighting the inadequacies of his performance, which he knows are caused by his inattention and lack of inner peace. The battle with the body is engaged in to beat the ego and free the mind. It requires great determination and consistency to fight, for it is a struggle without end.

Ki in Iaido

Iaido is not a practice that has been deliberately designed to stimulate the flow of ki or massage the internal organs. It is not a system of energetic exercise, yet like the iceberg it hides much of its vital nature below the surface of its forms. The development of power in the hara, or the abdomen, is the force that drives all action. At all times the swordsman must visualize the mind centred in the tanden and lead all his movements from this point. This one point is both the centre of the body's gravity and the generating source of ki. Breathing is essential to this process and the practitioner must learn to breathe deeply and evenly while synchronizing the breath with each action of the sword and body. In iaido practice, the mind, body and the sword are harmonized by the even flow of breath to become a unified expression of ki. This united power is witnessed in the kiai, the resonant shout that springs out deep from the belly when a cut with the sword is made. This forceful expulsion of breath need not be audible, but the breath is always pushed up and out from the hara as the cut is made.

Physical strength and a high level of fitness are not required to begin iaido practice. The pace of movement is slow and easy, marked only by a sudden step forward and a flash of the sword. At times its low, deep stances and kneeling postures put strain on the knees, but the practitioner learns to stretch out the legs and lower the body without tension or stress. Relaxation of the muscles, tendons and ligaments is necessary to the wielding of the sword, as it relies on gravity, balance and momentum, rather than strength, to direct it. In the same manner as t'ai chi forms, iaido kata reflect stillness in movement and take much mental and physical command to release tension and hold the body in the correct positions. This can prove to be both as demanding for the will and as stimulating to the flow of ki as any ch'i kung exercise and seeks the same spiritual outcome from its practice.

It is often said that iaido is the most philosophical of the Japanese martial arts. Untrammelled by battlefield relevance it is pursued entirely as a form of active meditation, dedicated to the spiritual path for enlightenment. No longer is there an enemy to cut down or external danger to face, for the practitioner's purpose has become entirely pacific. The sword has become *katsujin no ken*, the sword that cuts through delusion, attachment and fear to give life.

Seiza: preparing the mind

Koiguchi no kirikata: drawing the blade

Muso Jikiden Eishin Ryu: Seiza no bu, the first technique, *Mae*

Kiritsuke: the blade descends

Kiritsuke the sword cuts through to the centre

Nukitsuke: the blade springs free and makes the first cut

Kiritsuke: the sword is raised above the head

Chiburi: the sword is raised to the forehead

Chiburi: the swordsman stands to cast the 'blood' from the sword blade

Noto: the swordsman kneels as the blade is smoothly returned to the scabbard

Noto: the swordsman rests momentarily on one knee as the blade closes into the scabbard

Noto: the swordsman stands and adjusts his sword

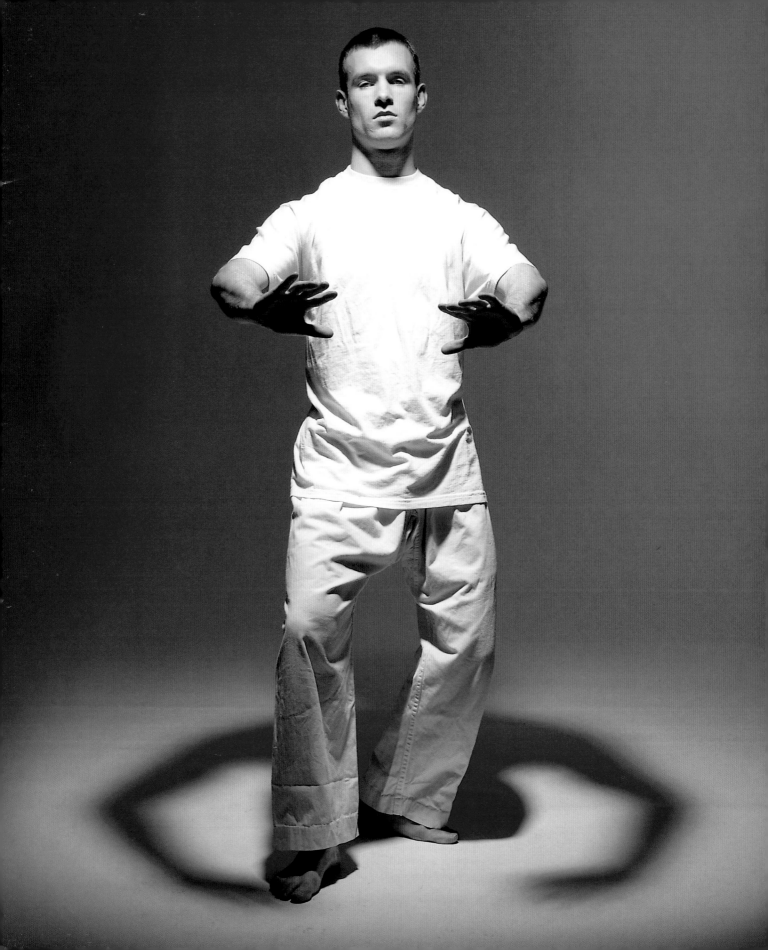

NATURE AND THE FLOW OF CH'I

The Dragon Veins

Throughout China, Japan and wherever the influence of Taoism has taken root, it is believed that the whole of creation is formed from one energetic substance: ch'i. This one energy is divided into two bipolar aspects, yin and yang, the negative and the positive. Between these two states there is constant flux, each state containing the embryonic seed of the other and each constantly in the act of transformation into its opposite.

Throughout this book we have seen that this Taoist-inspired cosmology has created the theoretical and philosophical foundation for all the meditative, medical, martial and cultural arts that we have examined. All these arts and sciences adopt the principle that vitality, health and spiritual peace can be actualized only when the mind, body and spirit are unified and harmonized with creation.

So far in our exploration of ch'i, we have concentrated on those disciplines that work directly with an individual's own psycho-physical condition. Any references made to the external influences of ch'i have largely been discussed within the context of each tradition, with only passing reference to the importance of setting and attunement to seasonal change. Logic dictates that as mankind occupies the realm where the pure cosmic downward flow of heavenly yang ch'i meets the upward flow of yin ch'i from the earth, we are profoundly affected by their influences. The fact that downward flowing yang ch'i meets upward flowing yin ch'i does not guarantee that at the point they meet they will necessarily be in a state of absolute balance. As with our own bodies there will be times when one state needs to be more predominant than the other, in order to restore and harmonize the organism over the longer term. The Taoists theorized that this bipolar flow of ch'i between Heaven and Earth must act in the same manner as the body itself, moving along unseen cosmic energy lines throughout creation. These energy lines, known as 'dragon veins', flow from the sky down through the mountains and into the earth, spreading out in a network of yang energy. Similarly, energy flows upwards from the earth towards the heavens. Between each individual star and planet this same process is at work, as each contributes its own yin or yang quality to sustaining the overall harmony of the cosmos.

It can be seen, therefore, that where we live, work and play we are directly affected by the qualities of this energetic exchange and their particular force and direction. Too much positive energy can be as deleterious to health as a preponderance of negative influences. Just as the acupuncturist and the shiatsu practitioner sensitively measure and adjust the yin yang flow of ch'i within the body to establish the optimum conditions for living the good life, so it is possible to work with the dragon veins. From the earliest times in Chinese history this concept has been at work in the design of their houses and temples, the laying out of their gardens and the orientation of their cities. This gave rise to the science or geomancy of feng shui. From a Western perspective many of the principles that may be observed within this science might seem far-fetched or merely a matter of aesthetic common sense. However, there can be no doubt that many buildings that conform to the principles of feng shui have an uncanny sense of being perfect in their place and purpose. What does feng shui give us that is comparable to all the other disciplines we have examined? It is a framework of thought and action that helps us focus on the way we live our lives in order to improve it. In this case it is 'where' and 'how' we interact with our surroundings that receives our concentrated attention.

Feng shui has, in common with other ancient traditions, both a mythological and an historical explanation for its origins. Feng shui literally translates as 'wind water', so it comes as no surprise to find at least one of these elements at work in the story of creation. Legend attributes the foundation of the science to the year 2005 BCE when a mysterious turtle emerged from the River Lo. The emperor at the time made many improvements to the agriculture of his domains along the River Lo by raising its banks to prevent flooding. He noticed that the area that enjoyed most prosperity had the River Lo on its east and excellent protection from the piercing energy of the north-east winds. One day as he sat on the banks of the river meditating he was brought out of his reverie by the sight of a turtle slowly climbing up the bank before him. The turtle is a creature of great spiritual significance to the Chinese, but this alone would not have provoked such interest. What amazed the emperor were the sets of dots, ranging from one to nine, laid out in a three-by-three grid upon its back. The arrangement was laid out in such a way that by adding any three squares together in either a vertical, horizontal or diagonal line the sum would always amount to 15. This 'magic square' is known as the *lo shu* and when superimposed upon the pa kua, the eight directions of the divination compass, they have the power to penetrate more of its sublime meaning. Since this time the lo shu and the pa kua have become the principal means of divination within the Compass School of feng shui, which we discuss in greater detail below.

4	9	2
3	5	7
8	I	6

What is historically certain is that the ability to read the classical texts and interpret the *I Ching* or *Book of Changes* was long a prerequisite for employment as an official of the imperial government. Feng shui formed part of this body of classical knowledge and was employed by these scholarly civil servants in the design of palaces and temples and in the harmonious layout of imperial cities. This planning took account not only of the flow of ch'i in the environment, but also how homes and people would affect and be affected by it. The acknowledged founding father of this learned tradition was Yang Yun-Sang who lived during the reign of the Tang emperor, Hi Tsang (circa 888 CE). Yang was the principal advisor at the emperor's court and wrote many books on the subject of feng shui that have remained the classical texts upon which feng shui theory and practice is based. This tradition has spread over time to Japan, Taiwan and other parts of the East and inevitably has been adapted and moulded to suit the culture within which it found itself. Today there are four major traditions of feng shui practised within the West. They are the Compass school, the Eight House school, the Flying Star and the Form schools. To these we may add a fifth, established recently in the USA to meet the needs of yet another cultural perspective, and called the Black Hat Sect Feng Shui. Of these schools, three, the Compass, Eight Houses and Form schools, use a compass to determine where the energy flow moves within a building and how this will affect people living or working there. In these schools a combination of the earth's magnetic field, the radiating energy of the sun and the planets are considered to be the principal agents affecting the flow of ch'i throughout a building.

The Schools of Feng Shui

The Form School

The Form School bases its principles on the classic texts written by the founder of feng shui, Yang Yun-Sang, and is the oldest of all the feng shui traditions.

Its precepts place the major emphasis on the features of the landscape, the configuration of mountains and hills, the flow of rivers and streams and the orientation of buildings in relation to the influence of their energies. Animal symbolism is an important element of Form School practice, where the landscape is conceived as holding within its contours the shapes and forms of black turtles, white tigers, dragons and many other celestial animals that move upon the earth. The most potent of these mythological creatures is the dragon in all the multiplicity of its incarnations, long revered by the Chinese as a manifestation of the overwhelming power and vitality of Heaven. When dragons angrily stir, earthquakes and floods can result, while the placated, happy dragon brings the comfort of rain for crops and the turn of good fortune.

To find the dragon's lair and divine his mood became a metaphor for Yang Yun-Sang's reading of the landscape and the most propitious circumstances for orientating and locating dwellings. Hills, mountains and other land features are identified by the celestial animal they most closely resemble in shape and character. The most auspicious feng shui would locate your home between green dragon hills in the east merging into white tiger hills in the west. Where the dragon lies is yang and the white tiger yin. Dragon hills are higher than the white tiger hills and a home should be located with these hills on the left as you look out from the front door. Solid black turtle hills should lie behind to give protection from the bitter northeast winds, while a red phoenix hill, symbolizing a footstool, brings comfort and wealth when situated in front of the house in the south. A cardinal principle of Form School feng shui is that the white tiger must never be disturbed as its nature is malevolent. A building on white tiger hills should be avoided at all costs!

Intuition forms an important part of Form School methodology and it is therefore considered to be more difficult to practise than the Compass School, for example, which lays down precise formulæ for its divination of energy flows. However, the influence of Form School animal symbolism and its categorization of landscapes has extended to other schools where it has been absorbed and incorporated into their own practice.

The Compass School

While the Form School and its landscape populated by dragons and celestial creatures provided the basis for the development of feng shui, a new school emerged that sought less subjective and intuitive processes. This second major tradition, the Compass School, based its analysis on the trigrams of the *I Ching*, arranged in the pa kua according to their compass direction. By making calculations using the trigrams and their compass orientation in relation to door directions and the astrological birth chart of the occupant, good or bad feng shui can be interpreted.

Each of the eight trigrams has its own individual characteristics, identified by colours, compass direction, family member and element associated with them. Thus, for example, the south has the number nine and its Five Element identity is Fire, its family member is the middle daughter and its colour purple. The energetic nature of each part of the home can be analyzed from this information and the house designed to suit its function and compatibility with the family member who may use it. The system seeks to harmonize the activity and individual needs of the whole of the family to gain the most auspicious feng shui for them all. This school has grown and spread out to form different branches that have developed their own formulæ for calculating good or bad feng shui. Some may emphasize numerology, while others will be more concerned with the influence of planets on the landscape.

Eight Houses School

This school uses a compass to orientate the front of the building with eight 'houses' or sections of the building, to determine their energy characteristics. Once this information is combined with the occupant's birth and Nine Ki astrological chart, each 'house' can be assessed for its positive or negative effects upon its inhabitants.

The Flying Star School

This is similar in concept to the Eight House method in that it combines the compass orientation of the front of the building with a birth chart. However, here the birth chart belongs to the nascence of the building itself, calculated from the date of construction. The building's birth chart is then superimposed over the compass chart and the features of the surrounding environment can be analyzed and their modifying effect on the birth chart worked out. Additional Nine Ki information for the year can also be gathered in order to divine the likelihood of impending problems.

The Black Hat Sect
Tantric Buddhist Feng Shui

The Black Hat Sect School is a departure from traditional feng shui in that it has elements of a specifically religious character incorporated into its practice. Brought to the USA in the 1980s and popularized by its founder, Thomas Lin Yun, its practice has become increasingly widespread throughout both the northern and southern continents of America. It owes its inspiration to the Black Hat Sect of Tibetan Buddhism which, after assimilating rituals and beliefs from the indigenous Bon shamanic religion, moved on into China. There its eclectic inclinations encouraged further assimilation of local beliefs and the Sect absorbed tenets from Taoism, the *I Ching*, Five Element theory, ch'i kung, astrological divination and feng shui. Thomas Lin Yun built on this tradition by incorporating concepts taken from modern 'Western' scientific disciplines such as medicine, psychology and ecology to create a new hybrid feng shui for the times.

The Black Hat School applies the pa kua without the use of a compass, according to its relationship with the flow of energy passing through the entrance or 'mouth' of ch'i into the building. This is always considered to be the building's main entrance irrespective of the frequency of its use. Within the building individual rooms or areas can be assessed on the same basis. The trigrams *ch'ien* (benefactors), *k'an* (career) and *ken* (knowledge) are aligned with the wall containing the entrance way. The other trigrams follow in their prescribed order around the pa kua.

Each of the trigrams represents the areas of family life and concerns such as *chen* for family, *sun* for wealth or *tui* for children. When the pa kua is positioned over a plan of the building, some areas of the pa kua may be found to be missing or exaggerated, according to its layout. Missing areas can be compensated for or rooms modified by making what is called *xie zi*, or minor additions to control or redirect the flow of ch'i. This may involve introducing mirrors, or the sound from wind chimes, or plants to mitigate the effect of bad feng shui or amplify the flow of positive ch'i.

The religious element of Black Hat Sect Feng Shui was derived from its Tantric roots and uses ritual to reinforce the diagnosis and strengthen the solutions adopted. Ritual hand gestures, known as *mudras*, are used in the same manner as martial artists of China and Japan to focus and project the power of ch'i from the body. This is followed by the chanting of mantras, adding the power of sound. Thirdly, the power of the mind is engaged to visualize through time and space the course of a solution and its consistency with the life aspirations of the occupant. While this method employs Buddhist ritual and chants, there is no reason why prayers or hand gestures from other faiths cannot be used. The essential principle is that there should be a genuine heart-felt spiritual belief that has the power and conviction to activate results.

As the Black Hat Sect methodology eschews compass alignments and calculations it can be more easily understood and applied than the complicated rule-bound calculations used by traditional schools of feng shui. This obviously leaves it open to misinterpretation and misapplication, particularly if the feng shui 'expert' has not been through a training directly transmitted by Thomas Lin Yun's school. Black Hat Sect, with all the force of new evangelizing ideas, is gaining ground in other parts of the world and seems set to enjoy great popularity in the West.

All these schools make their own particular contribution to a rich and interesting diversity of feng shui applications. The scope of this book precludes a detailed examination of the practice of every school and must content itself with those principles that come from traditional forms of feng shui divination. It is the Compass School and its branches, influenced by Form School symbolism, that enjoy the strongest representation in the public mind. Consequently our examination of the fundamental concepts of feng shui will be explained from this perspective.

The Principles of Feng Shui

The movement of ch'i within buildings is dictated by its own unique character. All of us have an intuitive sense of how an interior contributes to our feeling of well-being or, alternatively, drains us of energy. The purpose of feng shui is to discover within a building the most favourable circumstances that will sustain the emotional, physical and spiritual health of its occupants.

As we have already noted, ch'i flows both from the earth and to the earth from the planets of the solar system and the galaxy beyond. This two-way flow of energy directly affects the flow of ch'i within our own bodies and our ability to replenish the vital store of energy needed to sustain a well-balanced, happy, healthy life. These large-scale movements of energy correspond to the influence of a planetary body on our own planet. The geomancy of lo shu astrology is used to predict the movement of heavenly ch'i over time, and the likely effect this will have on an individual.

Ch'i flows through our environment in perfect imitation of the movements of wind and water. Just as the flow of water blocked by debris produces stagnant pools and a swift current produces clean, bright water, so the physical shape of the environment alters the course and temper of ch'i's passage. Buildings that have sharp, protruding corners cut across the flow of ch'i and result in spiralling whirlpools of energy. This 'cutting ch'i' can have unpleasant effects when the corner of an L-shaped room produces an area of disturbance and confusion in the home. It is these factors that feng shui addresses, relating the known patterns of ch'i movement to the unique circumstances of the building. It is the feng shui practitioner's task to find the blockages and sluggish runs of energy and offer solutions that will restore the harmonious flow of ch'i through the home or workplace.

Yin and Yang

As always, the flow of ch'i is conditioned by the internal bipolar dynamic, the relative states of yin and yang. We can recognize these same familiar states within the landscape and in the shape of buildings around us. For example, flat, featureless plains are too yin, while sharp, angular mountains with little vegetation or streams to soften them are too yang. Each needs components of its opposite to produce the most harmonious landscape. The plain requires trees, rivers and some undulation in the landscape. Whereas the mountains need trees clustered in high valleys echoing with the sound of running water to balance their stark grandeur with havens of quiet peace.

Balance and relative proportion are once again the rule and the most favoured environment is the one that obeys it. The best yin yang balance can be found in soft, rolling landscapes with good tree cover and running water that create a gentle, sympathetic environment in which to live. However, we are not all able to choose the ideal place to live, and so must content

ourselves with rebalancing the yin yang qualities in our immediate environment. Our own psychology must play a part in this process. We may find that the sun-filled room that is bursting with yang energy is too active a place for quiet study or reflection and seek out a more shaded yin room within which to think and work. If your home is too yang, with many angular surfaces and stark lines then plants, flowing curtains and softer furnishings will add yin aspects and slow down the swirling rushes of energy around it.

The Five Elements

Ch'i moves through an annual cycle of seasonal change governed by the transformational cycle of the five elements. The seasons are divided into winter, spring, summer and autumn with an additional season designated as late summer or early autumn sandwiched between summer and autumn. Each season is governed by one of the Five Elements, which alters

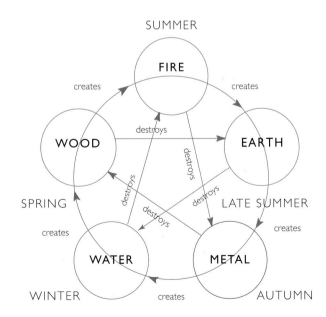

and changes the movement of ch'i during its cycle. The feng shui consultant uses Five Element theory to diagnose and treat blockages in the flow of ch'i within a house or room in the same way as the acupuncturist or shiatsu practitioner. Each of the Five Elements of Fire, Earth, Metal, Water and Wood is involved in both a destructive and a creative cycle of change. Wood destroys Earth and creates Fire, whereas Fire is controlled by Water and produces Earth. The qualities of each element predominate in its due season. Fire is summer and its colour is red. The compass direction with which it is orientated is south. Water governs winter and it has the colour black or dark blue and is orientated north. Wood is spring, its colour green, and direction east. Metal is west, its colour is white or gold and it comes to fullness in the autumn. Earth is the centre and its colour is yellow or brown.

The feng shui practitioner will use the Chinese system of astrology to determine which element was ascendant when their client was born and use that information to include features in the home that will be sympathetic to it. The rule applied here is that no home should have a preponderance of the element that is destructive to your own. For instance, if you were born in a Metal year then you should avoid bright red objects and too much lighting as Fire destroys Metal. To counteract the Fire effect the feng shui practitioner will encourage the introduction of more plants and greenery, as Wood creates Fire. By introducing decorative features or symbolic items into the home and placing them appropriately to encourage each element, a harmonious balance can be created.

The Pa Kua

The pa kua is the principal device employed in the practice of feng shui. The eight trigrams of the *I Ching* are placed around this octagonally shaped symbol corresponding to the eight directions of the compass. According to Chinese custom, south is placed at the top of the octagon and north below, although they remain the same magnetic north and south. Each trigram represents the symbolic virtues, directional influences and the elemental quality of ch'i that emanate from it.

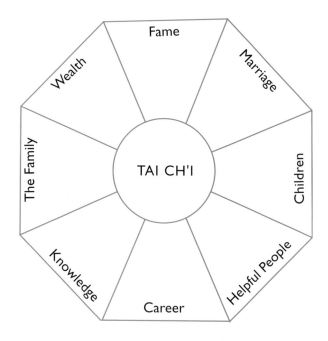

There are two arrangements of the pa kua used by feng shui practitioners, known as the Early Heaven and Later Heaven arrangements. In the Early Heaven arrangement the trigram ch'ien (Metal) is located at the top (south), while in the Later Heaven it is li (Fire). As these arrangements follow round in the same progression from li to kun, tui, ch'ien, k'an, ken, chen and sun the meaning of each of the compass directions is different in each of the arrangements. The Early Heaven arrangement is used in the diagnosis and design of yin dwellings such as graves and to hang in doorways to ward off malevolent ch'i, the so called killing breath of poisoned arrows. The Later Heaven arrangement of the pa kua is used for yang dwellings; the homes and offices of the living. The feng shui practitioner interprets the attributes and qualities of each of the trigrams, such as colour, element or directional influence, in each corner of a building to suggest the best feng shui solutions. This is done by using a compass to find true north and orientating the pa kua to it. Superimposing the pa kua over a plan of the building it can be divided into eight sectors where the influence of each trigram will have prominence.

In feng shui practice the trigrams are also associated with what are termed the eight life aspirations. These are, recognition and fame; marriage and romance; children; mentors and helpful people; career; education and knowledge; family and health; and wealth and prosperity. Referring to the pa kua chart each room and corner of the building can be matched to its life aspiration and compass direction and the most auspicious use of each space can be considered. By enhancing the flow of ch'i in the area of the house associated with the specific life aspirations you wish to activate, the practitioner hopes to increase the good fortune of the occupant. Therefore it may be appropriate, if arrangements allow, to place an office in the south east corner to encourage prosperity, or a bedroom in the south west to maintain your romantic happiness. Where the layout of the house precludes changing the use of rooms, plants, lights, aquaria, crystals and colours associated with a particular life aspiration can be introduced to enhance that quality within the space. The keynote is balance and the room should not be overloaded with enhancers. One tasteful element placed in the appropriate corner will stimulate the aspiration and add harmony to the space.

Unfortunately not all living or work spaces conform to a tidy square or rectangle over which the pa kua can be neatly superimposed. The building may be L-shaped with a missing life aspiration sector. In this case it would be necessary to compensate for the missing sector either by extending the building, using a large wall mirror to visually open it up or placing an enhancer in the appropriate corner.

There are eight categories of feng shui enhancers that can be used to activate the life aspirations of the pa kua. The first category is objects that introduce bright reflective surfaces such as lights, mirrors and crystals. Living things are important enhancers so plants, fish in ponds or aquaria and fresh cut flowers may be recommended. Instruments and objects that make melodious sounds such as wind chimes and bells add another dimension to the space and activate our aural sensitivities. Objects that revolve or have elements of circular motion like windmills, mobiles, fans and fountains encourage the flow of ch'i as do hollow objects such as bamboo and flutes. An element of natural solidness can be brought into the home by the use of boulders, stones, statues and other heavy objects. Colour is always important in creating the right atmosphere in a room and by referring to Five Element theory when choosing a colour scheme you can create a firm background for attracting good feng shui. Finally, objects that encourage and stimulate activity, energy and sound, which includes your music system, radio and television, will enhance your career prospects and encourage a happy family life.

Common sense and appropriateness need to be applied before filling your house with tinkling bells and great rocks in the middle of the room. It is the symbolic representation that is important and the overall harmony of the house when moving from room to room should be taken into account. The pa kua enables the practitioner to focus on each area or sector of the dwelling and assess its qualities. It does not imply that the layout of every space must conform absolutely to the ideal. The practitioner balances all the factors that he has observed and calculated in order to make judgments specific to the qualities of the space and the people who live within it.

The Lo Shu Magic Square

When the turtle emerged from the River Lo in front of the emperor 4,000 years ago, it carried on its back the numbers one to nine represented by dots and arranged on a three-by-three boxed grid. It was soon perceived that the grid pattern corresponded to the eight trigrams of the pa kua with a ninth point in the centre. When any three of the numbers are added together either horizontally, vertically or diagonally they always add up to 15. This is known as the lo shu magic square and is considered by the Chinese to have great 'magical' potency when linked with the Later Heaven arrangement of the pa kua. When the lo shu square is superimposed on the pa kua the number nine is matched to the south and the number one to the north. By consulting commentaries, numerology texts and almanacs relating to the numbers of the lo shu, deeper meanings in the trigrams can interpreted.

The feng shui practitioners of the Compass School use the lo shu magic square to view the feng shui of a dwelling across time by drawing up an astrological chart relating to the client's lo shu number. Every day, month and year has a lo shu number that moves through a 20-year cycle. By correlating the client's lo shu number to the lo shu numbers of the pa kua, the feng shui practitioner can calculate when it would be propitious to move, build an extension or redecorate. Conversely, bad periods can also be predicted and avoided. These calculations can be quite complex and time-consuming to undertake. Fortunately, the Chinese publish the annual *Tong Shu* almanac that indicates the best days in the coming year for important activities such as getting married or changing your job. With the assistance of the pa kua and the lo shu numbers, the practitioner can make a diagnosis that addresses the feng shui of the space currently and on into the future.

Feng Shui Today

Following the Communist revolution and the decampment of the Nationalist government to Taiwan, feng shui, along with many other of China's traditional arts, was discouraged on the mainland as primitive superstition. However, feng shui was kept alive wherever Chinese communities were able to maintain the practice of traditional customs without hindrance. Taiwan, Hong Kong and Singapore have all provided fertile havens where the art or science of feng shui has blossomed and re-established itself as a significant cultural concept. No modern business tycoon in any Chinese-influenced area of the East would consider erecting a new skyscraper or office block without consulting a feng shui practitioner. Good feng shui is considered essential to the long-term business health of any company or enterprise. The hot house atmosphere in these great financial centres requires a keen competitive edge and if everyone in that

4	9	2
3	5	7
8	1	6

enterprise feels the benefit of harmonious feng shui then it must be good for the company.

The increasing mobility of people, culture and ideas has brought feng shui to the West where it is currently attracting widespread interest and popularity. Just why a Taoist-inspired divination system based on a set of cultural values and beliefs so alien to our own should have colonized the Western imagination is still an open question. Perhaps feng shui offers a chance to bring back some control over our own space and a sense of well-being denied to us in the outside world. Despite our comparative wealth and technological triumphs, the West has not been able to insulate itself from the problems that economic success has created. Our cities and countryside are increasingly polluted and our senses continually assailed by the clamour and buzz of a high-tech world. We all need a place where we can shelter, take stock and replenish our energy and what better place for this regeneration than in the home? This, after all, is what homes are for: to provide a secure, comfortable resting place where family and friends can enjoy and support each other. Feng shui gives us the opportunity to examine the space in which we live for considerations that extend well beyond mere interior design. It is a means of looking at ourselves and our actions through the environment we have created around us. Disturbances in the patterns of our lives brought about by family tensions, ill health or spiritual disease will all be reflected in the way we use or misuse the space in which we live. Just as the body's meridians get blocked if you do not tonify them, so will the ch'i flowing through your home if you do not attend to its health. When we think about the sectors of the house from the perspective of feng shui we are really thinking about how human relationships work within the home and the conditions which will improve those relationships. This is good feng shui.

THE SPIRIT OF THE JAPANESE GARDEN

Wherever people have found themselves locked behind the walls of towns and cities, they have carried the memory of the countryside and open spaces with them. From the generous, suburban gardens of the West to the tiny spaces recolonized for nature in narrow Japanese city streets, the urge to bring the natural environment into the home is almost universal. It would seem that we all share the same instinctive impulse to draw away from the overstimulation of the yang energy that our frenetic urban existence brings and seek comfort in a quiet corner that is yin. In the garden, as with the home or office, feng shui can be the means of creating an area of balanced harmony that can replenish your body, mind and spirit.

As ch'i flows along the dragon veins across the earth its natural, even tempo can be halted in a blocked valley, accelerated through a narrow pass or slowed when clambering over obstacles. This complex picture of moving energy obeys the same natural laws as wind and water and can be seen working in the same way within the home as it does without. Our garden, if we are lucky enough to have one, is an extension of our home and it is just as important to ensure that it contributes to the harmonious balance we would wish to establish. The principles of feng shui we have examined are equally applicable to the garden and the same methodologies can be employed, including the familiar categories of feng shui enhancers. To bring harmony to the garden it must flow in gentle curves that meander through the space without being led into blind corners or funnelled through tight openings. As much as possible it should be a reflection of nature recreated within the space available. Nowhere is this principle of the universal expressed in microcosm more developed than in the gardens of Japan. Not only do these gardens exemplify a sophisticated naturalism, but they are often dedicated to the purpose of leading the mind to a spiritual encounter with nature.

The geomantic arts of divination and feng shui, called *eki* and *fusui* in Japanese, were imported from China via Korea along with the great philosophies of Taoism, Confucianism and Buddhism. In Japan the study of geomancy became known as the 'way of yin yang', or *on-yo-do*, and by the seventh century divination had become so important that a government department called the *on-yo-ryho* (ying yang bureau) had been set up to oversee its practice. During this period, the gardens of Japan used the Chinese principles of balancing the opposing and complementary forces of yin and yang, such as empty spaces and fluids with mass and solid features.

Although Chinese ideas of on-yo-do were important to the underlying structure of the Japanese garden, other spiritual forces were to influence their construction and design. Buddhism contributed its own concepts to the pattern of Japanese garden design, principally through the influence of its cosmology on

the imagination. The principal image was that of Shumisen, the central mountain of the Buddhist universe. Towering high above all that surrounds it, Shumisen stands in the centre of eight concentric rings of lesser mountains, with a sea enclosed between each successive mountain ring. The realm of man was thought to lie on the eighth and outermost mountain range beside the eighth sea. Japanese gardeners used this image as a motif in their design by setting up one arresting, upright stone surrounded by a ring of smaller stones.

Another important Buddhist image was of the Pure Land, ruled over by the compassionate incarnation of the Buddha, the gentle Amida. In this land of flowers the true believer would rest after death in the peace of Amida's love and gain freedom from the painful cycle of rebirth, suffering and death. The Japanese of the Heian period sought to recreate their image of the Pure Land in their garden designs. This paradise was imagined as an island surrounded by a sea, which, in the garden, was represented by a small island set within a pond planted with lotus flowers. Often this central island would be connected to the shore by a bridge or stepping stones, symbolizing the potential for all those who have faith to reach Amida's Pure Land.

Following the glories of the Heian Period and the early expressions of Buddhist influence on garden design came a period of turbulent political and military conflict culminating in the rise of the Ashikaga family. This was heralded by the establishment of a new military government in the Muromachi district of Kyoto by Ashikaga Takauji, who had usurped the Shogunate from the Hojo family. The Muromachi Period (1333–1568 CE) was an uncertain, tumultuous time when feuding samurai clans and powerful monasteries fought bitterly for power and influence. Against this backdrop of crisis and conflict, the life of the capital, despite the devastation of the Onin War, begun in 1467, showed great economic vitality and an opening of the creative spirit. New ideas in the arts, heavily influenced by the simple austerity of Zen Buddhism, were creating an aesthetic intent on seeing beyond the surface of things to reveal their 'inner truth'. This truth could be unlocked by recognizing how ki, the vital energy that is the mystery of life, works to form and shape the world in which our conciousness is formed. This aesthetic principle became known as yugen, written with the characters for 'faint/dim' or 'dark/mystery'. The word, borrowed originally from the Chinese, referred to anything that was too subtle and profound to see and was applied to poetry, painting, noh dramas and to garden design. The great Zen monastery gardens with their areas of white raked sand and islands of upright stones created abstract landscapes that served as allegories for the path to this spiritual insight.

While these Zen gardens were created for contemplation and spiritual inspiration, their purpose was not to serve as a place to meditate. The garden was too bright and open for this purpose. Seated meditation was conducted within the dark interior of the zendo, or the meditation hall, facing a wall and cut off from sensory distractions. However, while the garden was not created as a place for zazen, the act of gardening itself provided an opportunity to 'cleanse the soul'. Each day the monks worked quietly, sweeping and cleaning the temple and maintaining the gardens. By keeping both the body and the immediate environment clean and uncluttered the zen monk made this work a 'mindful' activity, expressing purity of thought in action. Once again the process assumes more importance than the product and gardening becomes a 'Way' of practice for spiritual development.

This Zen-inspired quest to express the inner nature of things can be found in a less abstract and more natural setting within the limited confines of the tea house garden. Here, in contrast to the aesthetic of yohaku-no-bi, or the 'beauty of extra white' which came with the large open areas of empty space and raked sand of the temple garden, was a desire to use plants and materials as they would appear in their natural setting. The tea garden was designed to evoke the quiet and stillness of a tiny glade within the mountains, far from the turmoil and disruptions of a society wracked by civil conflict. Everywhere the garden reflected the spirit of Sen-no-Rikyu's wabi cha, or 'tea of quiet taste', choosing evergreen trees and shrubs with only a few deciduous plants rather than obtrusive banks of colour. Although there was structure and formality in the design of the garden it should appear as if nature had created it almost without human intervention. Once the structure is set the garden must have life of its own and the gardener becomes an inspired 'tidier' attempting to tease out and reveal the inner beauty of nature rather than dictate to it. The tea house gardener worked with the rules of nature, balancing the yin yang aspects of the garden to provide contrasting areas of light and shade, open space and the impression of deep mountain recesses. Like his counterpart in the Zen monastery, gardening was also an element of practice providing a contemplative ritual for composing and quieting the mind before the tea gathering that would follow.

The Japanese name for the tea garden is roji, traditionally used to describe a path, but given a new, more profound meaning by the tea masters which translates as the 'dewy ground'. Conceptually, the tea garden is more path than garden, leading the tea guests through a spiritual passage intended to strip away concern for the outside world and prepare the spirit for the practice of tea. Entering the tea garden the guest walks from the turmoil of the town into the still heart of the mountain, where they find a simple rustic hut that promises shelter for the body and balm for the unquiet mind. The roji attempts to compress a journey from town to countryside into one short walk of the imagination, crossing from the world of attachment into the peace of the 'empty' spirit.

The guests' journey is marked by a series of gates or thresholds through which they must pass, symbolizing the gradual discarding of the outer world. When all have passed through the entrance gate into the roji, the last guest closes and locks the gate behind them. They are now separated from the outside reality and have translated themselves to a place that expresses the inner energy of life. To give the guests time to reflect and prepare themselves, they sit on a bench within a covered arbour, quietly awaiting the arrival of the host who waits discreetly until he senses their readiness. During this time they relax and re-energize their spirits in the contemplation of unobtrusive natural beauty. The garden is divided into two areas: the inner roji and outer roji, divided by a small middle gate, which may be roofed and hold a proper gate or of a more simple and symbolic construction. This gate is not flanked by a fence, holds nothing in and keeps nothing out. When the host summons the guests and they pass this threshold they enter a world of deeper meaning. The more open, lighter space of the outer roji is left behind as the guests enter the darker, more sheltered area of the inner roji, representing the mental transition they must make.

Passing the middle gate they find the *tsukaibai*, or stone basin, filled with water where they wash their hands and rinse their mouths in an act of ritual purification. Round the basin are set other stones on which other items may be placed for the comfort of the guests, such a bowl of warm water in the winter or a lantern to guide them through the roji at night. Close by is the well from which the water is drawn, always at dawn to ensure its purity and freshness. Moving through the inner roji they come to the thatched-roof tea house, the *soan*, where, close by the path they meet the *chiri-ana*, or dust pit. This pit contains a cut evergreen branch and two chopstick-like twig pickers arranged by the host. In this way the host signals to the guests that the garden and tea house have been properly cleansed and any lingering distractions they carry from the outside world should be left behind. Finally, they enter the tea house itself, passing through the last threshold, the narrow square opening they must crawl through. An action that signifies both humility and an acceptance of the equality of the tea house.

By the Edo Period, the merchant classes and townsfolk of Japan's bustling and thriving cities were experiencing a time of increased prosperity and social confidence. The arts, once the preserve of nobles and samurai, were addressing new mass audiences. Kabuki theatre and the burgeoning market for prints portraying popular life in all its fragile gaiety and melancholy-tinged richness, appealed to the sentiment of the times, Which could be summed up as: to live life to the full, for all beauty and happiness is ephemeral and there is only a brief moment before tomorrow. The new cultural assertiveness of town life encouraged many townspeople to look also to their own spiritual dimension and take up the study of the cultural arts once exclusively reserved for the samurai. Chado, the way of tea, was opened to this newly confidant bourgeois society and its practice became increasingly widespread. Soon the influence of the tea garden began to inspire the creation of small internal gardens set within the narrow confines of urban homes.

The *machiya*, or town house, fronted directly onto the street where the merchant's shop or counting-room would be located, separated by a tight open space from the buildings housing family and servants behind it. As one passed from room to room to the back of the house it became more private and contained, offering crowded but comfortable seclusion. Space was at a premium and gardens could not even extend to the modest limits of the roji. Nevertheless the idea of the tea garden inspired the development of the tsubo garden. Set within the narrow spaces dividing the machiya, the tsubo was a small garden intended to be viewed and contemplated through doorways or windows rather than walked or sat in. In the style of the roji, the garden would often contain water basins, lanterns and stepping stones covered with moss arranged within a miniature 'natural' landscape of evergreen shrubs and bamboo.

The name tsubo can be written with different characters that carry alternative meanings. One reading defines the tsubo as a standard unit of measurement for houses and small properties, approximately 3.3 square metres in area and equivalent to two tatami (straw mats) placed side by side. Alternatively, tsubo can be read as the name of a ceramic pot, similar to ones used by Chinese Taoist mystics for meditation. When applied to the garden, this identified its character as a small, enclosed space open to the sky, shaped by its surrounding walls and the overhanging eaves of the roof. Within this thee-dimensional space the garden sits contained within its pot.

This imagery has resonance with a third way to write tsubo, as a ki pressure point located on the meridian lines that conduct the flow of vital energy around the body. The configuration of a tsubo point is also characteristic of a pot, with a small 'opening' into a larger space. All the systems of medicine based on traditional Chinese theories of ch'i, or ki, apply needles, finger pressure or moxa to these tsubos of the body to unblock and rebalance the flow of energy when treating patients. Just as the body has energy flowing through the meridians, ki flows through the building and has its own tsubo points where energy can be stimulated.

Within the traditional Japanese home, tsubo points are identified with areas of special significance to the social life that animates and energize the inhabitants. Thus the tokonoma, or alcove, with its scroll painting or brushed charcters and ikebana arrangement give energy and stimulation to the creative mind. The door gives entry to the flow of ki and is the place for welcoming guests, bringing new social energy into the home. The tsubo garden is a container for ki, where by the cultivation of plants and the daily ritual of their care, ki is generated and flows back into the house through the open doorways and windows that surround it. In this way the family receives and maintains a constant source of rejuvenating energy through the beauty and delight that the garden bestows. As with the body, so with the spaces we inhabit. We should seek to balance all elements and maintain the constant, even passage of ki.

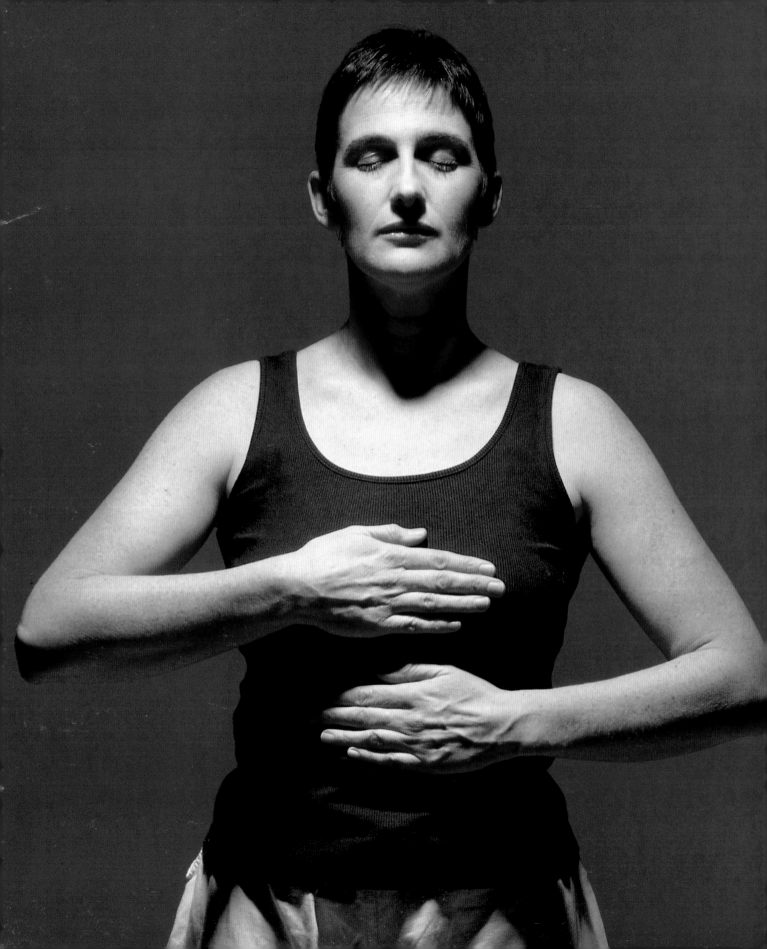

離

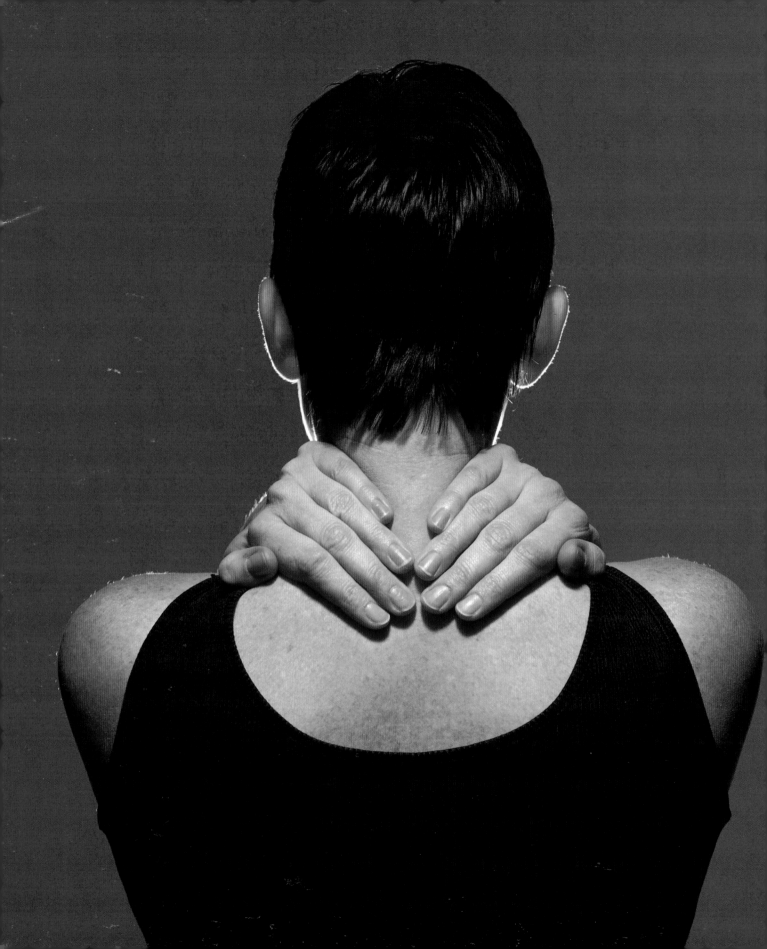

Ch'i, the transforming energy of life, is the vital essence that powers the universe and is the principal concept around which all the traditional Oriental healing, martial and cultural arts have framed their philosophy and practice. Largely Taoist in inspiration, yet owing a debt to Buddhism, the idea that ch'i, manifested through the dynamic of yin and yang, is the fundamental process that motivates all existence, is the bedrock on which Eastern culture is based. This world view sees all life as inter-connected and sharing the same vital universal energy. Although at birth ch'i is transformed into matter and we are gifted with our store of prenatal energy, it is not seen as being uniquely our own. Yes, it does come with inherited elements and it is obviously affected by the environment, but at its most basic level ch'i is ch'i and we all share it.

When we breathe in we take in the same universal energy that drives the whole planet and has created all the material of the universe. We are all the stuff of ch'i and because of this, no human process can be seen as independent of another. Mind, body and spirit are only constructs that we distinguish to give some sense of order to our human lives. In reality we exist only as an accretion of energetic particles formed from the one universal whole.

Our perception of this universal spirit energy has been clouded and hidden from us by the processes of our minds. The mind deceives us, and assails the clarity of our intuitive intelligence with a constant barrage of emotions, desires and pressing needs. Although we may learn to harness and direct ch'i throughout our bodies to maximize our potential for a long, healthy life, we are only staving off the inevitable dissolution of our material self at the moment of death. True peace and self-realization can only come when we surrender our ego-self and enter into the still heart of ch'i where we may find union with the universal spirit-mind, which the Chinese call the Tao.

The ultimate purpose of all the Oriental arts and Ways is the cultivation of the human body and mind to liberate our essential nature and reunite our consciousness with the universal spirit. We might choose to call this universal spirit God. We might see it as the passage to the bliss of nirvana or we might call it the Tao. The name matters little, or the imaginary shape we might clothe it in. In our un-unified condition it is unknowable and cannot be penetrated, rationalized or explained with the intellect – it can only be experienced and intuited.

Thousands of years ago the Chinese Taoist alchemists came to understand that there is no 'Great Pill' that can be taken to achieve earthly or heavenly immortality. If immortality can be grasped, it exists only in terms of the spirit and can only be found by transforming the energy of body and mind into spiritual energy. This process of transformation, the inner alchemy of the Taoist arts, does not come easily and

requires a lifetime of dedication and practice to achieve. There are no easy ways in or quick results. There is only what comes slowly by following a path with discipline, commitment and, above all, the patience to await the growth of understanding. These are not the messages that our modern, impatient, technocratic world motivated by performance and profit wishes to hear. Whatever the culture, East or West, the impulse to devote time to seeking spiritual peace is continually sapped by the culture of immediate gratification. If only we could invent a machine that we plug into overnight and wake up enlightened, all our needs could be instantly answered. Unfortunately, or rather fortunately, this is not an artefact that our technology can manufacture and the quest for a spiritual sense is still the prerogative of our human consciousness. The only machines that we can work with are the human mind and body, and somewhere within us are the connections that must be activated to make this real.

The arts and ways of the East all have their meditative aspect brought out through the process of absorption in the practice itself, whether the object is to heal, to promote internal strength or to reveal the beauty and energy of the natural world. An important part of this process is non-opposition to the flow of events and the desire to work alongside the natural order rather than tame it. It is the belief that the consequences of an action in this vast, inter-connected reality which we inhabit can never be clearly understood and may have wider ramifications than we could possibly imagine. Therefore, rather than being obsessed with changing how things work, we must harmonize our mind, body and spirit with this natural order and balance our desires if we are not to become frustrated and ultimately disappointed. The lessons of practice within the Ways reveal this truth through the doing. They are felt through the body and mind and make the first pyscho-physical connections in our consciousness that lead to the realization of the spirit. While the arts that require action will take us forward, Taoist sages and Buddhist clerics have always believed that only meditation can reveal our spiritual centre to the present mind. Meditation is the complement to the pyscho-physical exploration of ch'i and is the training ground of the soul. To complete our examination of the phenomenon of ch'i we must turn to the arts developed in the monasteries and hermitages of ancient China and Japan where monks and priests sat still under the roof of Heaven.

The Taoists have long used meditation as a means to cultivate long life and health by directing the internal flow of ch'i with the mind. Health, vitality and longevity are not complete ends in themselves, though they are laudable and necessary objectives. For those who wish to go deeper into the still heart they serve as a platform from which we can reach deeper understandings of the human self. Ultimately the goal is liberation from the self in union with the Tao.

Meditation is a progressive practice within Taoism, taking the practitioner through ascending levels of experience and revelation until this union is reached. The lower levels of the meditative experience teach the practitioner to circulate ch'i, clear the mind, subdue attachment and control the emotions. At the highest levels ch'i is transformed into spiritual energy which unites us with the Tao, the undifferentiated source of existence.

Meditation is common to many faiths and even considered to be beneficial by those who have none. Each faith has given birth to many different forms of meditation, distinguished by both doctrine and practice, yet at their heart is a commonality of purpose involving suppression of the ego. Whether you describe this as surrendering to the loving will of God or attaining the Buddha mind, the objective remains the same: the reunification of the separated self within the universal other. Within Taoism there is no single meditational practice that will guarantee this end. Each sect has its different methodologies and levels through which the student ascends on the pathway to spiritual development. Eva Wong in her book *Taoism* identities 12 styles of Taoist meditation that are practised today. Four of these styles can be learnt relatively easily and safely performed without undue stress or strain to the body. While teaching and guidance in their use should be sought before embarking on practice, they can be used without supervision in the home. One of the lower level forms, Shang-ch'ing sect's 'The Method of Holding the One', does require the strength and the stamina to hold a completely still posture, but it can be safely practised on your own. The remaining seven forms of meditation represent much higher levels of practice, requiring strenuous physical training and mental preparation under the guidance of a master teacher. These meditational forms are often combined with an exercise regime dedicated to strengthening the skeletal structure and regulating the internal organs of the body. They require an exceptional dedication and a commitment to training that is usually found only within a monastery or during a long-term guided retreat.

The five early levels of meditation practised by Taoists share many of the characteristics found in T'ien-tai and Zen Buddhist forms. With one exception, 'The Method of Holding the One', these forms demand no special physical postures, stamina or physical strength. Most of these forms encourage practitioners to sit in the full or half lotus cross-legged position. However, excepting 'Holding the One', all these lower level forms can easily be practised while sitting upright in a chair. A full examination of all these forms is the province of specialist books on meditation and Taoist practice, instead we will limit ourselves to a description of two of the forms that illustrate the differences between lower and higher levels of practice.

'The Method of Internal Observation' can be practised while sitting in a chair or even when walking, but most practitioners do prefer to sit with legs crossed and the back straight. Influenced by T'ien-tai Buddhism, the Internal Observation method evolved during the T'ang dynasty. Inside the mind the practitioner monitors the 'rise and fall' of thoughts, emotions and physical sensations. Initially the practitioner makes no attempt to dictate where thoughts go or interfere with their passage, but attends only to mindful observation. Gradually the process leads to an evaluation of this mental and sensual activity and the practitioner realises that their existence only brings problems and disharmony. If the mind can be 'stilled' and the mental activity suppressed there can be no basis for disharmony.

Moving on from this mindful state, the meditator seeks to stop all thoughts and sensations before they arrive. The mindful vigil has enabled the practitioner to identify and anticipate when thoughts and responses to sensations are likely to arise. Now they can be stopped before they occur. With the mind stilled and cleared of extraneous activity it becomes 'bright'. Within this brightness the practitioner perceives the light that is the Tao and is unified with its energy.

Conversely 'The Method of Focusing on the Cavities' represents one of the higher levels of practice and requires a long apprenticeship of physical and mental training before it can be safely embarked upon. The postures of this method are very strenuous and must be held for lengthy periods of time to facilitate the transformation of ch'i within the body. This form is never taught to beginners and the practitioner must accept routine supervision and direction from an experienced teacher. The Focusing on the Cavities method is used by those Taoist sects that practice inner alchemy to direct the flow of ch'i through energy gates and elixir fields of the body.

There are two stages of practice. The student begins by focusing the mind on a cavity inside the body. This concentration and mindful focus quiets thoughts and emotions and diverts attention away from physical sensations. When this stage is confidently secured the practitioner focuses on moving ch'i internally to an area or organ of the body. If there are imbalances or blockages in meridians and organs these can be cleared or ch'i can be gathered and stored for refinement in the tan t'ien. The practitioner's focus is directed towards different cavities according to the needs of the body and the stage of spiritual development he or she has reached. A hierarchy of progression begins with the practitioner focusing on the *ming-men*, or life gate. This is followed by the direction of focus attending to the lower, the middle and the upper tan t'ien in their turn. As the focus passes through each of the three tan t'iens, or inner elixir fields, essence is transformed into energy, energy into spirit and spirit into union with the all-pervading Tao.

Taoist meditation seeks to cut the mind off from the exterior world and the narrow interior world of the preoccupied self. This is not as an end but a beginning. The essential first step in opening the spirit to the Tao where distinctions between interior and exterior no longer exist. Finally, through the cosmic breath, a cosmic union is achieved, not by listening with the ears, or with the heart and mind, but by listening with the breath. The transformation and distillation of ch'i through all its elemental stages incubates ling-tai, the spiritual embryo. With death the ling-tai conveys the consciousness to spiritual immortality within the heart of the Tao and is the ultimate purpose of all Taoist meditation.

The Mahayana Buddhism that spread throughout East Asia was heavily influenced by Taoist concepts, which saw man as being in an organic relationship with Heaven and the universe, and considered that all matter was created from the primordial formlessness of the Tao. These teachings became identified with the

Buddhist concepts of *dharmakaya*, the absolute Buddha essence, and of *sunyata*, or emptiness. For all practical purposes these became the Buddhist forms of the Tao.

Ch'an, or Zen has the closest relationship with Taoist doctrine and practice. It adopted much of the Taoist language that prized the intuitive over the rational, saw silence as true eloquence and knew that it was impossible to express the deepest meaning through words. The Zen monk seated in silent meditation felt the oneness of reality through his abdomen and drew in ch'i with each intake of his breath in just the same way as his Taoist counterparts. While both Buddhist and Taoist clerics shared a similar philosophical outlook, their meditational practices were dedicated to different purposes. The Zen monk did not sit in formless, objectless meditation or wrestle with the meaning of his mind-puzzling koan for the purpose of inner alchemy, but to gain the Buddha mind. Despite its debt to Taoism, Zen largely confined its practice to the simpler forms of meditation that emphasized the emptying of the mind without recourse to mantras, visualization techniques or special, energy-moving postures.

Although not as close philosophically as Zen is to Taoism, esoteric Buddhism did attach great importance to the use of mantras, visualization and the control of the flow of energy around the body. Heavily influenced by Tibetan and Tantric practice, the Japanese Shingon meditator also sought to direct the flow of ch'i, or ki, to the energy centres of the body and refine the lower forms of internal energy into the pure energy of the spirit. In *shinto-ho* visualization, when the meditator exhales, the breath leaves his body through every pore of his skin and spreads out into the universe. When he inhales the process is reversed and the universal life energy floods back through the same pores to fill every part of the body with its sustaining power. By using this technique the Shingon meditator seeks to unite with the cosmic energy that permeates all things.

The higher or more esoteric levels of meditation practised by Taoists and Buddhists can only be reached by those who have undergone years of intense application. They are not easy to undertake and must usually be accompanied by other forms of moving meditation and physical exercises. If mastered they offer the greatest of gifts, for the body is no longer bound by the need to perform a t'ai chi set or ch'i kung exercises to maintain health and vitality. Now the meditator, in union with the Tao, can circulate energy by the power of the mind alone.

The creative energy of sound, expressed through music and the chanting of mantras and prayers, has always played an important part in the practice of the World's spiritual traditions. Invoked to heal, or to calm the spirit, or to overwhelm an enemy, the vibrating energy of the human voice embodies the creative power of the universe.

Within the Christian tradition creation is said to have begun with the 'word' and the universe given shape and substance when the 'word' was made into flesh. For the Hindu, the resonating power of the single syllable 'aum' is the source of all existence. Just as ch'i is breath, it is also the sound that can be channelled, projected and given note by the breath. This vital energy, pregnant in the pitch and tenor of the human voice, was used by the early Chinese shamans to summon guardian spirits and induce the trance that would take them on their journey to other worlds and dimensions. Later both Taoist and Buddhist priests would use chant and music to awaken awareness of the primordial energy alive within their bodies and to serve as an aid to meditation and reflection.

As we have described in earlier chapters, the power of sound can also be utilized in the martial world. In Japan this is focused through the kiai, or spirit shout, which gives vocal expression to the synergy of the practitioner's body and mind unified in decisive action. No one can be certain of the origins of the kiai or when it came to be a feature of the practice of Japanese martial arts. However, stories abound of the supernatural powers of voice enjoyed by the *yamabushi*, devotees of a seventh century religious cult known as Shugendo, which combined elements of Shinto, Taoist and Buddhist beliefs. These yamabushi, or 'those who repose in the mountains', lived an isolated and lonely life, wandering the mountain trails meditating, chanting and practising acts of purification in their quest for spiritual union. Part shamanic in ritual and practice, the yamabushi were able to drive out evil spirits with the magic power of the kiai and return the possessed to good health and vitality.

In China and Japan sound was not only recognized as a source of inspiration and a tool of spiritual practice, but as a healing power that could act directly on the energetic balance of the body. This knowledge became an important element of ch'i kung practice and was used in conjunction with physical exercises and breath control techniques to harmonize and restore the ch'i balance of the body. Ch'i kung practitioners learn to emit sounds pitched to different frequencies of sound waves. These, in turn, produce characteristic pulses of electromagnetic current that have a beneficial effect on specific tissues, glands and organs of the body. By this means healing energy can be directed to specific organs or glands to disperse blockages and release the flow of ch'i.

The specific healing quality of the sound produced is conditioned by the level of control the practitioner is able to exert over the body's respiratory system. In combination with deep abdominal breathing and a pattern of rhythmic exercises, the ch'i kung practitioner is able to add power and energy to the expression of the voice. Certain syllables are chosen for their ability to encourage the exact timbre of the voice that will find an affinity with the heart, the lungs or any other of the organs to which it is directed. This vibrating energy is converted into electromagnetic pulses via the bones and the connective tissues. The crystalline structures of these bones and connective tissues have piezoelectric properties which are able to transform and transmit the healing energy of sound to the heart, the liver, the lungs and any other organ that requires rebalancing.

The Tang dynasty physician and ch'i kung master Sun Si Miao elaborated the six sounds used in ch'i kung therapy. Voiced through the syllables, '*xu, he, hu, si, chui* and *xi*' (or 'shu, he, hoo, sss, chway and shee'), therapeutic energy can be directed to the heart, spleen, lungs, kidneys and triple burner respectively. The six syllables can also be used for more general therapeutic effects. 'Xu' banishes malaise, 'he' releases pent up anger, 'hu' expels cold while 'chui' expels heat, 'si' rebalances the flow of ch'i and restores general equilibrium and 'xi' releases tension in the body and mind. The ancient practice known as the 'Six Syllable Secret' combines the exhalation of these sounds with physical exercises and controlled diaphragmic breathing to revivify and harmonize the flow of each of the organs in turn.

Although the health benefits of sound therapy are important to the practice of ch'i kung, the spiritual energy transmitted by sound has its own contribution to make to creating a harmonized body, mind and spirit. The basis of this practice is the voicing of tones, known as *fa yin*, to vibrate the chakras, or the spiritual energy centres of the human body. This vibrating vocal energy opens them to the most subtle and profound primordial forces of the universe. As the chakras are vibrated by the practitioner's tone of voice, the flow of prana, or ch'i, builds and powers the transformation into psycho-spiritual energy. Each of the seven psychic centres is associated with particular qualities of the spirit-mind, such as creativity, the capacity for compassion or the development of wisdom and insight. By intoning different syllables at a pitch sympathetic to each individual chakra in turn, the energy centres are opened and the spiritual faculties of the human mind alerted and sustained.

Although ch'i kung practitioners use the same syllables and direct their voice to the same chakras, the actual pitch of the voice will vary according to the physical, emotional and energetic characteristics of each individual. It is not easy to find the right pitch to intone without the direction of an experienced teacher. As the student is guided through the postures and vocal exercises the teacher is able to intuitively assess the response of each chakra and encourage the student to reach the pitch most suitable to their condition. Together, sound, breath and the rhythmic movement of the body make a powerful energetic combination that adds spiritual power to meditative practice. With this spiritual energy the chakras can connect the body to the mind and unify the spirit with the primordial voices of creation.

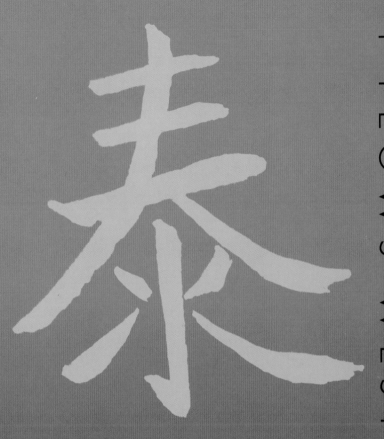

CH'I FLOWS WEST

The Oriental arts and ways we have described in this book are no longer as mysterious and exotic as they once were. Travel and trade as well as the constant shifting inter-change of people between East and West to work, study or settle has brought greater insight into each other's culture.

Eastern philosophies, medicine and martial arts attract growing numbers of Western adherents who have found new pathways to self-discovery through their practice. No major city or town is likely to be without its complement of t'ai chi teachers, acupuncturists or feng shui consultants. Driven by the impersonality of much Western medicine and health care, people everywhere are looking for more holistic and integrated answers to their problems. Many now accept that true health and vitality come only with a balanced integration of the mind, body and spirit and are increasingly willing to explore Eastern arts that exemplify this purpose.

The sympathetic audience that the Eastern energetic ways have found in the West should not surprise us when we remember that European culture has its own long association with natural herbal remedies and spiritual healing. Founded on Classical and Pagan models, the Judaeo-Christian tradition has always made a close association between the healthy body and the healthy mind. When Christ's hands reached out to heal the sick

WESTERN ENERGETIC WAYS

we know that he sought to bring more than physical rejuvenation. His real purpose was to heal the human soul by bringing it in direct and personal contact with the Holy Spirit. Health and vitality is a gift from God and maintaining a healthy body is an act of faith that recognizes its importance as the temple of the spirit. When Christian healers lay their hands upon the sick they act as a conduit for the compassionate energy of the Holy Spirit, using a therapeutic strategy only distinguished by faith and philosophy from their Eastern counterparts.

Latterly 'New Age' philosophies have sought to revive pre-Christian Pagan traditions and regain the connection between spirit and health by recognizing the importance of internal balance and living in harmony with nature. The more we have explored the world and its cultures, the more we have seen this common theme evident in human beliefs and therapeutic practices. There seems to be an almost instinctive belief in a 'life force' that is undisturbed by scientific rationalism and the burdens of proof. Yet, from where this life force stems and how it may be explained are questions that cannot be avoided in a Western context. While it may have been possible to accept a therapy purely on trust, tradition and personal witness in a less sophisticated past, we are all now shaped, consciously or unconsciously, by the need to 'prove' how it works, even if only to ourselves. In order to do this satisfactorily, Western healers and researchers have had to invent a new language to explain the concept of vital energy in ways that may be understood and debated scientifically. Terms such as biofield, bioenergy, biomagnetism and subtle energy are substituted for Eastern metaphysical terms such as ch'i or prana, and their flow is described as energy generated by the body's electromagnetic or electrostatic fields.

This interest in establishing the scientific validity of vital energy is not, of course, confined to Western researchers alone. The Chinese government has promoted research into acupuncture and ch'i kung and is sufficiently convinced of its efficacy to fund both training schools and hospitals practising Traditional Chinese Medicine. In Japan, Dr Hiroshi Motoyama has developed a machine capable of detecting the flow of energy through the meridians. Called the AMI (apparatus for meridian identification) it measures the flow of ions through the interstitial layers of tissue lying just below the surface of the skin. These 'ionic stream beds' are not thought to constitute the flow of ch'i itself but are seen as a parallel electromagnetic effect that indicates its presence. The strength of the flow of ch'i through any of the acupuncture points or meridians is thus indirectly measured by the intensity of the ionic stream. Dr Motoyama's AMI device was able to establish a close correspondence between the ionic stream beds detected and the traditional map of the meridians familiar to Traditional Chinese Medicine. Hiroshi Motoyama also found that by placing copper electrodes a short distance from the skin, he could detect the presence of energy emitted from the areas of the body where the chakras are located. This experiment was repeated by Dr Valerie Hunt of the University of California, Los Angeles using electromyograph (EMG) electrodes placed directly on the skin. Her experiments showed that regular, high-frequency signals could be detected emanating from the chakra points.

Electromagnetic energy may hold the key to a scientific understanding of ch'i and how it affects the human body. Currently much interest is being shown in what is termed 'magnetic therapy' and the use of electromagnetism in the treatment of depression and other illnesses. Pulse magnetic therapy is a practice already used extensively to heal bone fractures that will not knit together under plaster. Remarkably, published reports indicate that pulse magnetic therapy has an 80% chance of working successfully in these cases.

Electromagnetic therapy is also being trialled for use in the treatment of chronic depression. Using a technique called magnetic nerve stimulation, patients are given a 300 millisecond burst of magnetic energy, powered by two hand-sized batteries. When this short burst of magnetic energy connects with tissue it converts into an electrical pulse, which, depending where it is targeted, may produce a twitch in a muscle or nerve ending, or elicit a flash of colour before the eyes. Research supports the hypothesis that TMS stimulates the release of chemicals in the brain that ameliorate the symptoms of chronic depression. Trials are currently being conducted by Dr Mark George of the Medical University of South Carolina and in Israel. So far results suggest that patients receiving TMS improve by 50% on mood rating scales, as opposed to 28% receiving placebo treatment. Within the world of psychiatry and neurology this percentage of success compares favourably with more conventional therapies used to treat patients with this condition.

Great claims are also being made for the effects of much lower intensities of magnetic field, which involve no electromagnetic stimulation of tissue at all. Dr Ronald Lawrence, a Californian neurologist, suggests that moving the body through a magnetic field can generate low levels of electrical activity within blood cells that enhance the circulation of blood. A study he conducted where a patient wore a magnet on the wrist detected a 300% increase in blood flow to the fingers when the wrist joint was moved only slightly. The theory behind these new experiments postulates that magnetic fields raise the temperature of the blood and promote an increase in the blood flow, which washes away harmful toxins and stimulates the production of white blood cells that combat disease. This improvement in blood circulation establishes a rebalancing of the body as the increased flow washes clean the areas where harmful toxins have accumulated.

Research into vital energy is still in its infancy and cannot match the resources poured into drug research by the big pharmaceutical companies. If acupuncture, massage, breathing and exercise also stimulate the body's electromagnetic field in similar ways it is likely to be at lower intensities than those presently being tested. Scientists remain sceptical of claims for the influence of such low levels of magnetic energy and we must await the results of more research before we are likely to see any conclusive evidence. At the moment we are in the realm of 'There is no scientific evidence to suggest that ...', a phrase that is being treated with increasing public suspicion. We have come to suspect that this phrase really translates as 'We haven't found anything yet' or 'We don't know, because we haven't looked.'

Ultimately, the scientific case for the existence of ch'i, or vital energy, matters little to the thousands of healers and their patients, or t'ai chi and aikido practitioners who believe that they have felt this energy and that it works for them. Practice and practical experience offers confirmation enough. This is also true for the two Western energetic therapies that we explore in this chapter, Therapeutic Touch (TT) and reflexology. Both these therapies employ theoretical frameworks for their practice that have been heavily influenced by Eastern concepts of vital energy and the need to balance energy within the body. Both TT and reflexology enjoy a comfortably high profile within the complementary health community and have therefore been chosen to represent how Western healers have adapted Oriental practice to fit more closely to Western cultural expectations. Unlike Chinese or Japanese energetic ways, TT and reflexology are not presented as a 'way of life' with a spiritual and moral dimension that involves both practitioners and receivers. However, each of these therapies does require commitment and compassionate action from practitioners and the willing co-operation of patients in the healing process.

Therapeutic Touch can claim to be one of the most widely practised complementary health therapies in the Western world today. Unlike many other complementary therapies it has enjoyed strong support from nurses and other members of the medical profession and it can be studied academically in more than 80 colleges in the USA. Therapeutic Touch is a modern form of touch healing or laying on of the hands. It was devised by two eminent women, Dora Kunz, a noted spiritual healer and metaphysician, and Dr Dolores Krieger, Professor of Nursing at New York University during the 1960s. The therapy is based on research conducted by Dora Kunz into ancient health practices in both Europe, Africa and the East. She came to the conclusion that the laying on of hands has a history as old as mankind itself, and cited much evidence to support her view.

Dora Kunz found that cave paintings in northern Spain, dating back some 15,000 years depicted a similar practice. Research into the early Christian and medieval periods in Europe revealed that healing by touch was commonly practised by both the clergy and royalty. The miraculous qualities of the 'King's touch', was a persistent superstitious belief held by many of the people of Europe right into the 20th century. Christianity has a long association with the laying on of hands, despite the disapproval of church authorities, beginning with Pope Alexander III's ban on priests and clergy practising it in the 12th century. Although it has never received true sanction from Christian religious authorities, its association not only with Christ himself, but with saints as prominent as St Patrick in Ireland and St Bernard in France, has ensured its survival as an element of Christian ministry.

As a healer who also sought spiritual insight, Dora Kunz researched many of the world's faiths, including those of India and the Far East. Drawing from this research she concluded that human health and vitality is determined by the relative condition of an energy field that both surrounds and emanates from the body. Dora Kunz based this thesis on the ancient Hindu theory of prana, the equivalent of ch'i, which forms the conceptual basis for the practice of yoga and Ayurvedic medicine. Why a therapeutic system that assumes little difference in philosophy, outlook or practice from Eastern models should receive such generous acceptance by Western medicine, while its Oriental counterparts are viewed with suspicion, is open to question. One answer may be found by examining the contribution made by Dr Krieger.

In the late 1960s Dr Krieger became increasingly concerned by what she saw as a decline in the quality of care being given by the nursing profession. What particularly concerned her was the impersonal nature of modern hospital care and the lack of attention to the emotional comfort necessary to support recovery. Dr Krieger learned laying on of the hands techniques from Dora Kunz and became convinced that this was an avenue worthy of scientific examination. Together they

collaborated on further research, refining the system and naming it Therapeutic Touch. From the beginning of her association with TT, as it is often referred to, Dr Krieger's academic and medical background enabled her to subject its practice to rigorous scientific scrutiny. In many subsequent controlled studies she found that there was strong evidence to support the efficacy of TT in the treatment of patients.

Dr Krieger's early experiments focused on the effect the practice of TT had on the blood and particularly the levels of haemoglobin found within it. Haemoglobin binds oxygen molecules to red blood cells so that it can be distributed efficiently around the circulatory system to power our metabolic functions. She reasoned that if haemoglobin levels were increased by TT therapy oxygen levels in the body's cells would increase and promote faster healing. By comparing patients receiving treatment to a control group, Dr Krieger was able to report that patients receiving TT showed significant increase in haemoglobin levels. In further studies conducted in the 1980s TT was found to be more effective in relieving tension and anxiety than simple touching. More evidence came to light in 1997 when a US study found that TT could limit the effects of stress on the body's immune system. With evidence such as this to support claims for the effectiveness of TT, Dr Krieger has been able to publicize and promote its use among the nursing profession, where she is regarded as a leading educator. Currently, it is estimated that over 30,000 nurses in US hospitals and clinics use it to ease the discomfort of their patients and contribute to their recovery.

The Principles of Therapeutic Touch

According to Dr Krieger, Therapeutic Touch exploits an innate potential to heal found within us all. In common with many Eastern therapies this potential can be easily realized by a compassionate, focused intention to patients and the willingness to undertake a disciplined approach to learning. Therapeutic Touch bases its practice on two fundamental principles. The first regards each human being as an open energy system engaged in a dynamic exchange with the surrounding environment. Just like prana, or ch'i, this energy enters through source points, circulates round the body and exits. TT bases this principle on the Indian medical theory of prana, a vital universal energy, and its circulation and distribution around the body through the chakras. Prana enters through the spleen chakra and then passes in succession through six major chakras and the 72,000 *nadi*, or energy channels, in a manner similar to the distribution of ch'i through the meridians. Eventually, it travels out of the body via the shoulders, arms and the palms of the hands. For this reason the palms of the hands are considered to be secondary chakra and become potent tools for healing.

The second principle of Therapeutic Touch maintains that within the body this energy has bilateral symmetry, with each side of the body reflecting the other. By making comparisons between the energy levels on both the left and right side of the body the practitioner can detect areas of imbalance. Imbalance in this energy flow, in common with traditional Chinese medical practice, is considered to be the root cause of dysfunction and disease. The task of the healer is to unblock, rebalance and restore the flow of energy in the patient, referred to as the 'receiver' or 'healee' by TT practitioners, by transferring energy to them. As with reiki, this involves no loss of energy from the healer, who acts as conduit through which energy passes to the receiver, imprinted with the healer's own model of wholeness.

Dr Krieger believes that beyond the surface of the skin we are surrounded by electromagnetic fields of energy that permeate the body and that it is possible to influence these energy fields for the benefit of the receiver. Although named Therapeutic Touch, Krieger and Kunz's system works with the hands over the body, a few inches from the surface, rather than by actually touching it. This has obvious comparisons to similar concepts that we have explored throughout this book, and despite Chinese and Western medical research, are still thought unscientific by the majority of the medical profession. However, all orthodoxies are in a state of transition as the new science of quantum physics continues to overturn our Newtonian view of the world. Where there was once a world delineated by the law of cause and effect, we now have a science that sees the universe as a shifting pattern of energetic relationships. Within this universe the respective elements come together to participate in creating the whole in an ever-changing state of flux.

Therapeutic Touch Treatment

Therapeutic Touch treatment takes 20 to 30 minutes to perform. The receiver sits in a chair or lies upon a therapy table fully clothed, as the TT practitioner has no need to make direct contact with the body. Holding his or her hands two to five inches away from the body, the practitioner works with the encircling field of energy to restore balance to the whole system. The process of Therapeutic Touch treatment is divided into four distinct stages described as centring, assessing, unruffling or clearing, and transferring energy.

Centring

Before embarking on the treatment it is vital that the practitioner focuses his or her intention to heal and attunes his or her own 'inner wisdom' with that of the client. Sitting next to the client, the healer centres her mind by controlled, deep, rhythmic breathing, the visualization of a peaceful image or the silent repetition of a sound in the manner of a mantra. This allows the TT healer to empty the mind of distractions and to adopt an alert mental stillness that will be able to sense the areas of imbalance and diagnose how to restore them to healthy levels. The receiver should also try to centre, as compassion and empathy flowing between both the healer and the receiver are necessary if a deep level of healing is to be reached.

Assessing

Once the practitioner feels completely centred and the receiver is calm and comfortable, the practitioner begins to make an assessment of the patient's energy field. This is done by the practitioner standing, then kneeling in front of the client while making gentle rhythmic passes with the palms of the hands about two to six inches above the receiver's body. When the front is completed, the practitioner moves to the back of the patient and continues the same exercise from the rear. The practitioner feels imbalances in a variety of ways, but they are most often experienced as areas of warmth or cold, or areas that produce tingling or buzzing sensations. As with acupuncture or shiatsu practice, TT adopts a holistic view of the human energy system. This often means that the area that is causing pain or discomfort is not the source of the imbalance and the practitioner must be able to detect which areas are provoking the receiver's symptoms. TT practitioners claim that holding their hands away from the body facilitates their attunement to the human energy field by avoiding distractions caused by the patient's clothing, body movement or contact with the receiver's skin.

Unruffling

The practitioner clears the patient's energy field by making gentle, sweeping movements of the hands over the receiver's body, passing downwards from the head to the feet. This has the action of ironing out, or 'unruffling' the blockages that he or she has identified and restoring an even flow of energy around the receiver.

Transferring Energy

When the practitioner is confident that the client's energy field is flowing smoothly and evenly, the next step is to transfer energy to those weak spots that he or she has identified as deficient. This is done by holding the palms of the hands over the spot chosen for treatment and regulating and directing the flow of energy towards it. In a similar manner, the ch'i kung therapist emits ch'i through the palms of the hands towards the client. Both systems believe that there is a natural tendency towards a healthy balance which is evident in all life. When the patient receives this new energy it carries a template imprinted within it, with which the body can remodel its own pattern of healthy balance. The TT healer and reiki practitioner share the same belief that they act as a channel through which the universal energy passes to restore and harmonize the internal energy of the receiver. This not only recharges the receiver but also invigorates the healer who shares in the benefit brought by the inflow of universal energy.

Therapeutic Touch theorizes, in common with all Oriental energy-based therapies, that the actual location of pain symptoms does not necessarily have a direct correspondence with the areas of imbalance the practitioner has identified. The actual seat of the imbalance is very likely to be far from the place where the patient is experiencing tension or pain. Once

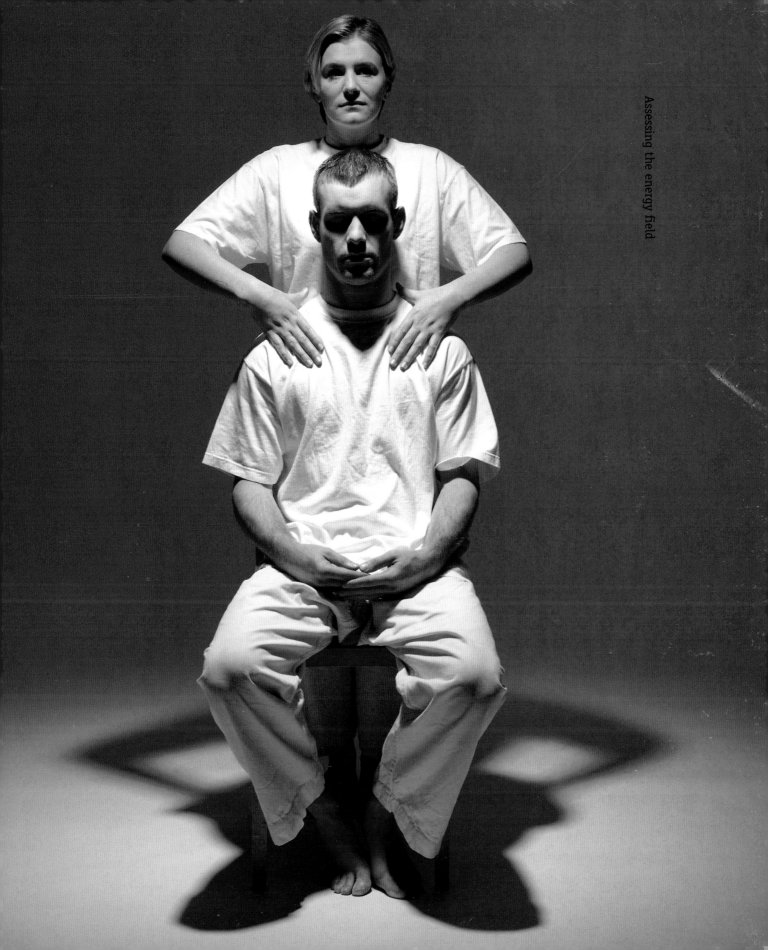

again, if we make a comparison with reiki, the TT healer makes no medical diagnosis of their client's condition. He or she is led to the areas that require the transfer of energy by sensitivity to the electro-magnetic activity encompassing the client. Surges and disturbances are signals felt through the hands and interpreted intuitively by the healer, who will know where to channel the energy flow. Experience and intuition will also determine how long he or she may transfer energy in any one area of the field. Too much energy is as unhealthy as too little.

Although TT is essentially a 'hands-off-the-body' therapy, some practitioners will provide shiatsu or similar massage to the neck or shoulders in the early stages to help the patient to relax. The patient may also be encouraged to assist the transfer of energy by visualizing the process. Treatments can result in the release of pent up emotional distress and a practition-er takes great care to be sympathetic to the client's needs. If issues are raised that require longer-term and more specific emotional support the practitioner may advise the patient to seek counselling. The power of a treatment can be dramatically increased by two practi-tioners working together, co-ordinating their move-ments as they work around the receiver's energy field. The emotional power of such a treatment is strong, for both client and healers, as it helps to build empathy and compassion, the essence of good nursing.

TT makes no extravagant claims to be able to cure any specific disease or medical condition, although many patients may feel it has been the key to their personal recovery from illness. The purpose of TT is to help the patient attain a sense of well-being, which will encourage their own internal fight against dis-ease. In the case of terminal disease the support that TT offers works on both the mind and body to induce relaxation and the easing of stress. By promoting a feeling of calm and peaceful serenity the patient's

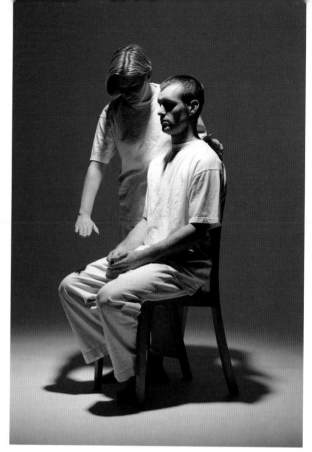

Repatterning the energy field

quality of life can be lifted and the passage towards death made more comfortable. Evidence from studies has shown TT to be effective in helping patients over-come the feelings of nausea that accompany chemotherapy. TT can also assist the control of pain and, remarkably, has been shown to speed the heal-ing time of fractures and wounds.

Many Western critics of TT and, by inference, of shiatsu, reiki and other energy therapies, suggest that if these systems work at all, then it is because of a placebo effect. This is partially confirmed in the case of TT in a study which indicated that people who were critical of treatment and highly sceptical of its effect felt no measured benefit from treatment. This does not worry Dr Krieger or her followers. The point is that it does work for many people and if this is merely the consequence of the patient's own mind being mobilized to fight disease, so much the better, because this is an intention of treatment. If ch'i or prana is the dynamic of all life, we are far from finding an answer. In the present it matters little whether it can be proved to exist scientifically or not as long as patients believe in the treatment and believe that it has helped them. Medical treatments far more harmful than any we have described in this book have been used regularly in the past by Western doctors until discoveries in scientific research found them wanting. TT has on the other hand much continuing testimony to suggest it makes an effective contribution to the care and treatment of the sick. For nursing it has also provided confirmation of the vital role that human touch plays in relieving patients' pain and emotional distress.

As a complementary element of the total care that can be provided to those who are sick, TT can be employed by almost anyone, provided they have been trained. Initial training in the basic techniques takes a matter of six hours, but a serious practitioner would have worked through therapeutic support groups and with other healers to develop the intuitive qualities necessary to good practice. In the USA training can be sought through the Nurse Healers – Professional Associates Inc., the only organization sanctioned by Dr Krieger, and in the UK through the British Association for Therapeutic Touch, formed in 1994. Many nurses and lay healers make up a growing community of healers, estimated to be as many as 100,000 strong. While many in the West are attracted by Eastern philosophy and ritual, there are thousands of others who feel uncomfortable with the culture and practice associated with therapies such as shiatsu and reiki. TT offers those who believe there is something in the concept of a subtle, universal energy, a bridge between Eastern and Western therapeutic practice with which they can feel comfortable.

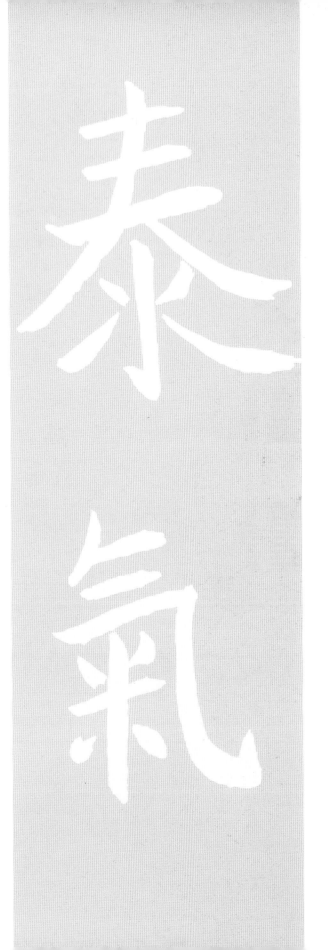

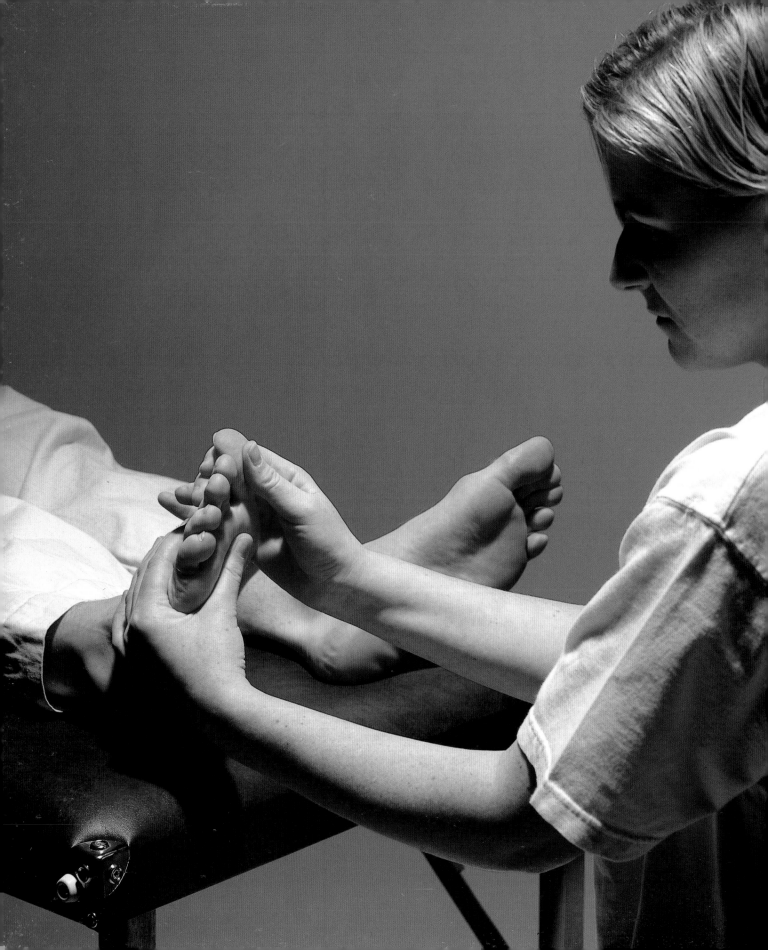

REFLEXOLOGY

Reflexology is one of the most popular forms of complementary health care practiced in the West. In common with Traditional Chinese Medicine it shares the belief that areas of the body, called reflex zones, are energetically linked to other parts of the body such as the organs and glands. By manipulating these reflex zones, primarily on the feet but also on the hands, ears and the surface of the skin, corresponding limbs or organs within the body can be treated to improve the energetic balance of the body. The feet are a particularly important reflex zone, for they contain over 7,000 nerve endings and almost a quarter of the body's bones. Reflexologists believe that the whole body can be mapped on the feet, and that by applying pressure to specific points of the foot they can influence any body part in its corresponding reflex zone.

The origins of reflexology date back at least 5,000 years to ancient Chinese foot massage techniques that later matured into the comprehensive practice of acupuncture. However, it is certain that other ancient cultures as widespread as Egypt, Russia, Japan and the native peoples of Pre-Columbian America shared similar foot massage practices. Egyptologists have provided us with evidence of the antiquity of reflexology when they uncovered a wall painting in the tomb of Ankmahor, known as the physician's tomb, which clearly depicts the practice of manipulating and massaging the feet.

Although reflexology can claim ancient roots, the modern practice of this 'science' or 'art' owes its inspiration to the work of Dr William H. Fitzgerald, an American physician and surgeon from Hartford, Connecticut. His interest in zone therapy was prompted while he was working at the Central London Ear, Nose and Throat Hospital in 1902. During his stay in the UK he became familiar with the work of many European researchers in the field of zone therapy. Prominent amongst these researchers were figures such as Per Heinrik Ling, the founder of Swedish massage, and the British neurologist Sir Henry Head. In 1834 Ling's researches led him to conclude that pains associated with particular organs had referral points on unrelated areas of the skin's surface. Later in the same century, Head offered the first map of reflex zones outlined on the back and known as Head Zones as his contribution to the developing theories of zone therapy.

After returning to America, Fitzgerald continued his zone therapy research and began to use reflex techniques in the treatment of his patients. At this point, Fitgerald was more interested in the reflex zones of the hand and how they could be used to anaesthetize pain during minor operations. He found that by applying pressure to certain points on the hand, pain could be inhibited in other areas of the body. Through empirical observation, he meticulously traced these correspondences and proposed a theory of reflex zone reference that divided the body into ten longitudinal zones of equal width, extending through the body from front to back. Each of these zones related to the digits of the hands and the feet, and divided the body into five matched areas on either side of a central line. As well as using the hands to apply pressure, Fitzgerald and his followers used combs, clothes-pegs and elastic bands.

Fitzgerald's pioneering work was continued by other physcians, such as Dr Edwin Bowers and Dr Joseph Shelby Riley. However, the honours for the creation of foot reflexology as it is practised today go to Eunice Ingham (1889–1974) who worked as a physical therapist in Dr Riley's clinic. Ingham became interested in zone therapy and began an extensive period of experimentation through trial and error. She kept extensive notes of her patients' reactions to pressure applied to different positions on the feet. As a result of her observations, Ingham was able to produce a comprehensive map which linked specific areas of the foot with a corresponding organ, gland or part of the body. In 1938, her book *Stories the Feet Can Tell* was published, in which she described and explained her findings. Later she was to set up the International Institute of Reflexology to teach the Original Ingham Method of Reflexology and assure its continuation as an effective therapy into the future. Throughout her life, Ingham devoted herself to teaching the principles of her method and promoting its use throughout America until her death at the age of 80. Today the Institute is led by her nephew, Dwight C. Byers and claims a current membership of some 70,000 former students.

In the UK, reflexology was brought to public attention through the dogged efforts of Doreen Bayly, who studied with Dr Ingham in the 1960s. Struggling against public apathy and at times open derision, she won adherents in both the UK and other parts of Europe. Eventually she was able to build both a flourishing practice and the famous Bayly School of Reflexology that continues to train practitioners to this day.

The Theory of Reflexology

Zone theory divides the body from head to toe into ten longitudinal zones, five each side of a median line on the right and left sides of the body. The zones are of equal width and section the body from the front to the back. Each zone runs from a digit on the foot up to the brain and down the arm to a corresponding digit on the hand. As the zones do not cross over in the brain, as does the nervous system, the right side of the body is represented in the reflex area of the right foot and the left side of the body is linked with the left foot. All the organs, glands and body parts within a zone are energetically connected to the reflex areas on the palms and backs of the hand and the sole, top and side of the foot with which they are associated. By working on these reflex areas the reflexologist can affect energy in another part of the zone to which it is connected.

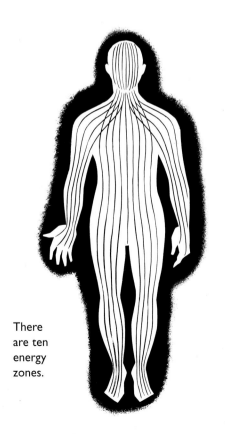

There are ten energy zones.

The ten longitudinal reflex zones are crossed by additional transverse zones, distinguished by lines drawn across the upper shoulder girdle, the waist and across the lower body level with the bottom of the pelvis. These lines are reflected in the feet and are defined by its skeletal structure with a line crossing the base of the phalanges, or the bones of the toes, the second line crossing at the base of the metatarsal bones and the third across the tarsal bones and up to the bones of the ankle. In this way the reflexes of the head and neck are found in the toes, those of the thorax and upper abdomen are found in the area over the metatarsal bones, and the reflexes of the pelvis and lower abdomen are located over the tarsal bones and around the ankle.

Reflexologists maintain that the foot has the appearance of the human body with the toes forming the head, the balls of the foot parallel the shoulders, the instep becomes the waist, the front of the heel becomes the pelvis area and finally the feet are represented at the bottom of the heels. The five lines of the reflex zones on each side on the body cross each foot from the heel to the toes and, together with the transverse zones, form a grid within which all the organs, glands and limbs of the body are positioned. With this map the reflexologist is able to guide energy to a particular area that requires balancing. For example, when pressure is applied to the middle of the foot, energy in the stomach and the abdominal organs will be affected, while working on a big toe can relieve the pain of a headache. This same representation of the body can be transposed to the hands, where the referral areas are similarly mapped and associated with organs and major parts of the body within their reflex zone.

As yet there is no definitive scientific explanation for how reflexology might work. Reflexology bases its 'proofs' upon the empirical evidence gathered by practitioners in the course of treating their clients.

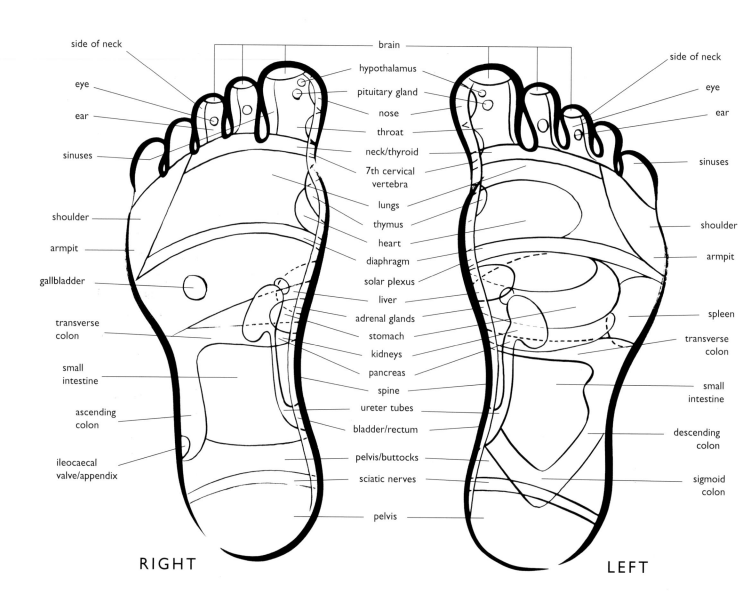

side of neck

eye

ear

sinuses

shoulder

armpit

gallbladder

transverse colon

small intestine

ascending colon

ileocaecal valve/appendix

brain

hypothalamus

pituitary gland

nose

throat

neck/thyroid

7th cervical vertebra

lungs

thymus

heart

diaphragm

solar plexus

liver

adrenal glands

stomach

kidneys

pancreas

spine

ureter tubes

bladder/rectum

pelvis/buttocks

sciatic nerves

pelvis

side of neck

eye

ear

sinuses

shoulder

armpit

spleen

transverse colon

small intestine

descending colon

sigmoid colon

RIGHT

LEFT

Reflexology points on the soles of the feet

However, there are various theories that suggest plausible explanations which future research may confirm or deny. At the most basic of levels reflexology can be seen to have an effect on the nervous system and the circulation of the blood. The healthy circulation of blood carries nutrients to the tissues and conducts away waste deposits formed by the metabolic process. By stimulating the referral areas the reflexologist can increase the efficiency of the circulatory system in any of the reflex zones and contribute to the overall health and well-being of the client. Reflexology works beneficially on the nervous system, helping the body to relax and easing the unpleasant effects of stress and tension. Massage of the appropriate referral areas can also stimulate the release of endorphins in the brain, which are known to act as the body's natural anaesthetic for the relief of pain.

Another possible explanation for the positive effects of reflexology on general health may lie in its ability to disperse the crystalline deposits formed by uric acid and other toxins that accumulate in the feet. The feet are a potential dumping zone for toxins and the calcium carried in the blood. Blood is assisted by gravity on its downward flow but requires more effort to pump itself up through the body. At this mid-point in the circulation cycle, toxins move sluggishly and easily coalesce into gritty deposits beneath the skin. The action of massaging the feet breaks down these crystalline accumulations and enables the circulation to disperse them more easily. Some reflexologists believe that crystals will always be found in a referral area connected to a zone where there is an imbalance of energy. Consequently, if the crystal deposits are dispersed, energetic balance will be restored to the affected area. The determinism of this view is not, however, universally accepted, for reflex areas can show signs of imbalance without the reflexologist finding any crystalline deposits to be present.

Whatever the outcomes of future research may be, reflexology, alongside other therapeutic massage and touch therapy systems, can claim an increasingly large number of clients who clearly believe that it has worked beneficially for them. The common factor in all these approaches to restorative health care is the belief that the therapy adopted restores homeostasis, or the natural balance of the body's energetic system. All these therapies claim to improve the circulation of the blood and enable an increase of flow to areas of congestion or imbalance. When body temperature is raised it causes vasodilation or the expansion of the blood vessels, and promotes circulation. This has the effect of washing away harmful toxins and raising anti-inflammatory white blood cell levels which help to reduce pain. Research has shown that this effect can be stimulated by electro-magnetic fields, and current research into the use of magnetic nerve stimulation by Dr Mark George at the Medical University of South Carolina suggests it may also be effective in treating depression. It may be that acupuncture and reflexology act in similar ways by stimulating low-level charges or pulses of electro-magnetic energy which produce beneficial discharges in the brain, such as the release of endorphins, and cause an increase in the flow of blood around the body. While evidence from scientifically conducted trials suggest that these claims have validity, the research has been on such a small scale that as yet it can offer no definitive proofs.

What reflexologists can point to is that the feet are known to be particularly sensitive areas with more than 7,000 nerve endings in each foot. It is therefore more than likely that by working on these nerve endings, signals will be referred back through the complex, interweaving network of nerves to other areas of the body. Working with these assumptions, reflexologists have been able to develop a therapeutic massage

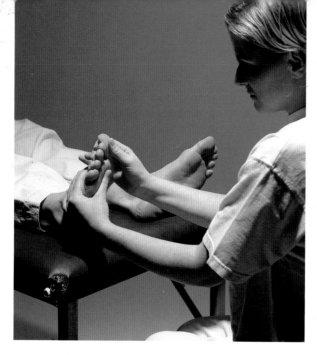

From the base of each toe the thumb is 'caterpillar' walked towards the tip for the sinuses

Each foot is massaged with the thumb below the first three toes for the neck and thyroid gland

system that offers an observable consistency in both treatment and results.

The Practice of Reflexology

Reflexology treatments usually last from 30 minutes to an hour and are conducted with the patient seated in a reclining chair, with their footwear removed. The back and the lower leg from the ankle to the knee should be comfortably supported so that the feet remain relaxed throughout treatment. New clients will be asked questions about their previous medical history to assist the reflexologist in directing treatment and to make sure there are no contra-indications that must be taken into account. Where there are serious illnessess that might be affected by increased circulation spreading infection or if there is damage to the feet themselves, then reflexology is not appropriate.

The reflexologist begins a treatment by examining the feet for such things as the colour, temperature and the texture of the skin. Cold feet, together with a blue or red tinge to the skin will indicate poor circulation, while perspiring feet might signify imbalances in the glands. The reflexologist will avoid treating areas where there are verrucas, corns, blisters or athlete's foot to prevent the spread of infection and avoid transmitting infection to their hands. If the foot is too infected to touch then the reflexologist will treat the corresponding reflex areas of the hand.

When the examination is completed, the reflexologist will apply a small amount of talcum powder to the foot and massage to induce relaxation. The feet are massaged with the sides of the fingers and thumbs moving slowly up the foot: this is known as finger or thumb walking. After the initial relaxation massage has taken place, the practitioner will apply pressure to the reflex areas that have been chosen for treatment.

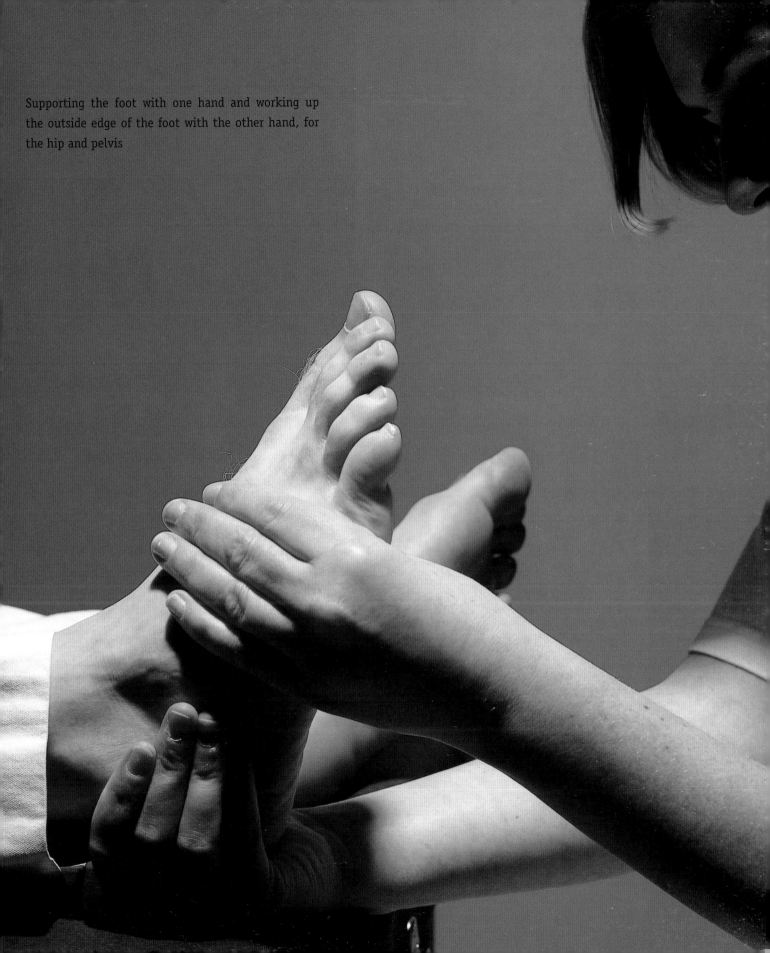

Supporting the foot with one hand and working up
the outside edge of the foot with the other hand, for
the hip and pelvis

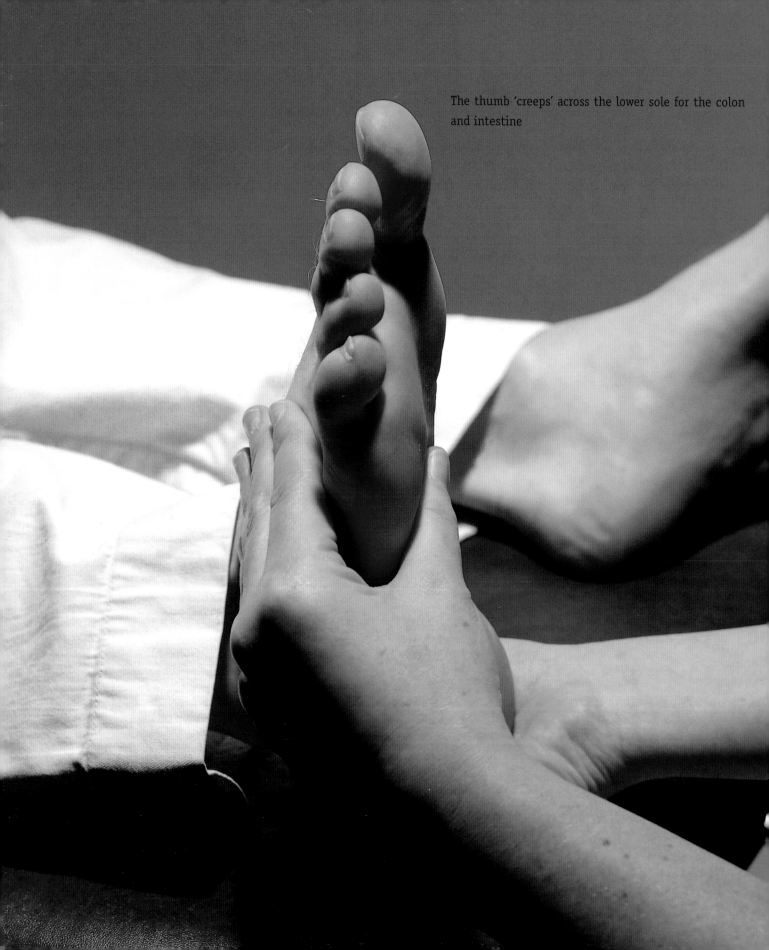

The thumb 'creeps' across the lower sole for the colon and intestine

Pressure is generally applied with the thumb, although the fingers may also be used. The thumb is held bent at a 45 degree angle and drawn back slightly when pressure is applied to prevent the practitioner's finger nail contacting the foot. Within each reflex area there are many reflex points and the reflexologist must take great care to align the side and end of the thumb with each point precisely to ensure effective treatment. Where there are tender areas in the foot not related to any localized condition there is a good indication that this relates to an area of imbalance or congestion in a related organ or gland. Always the reflexologist is concerned to ensure that the patient is relaxed and comfortable throughout treatment. Consequently, the pressure applied by the reflexologist is firm and deep, but should not be painful. When the treatment of both feet is completed the practitioner will finish by gently manipulating the feet. This includes rotating the toes and ankles and kneading the sole of the foot with the fist. The session ends with a breathing exercise to further relax the patient and encourage the flow of breath and energy. The practitioner places her thumbs on the reflex points of the solar plexus and applies pressure as the patient breathes in and simultaneously pushes the feet gently up towards the body. When the patient breathes out the pressure is relaxed and the feet pulled gently away.

Reflexology is often applied in combination with other therapies by complementary healers, although it is important that a full treatment is given to ensure that the body is rebalanced properly. Healers may also use the feet to diagnose areas of imbalance before applying other therapies. From the client's viewpoint it is essential to check that the practitioner has been properly trained and has a professional understanding of the treatment. There is much variety in the standards and length of time taken in training; an unsatisfactory situation which is likely to continue as long as governments take a relaxed view of complementary health care regulation. Within the European Union there is some momentum for the agreement of common standards and competencies, but it is likely to take some time to develop. In the USA Eunice Ingham's International Institute of Reflexology is the oldest school and has set standards for others to follow. Doreen Bayly set up an equivalent institution in the UK in 1968, called the Bayly School of Reflexology, which runs courses at home and abroad and has trained many practitioners. Reflexology offers a comfortable and easy entry into energetic therapy treatment, where a patient may feel more comfortable and less vulnerable than lying on a futon or massage couch.

Reflexology is particularly effective in the treatment of stress-related illness, lower back pain, high blood pressure, headaches and chronic digestive disorders. Emotional disorders, sexual problems and addictions such as smoking and overeating may also be usefully treated by reflexology. Patients report a variety of responses to treatment, which vary from a sense of lingering tiredness to feeling more creative, alert and alive. In all cases reflexology is a completely non-invasive and comforting therapy that can induce a sense of positive well-being. It is one of a growing number of Western adaptations of Eastern medical philosophy. All these therapies recognize that true health can only be achieved by balancing both the mind and the body.

THE MIND OF CH'I

This book has been an exploration of ch'i, the vital cosmic energy from which all life and consciousness emanates. It described how a belief in this energy moulded and shaped the medicine, callisthenics, cultural, creative and martial arts of China and Japan. Indeed, every aspect of Chinese and Japanese culture is so permeated by this concept that there is no traditional craft, skill, intellectual, creative or spiritual practice where its motivating power is not acknowledged. We have inevitably left out many other arts and disciplines where ch'i is central to practice.

To include every system of exercise, therapeutic system or school of martial arts would break the bounds of this book and lose everyone bar the most dogged reader. We have been content to illustrate the diversity of the human expression of ch'i through those arts and Ways that are more familiar and practically accessible to people in the West. Each of the disciplines we have reviewed can be studied, practised or consulted in almost any major urban setting across the globe. As the internet and the communications revolution open up more corners of the world, these ideas and

STEPPING OUT ON THE WAY

concepts and the systems built around them find even wider audiences. Day by day and year by year, the participation levels in t'ai chi, ch'i kung, aikido, shiatsu and other arts go on climbing. They are just as likely to be found in your local sports centre or health club as basketball, fitness training or aerobics. Why have these arts become so popular and what is it they offer that cannot be found in Western sport or health and exercise systems?

It is clear from the survey we have made that all these Oriental arts come with a philosophy that cannot be supplied by our own Western traditions of health, sport and exercise. They are all intimately concerned with the spiritual condition of the individual and are dedicated to the purpose of improving it. Whether this involves compassionate action through healing, or self-development through ch'i kung, the martial arts or calligraphy, the path points towards a spiritual enlightenment that reconciles the ego-led self with the cosmic self. While playing football may teach you much about co-operation, human relationships and dedication to effort, these lessons are largely implicit and not the declared purpose of practice. The modern tennis player or athlete may call the 'no-mind' of the martial arts the 'zone', and borrow the techniques of Zen meditation, but there is no way that sports so dedicated to competitive reward could lay claim to being spiritual disciplines.

This is not to imply that within the Oriental martial arts there is no competition, although the 'soft' martial arts we have chosen to illustrate generally avoid it. Competition is there, but it is regarded as having an entirely different purpose. The stereotypical English gentleman's view that the spirit with which you play the game is more important than winning may have the same frayed edges as his old tweed jacket in the charity shop, but it is a useful parallel. If your motivation for winning is self-conceit and

supposed glory, then, from the perspective of the true martial artist, you have already lost without having ever fought the battle. The real struggle is always with yourself, your emotions and the attachments you are conditioned to. When you are truly integrated with the practice of your art, such things as winning or losing become irrelevant and fall away. The martial artist 'wins' when there is no desire to win and consequently no fear of losing. Untrammelled by this burden, the mind and body can centre on the performance to realise the individual's fullest potential. Ultimately, the winning of a competition is not the vindication of innate superiority but a demonstration of the physical, mental and spiritual progress the martial artist has made.

Throughout all the energetic arts this same lesson is apparent and the process is much more important than the product. Neglect the process and forget to treat each element as an essential part of the whole and the product will be tarnished and incomplete. Apply yourself to dedicated, consistent practice with an appreciation of the intrinsic worth of each stage of the process and your skills and insight will improve, almost of themselves. For the value of the 'Way' is not to be judged by your prowess or natural creative ability, but by your application to the task and the lessons you have drawn. In this way the student and the teacher gain as much from the process as each other. They are only differentiated by their place along the continuum of potential experience. Provided they keep to the task and practise with the right spirit then all can become 'masters' however long it may take. It is the virtue of this principle of neo-Confucian inspired learning that no-one is excluded from a judgment of success. Each gains value and virtue from the effort that is put in.

Patience is also a great principle here, for there can be no rush to learn what cannot be taught. All understanding of the Way is experiential and cannot be crammed. Each student can proceed at their own pace as they will be judged according to their individual merits without reference to the achievements of others. The teacher's role is to encourage, draw out the lessons and pose the challenges that will get the best out of the student, not to trip him up gratuitously or defeat his will to succeed. This is not an ideal of education out of sympathy with Western traditions. It formed the basis of our own apprenticeship system where each craftsman expected to pass from apprentice, to journeyman, to master, in the due passage of time. It is still the classic educational ideal despite the sustained attack from a world obsessed with performance measures and outcomes. From the moment a student first joins a ch'i kung class to the time when he or she has become a teacher, he or she is allowed to fail. Indeed, the student is expected to fail, for how else is it possible to learn? What lessons about fortitude, or courage, or resolution can be learnt from an activity that sets no challenge and requires no personal effort to perform? If only we had the same perspective in our classrooms and workplaces we might have more well-adjusted people than we have now. Unlike the performance-target-obsessed boss, the teacher of a Way is not looking over your shoulder to find you out but to see how to guide you further along the path.

Once again, this represents an ideal. Not all teachers of the Ways are infallible or could be described as enlightened. Just as in every other human activity there are both charlatans and saints and it is important to judge between them. But becoming a student of a Way cannot be accomplished on your own by trips to the bookstore or watching videos. It requires the close personal attention of a teacher to tease out every detail and reveal every nuance of technique through instruction and example. The teacher is simultaneously instructor, mentor and spiritual guide and must believe in your sincerity to learn before making an investment of his time and effort. To stand in such close relationship the student must have complete trust and confidence in the teacher, for he has no foreknowledge of where the learning will take him. Yes, the target may at first seem clear – become a shiatsu practitioner or get that coveted black-belt – but by the time you get there you will know there is so much more to be gained and understood. A good teacher will be open, modest and sincere and above all will demonstrate quiet authority and compassion, without these qualities it is unlikely that he will point you in the direction you would wish to go.

The importance of trust is paramount to the learning of a traditional Chinese or Japanese Way because its methodology is centred so closely on the role of the teacher as a model of the Way. In Japan this is described as *shu, ha, ri* – keep, break, leave. At first the student has only the teacher to emulate and must imitate, or 'keep', each of his actions and movements and become as close a replication of his teacher as he can. All learning of the Ways is ultimately experiential at this stage in the student's training, as little beyond technical detail and the outward intention and shape of forms can be explained to the student. After years of diligent practice and close identity with his teacher's model, the student begins to absorb the lessons of the Way into his own body. Gradually, with the growth of intuitive perception, the student gains the confidence to adapt or 'break' the model to fit his own mental and physical character. Eventually, after many years of training he comes to maturity in the art and can 'leave' to found his own school and teach the 'Way' with his own insight and understanding. This is not a three-year degree course or even a long-drawn-out doctorate, it is a lifetime's journey.

It can be seen that this traditional model of learning has immense difficulties for those of us who are used to a pedagogy that invites questions and expects answers to be subjected to analysis and debate. This is not the traditional Eastern way, and our interrogative approach to learning has little relevance here. We might get a good verbal description of the condition of our minds when they are in deep meditative states, but we will not 'know' it until we feel it. The Ways we have described in this book are holistic and require that understanding be an integrated process learnt through the body, mind and the spirit. This cannot be short circuited by reading teaching manuals or ploughing through books on Eastern history and philosophy. Study will be encouraged and does help to feed the mind, but the Way cannot be grasped on the intellectual plane alone – the Way must be done. For the impatient, inquiring Westerner this means he must wait for his body to catch up with his mind. When it does, the student often finds that he was asking the wrong questions in the first place.

Not every student has the time, application or devotion to become a 'master' in his own right. It takes a degree of commitment and single-minded purpose beyond the ordinary, just as it does to become an acknowledged writer, artist or musician. At each stage along the Way a regular commitment to training brings benefits to the mind and body that help to repel the mental and physical stress of modern living. The Way provides a refuge where the mind and body become lost in the process of doing and all distractions and anxiety begin to fall away. Just as we might shower in the evening to wash away the detritus of the day, the hour or more we devote to training promotes the flow of ch'i and washes the toxins from our minds and bodies to refresh the spirit.

The Benefits of Ch'i

All medical science, be it Western or Eastern, acknowledges the importance of general fitness in resisting disease and maintaining the agility of our minds. The ability to convert the breath efficiently into a steady, oxygenated flow of blood through the body and the brain keeps us functioning and alert. Good diet, regular exercise and mental stimulation are all recognized as important aspects of maintaining a happy, balanced life. These sustaining qualities can be found to some degree in all sporting and recreational pursuits, so what more can t'ai chi offer than aerobics or playing the piano? At the most superficial level, the answer would be none. Aerobics, or golf or playing an instrument will exercise the heart and keep coronaries at bay. Feeding the mind with intellectual stimulation and an aesthetic appreciation of art and beauty will increase the quality and savour of life. No student or teacher of the Way would deny the benefits that are to be gained from pursuing any activity that provides healthy exercise, mental stimulation and relaxation for the spirit. What is suggested is that by establishing the vital balance of ch'i within the body, you will be able to gain more from any activity or pursuit that you wish to follow.

The energetic Ways maintain that by concentrating on only one aspect of training, such as lowering blood pressure, or increasing your muscle strength, you will fail to realize your full potential. This will leave the body forever condemned to firing on two or three cylinders without the engine ever ticking over harmoniously. An over-concentration on any one aspect will overload the system and throw it out of balance, putting pressure on other parts of the body or mind as they attempt to compensate for the distortion. Bodhidharma discovered this at the Shaolin Temple. He realised his monks needed exercise and fitness training to equip them to sit still and focused through long hours of silent meditation. Enlightenment was unlikely to come to a tired brain in an exhausted body. The student of chado will still need to exercise and the t'ai chi teacher will need to have interests beyond the limits of his discipline if he is to remain a balanced human being.

It has not been the intention to provide scientific proof for the existence of ch'i, but to let the energetic Ways we have described speak for themselves. However, running like a central thread through the core of all these disciplines is the claim that by gaining the ability to summon the energy of ch'i you may extend the vitality of your life beyond the ordinary. Many amazing reports from travellers to Tibet relate how monks in deep meditative states were able to sit long nights outside in the snow, and endure extreme freezing conditions without succumbing to frostbite or hypothermia. There is no doubt that meditation enables the mind to change the physiology of the body. Research conducted by Dr Ratree Sudsuang and colleagues at Chulalongkorn University in Thailand found that when meditating the heart rate, serum cotisol levels, blood pressure and lung volume all decrease. As an increase in these functions is associated with the symptoms of stress, Dr Sudsuang and his colleagues concluded that meditation can be used to relieve stress. The research also found that EEG readings of brain activity showed that alpha brain waves have a tendency to increase during meditation and help to promote a state of tranquillity. This type of brain activity is similar to that operating during desynchronized sleep, when dreaming is most likely to occur. Trained meditators do not, however, fall asleep, they remain alert and fully awake but without the distraction of thought. The brain is quietened through the breath. By breathing very slowly, taking fewer breaths per minute, the rate at which nerve cells fire in the brain is reduced and produces a calming sensation in the body and the mind. A skilled meditator is able to slow her whole metabolism to almost a standstill and yet remain mentally alert and physically stable, running on the internal energy of ch'i.

This state of inner stillness and calm has an active as well as passive character. In the Japanese martial arts this is described as mushin mugamae, or 'no-mind no-posture', a state of alert openness in the body and mind that reacts spontaneously and appropriately to events without conscious direction or prejudgment. In the martial arts this alert spontaneity enables the practitioner to react instantly to an attack almost before it has been launched. It is a meditative state that is learnt through the arduous practice of drills and sequences that simulate scenarios of attack and defence. The movements of these forms are absorbed through the body and locked into the memory so that they become as natural to perform as riding a bicycle or driving a car. The transferability of this state to everyday life is not automatic. To some extent it is 'switched on' by a situation the practitioner has trained to meet, but it does give a reserve of mental and physical energy that can be relied on during times of stress and crisis. The martial artist knows that by adopting a particular defence stance he betrays some of his intention to an enemy and has potentially escalated the nature of the conflict. Better to stand in neutral stance and be ready to move in any direction when the attack is delivered. When you know its timing, shape and direction then you can make the most appropriate move to meet it. Spontaneity is the ideal here, but it is not arbitrary, wilful, anarchic or destructive. This spontaneity is trained and can only come when the martial artist has learnt to harmonize body, breath and mind and 'blend' with life around him.

Mushin mugamae can also be translated as 'open heart open mind', implying that the character of a practitioner should reflect the mental and physical openness practised in the dojo. It is, or should be, a quality of compassionate, non-judgemental frankness, of open dealing, flexibility and the search for consensus rather than conflict. If we are all animated by ch'i and the object is to find balance and harmony in the body then we must also strive for balance and harmony in our everyday lives. You cannot expect to reap the benefits of energizing your body without also understanding that you must harmonize the mind with the cosmic energy that surrounds you. This cosmic ch'i seeks equilibrium by balancing the opposing forces of yin and yang, and looks for stability rather than violent surges from one to the other. Just as our bodies need training to stimulate the flow of ch'i we must also train the mind. Although this is primarily undertaken by physical practice in the belief that this will inevitably lead to the flexible, open mind, it is also clear that training in the energetic ways requires the acceptance of certain spiritual values. Training in the Oriental energetic ways can be pursued entirely on the physical level without any real belief in the scientific truth of ch'i, but it would be entirely empty without commitment to the spiritual lessons that can be drawn. At its simplest level this is a belief in co-operation, the avoidance of conflict and the establishment of accord. This contract of accord extends to all things, covering our dealings and relationships with others and our responsibilities to the natural world. It implies bend, deflect and redirect rather than break, block and oppose. It means finding solutions to problems that try to take account of all the interests and consequences and seek the least harmful and most beneficial resolution. A little saccharine sounding perhaps, but nevertheless a practical ideal to strive for for those who need to find an everyday spiritual dimension to their lives. While the spiritual philosophy of the arts and Ways of ch'i has been founded on the teachings of Taoism and Buddhism it is not necessary to believe in these faiths to develop ch'i. However, ch'i is a conception that holds that all things are part of a universal oneness. A Christian may name this oneness as God. A Muslim may name it Allah. The faithless may accept it intellectually as a philosophical principle that represents an ideal to be striven for. But without a belief and identification with this oneness and the determination to reach and experience it you will be practising the energetic arts superficially and eating only half the cake.

Constancy is another aspect of the mind of ch'i. To benefit from any of the arts and ways we have described requires a long-term commitment. This is not a six-week fitness programme or a recreational pursuit that you take up when you feel like it. An engagement with ch'i needs regular, sometimes grudging, training. Indeed often it is just when you feel least like standing in a ch'i kung posture or giving a massage that it is likely to do you most good. The Japanese called this learning keiko, where understanding arrives through the repetition and polishing of the technical forms. It is positive experiential learning as opposed to passively absorbing knowledge from a book or a lecture. Confucian and Buddhist thought gives an added spiritual interpretation for keiko which is seen as the means 'to learn the proper way of living (do) through mastery of one's art form.' When that mastery arrives you are on the threshold of true harmony with the spirit. This is the life affirming energy of ch'i.